RISKY BUSINESS

Private Management of Public Schools

RISKY BUSINESS
Private Management
of Public Schools

CRAIG E. RICHARDS

RIMA SHORE

MAX B. SAWICKY

ECONOMIC POLICY INSTITUTE

Library of Congress Catalog Card Number: 96-84458

ISBN: 0-944826-68-7

Printed in the United States of America

To Eileen, Janet, Rochelle, Judy, John, and Patty,
foot soldiers in the trenches of public education.

MAX SAWICKY

For my mother, Florence Shore.

RIMA SHORE

To my wife, Diann, for her endless patience and support,
and to my son, Michael, for the sheer joy he brings.

CRAIG RICHARDS

TABLE OF CONTENTS

ACKNOWLEDGMENTS

MAX SAWICKY would like to thank Elliott Sclar, Bruce Fuller, Craig Richards, Alex Molnar, Jewell Gould, Martha Matzke, Judith Stern-Torres, Anita Summers, and EPI staff economists for their helpful and often bracing comments on the manuscript. He would also like to acknowledge the assistance of Carl Stokes, Judson Porter, Irene Dandridge, Loretta Johnson, Robert Slavin, Lawrence Howe, Les Linaberg, Linda Prudente, and Stephen Ruffini of Baltimore, and "Teacher of the Year" Rochelle Holder of Hartford.

CRAIG RICHARDS would like to express his deep appreciation to his academic colleagues, Max Sawicky and Helen Ladd, for their thoughtful comments on earlier drafts of Chapter 2. He is also deeply indebted to Bruce Baker and Miriam Cilo, doctoral students at Teachers College, Columbia University, for their invaluable research assistance in developing the data for the analysis and for making thoughtful observations on how it should be interpreted—even though he did not in the end always agree with them. Finally, he would like to thank his partner for 20 years, Diann Richards, who granted the time away from family necessary to complete the work. Absent her support, he could not have found the time for the study.

RIMA SHORE would like to thank Barbara Shore, who contributed substantially to the research for this chapter and offered valuable insight into the phenomenon of privatization; Rachel Smith, who helped with library legwork; Richard Guttenberg, who dug 25-year-old reports out of cartons in his basement and shed light on the origins of performance contracting; Sharon Lynn Kagan, who suggested directions for research; and Madeleine Grumet, Florence Shore, and Judy Torres, who read the manuscript and made very helpful suggestions. She is also grateful to the numerous individuals who were willing to be interviewed for this project.

Introduction

BY MAX B. SAWICKY

Doubts about government efficiency have embraced local public education, which in today's global economic environment is viewed as a near life-and-death matter for the nation's youth. While such doubts can be attributed in part to disappointment with the general shape of the economy and to anxiety over federal budget deficits, there can be no question that the public sector, including public schools, could benefit from ongoing trials of reform. This book examines one idea for education reform that has attracted the attention of local officials: hiring business firms to manage public schools or public school systems.

Contracting in public education is not new. Assorted tasks within schools, such as specialized instruction or food services, have been contracted out for decades. Moreover, public administrators have long relied on the services of consultants in the management of public schools. The projects examined in this book take contracting a giant step further, by transferring the management of entire schools or school systems to private firms.

The key findings that emerge from this study are the following:

- Actual experience in contracting out the management of public schools to business firms is rare. Business firms seeking such business are startups that have yet to demonstrate expertise. There remains no empirical evidence that such arrangements can improve public education, while failed experiences to date have cost communities money, time, effort, and morale. For reformers in search of *proven* innovations or demonstrated cost savings, contracting is the wrong option. It can be approached only as an experiment.

- We have yet to see genuine competition in the market for education management services. For contracting to provide the economic benefits commonly ascribed to it, governments must have a variety of choices and organize the contracting process to exploit competitive forces. Local governments have not been sensitive to the prerequisites for competition in education contracting, thus raising basic questions about their capacity to master the education market.

- A basic requirement for any educational reform, including contracting out, is establishment of an information system that will gather and report baseline data on student achievement and make possible rigorous evaluation of educational practices. To date, the limited efforts at contracting out have not placed a priority on information gathering or evaluation.

- There is no evidence that education contractors possess proprietary approaches to instruction that are superior to proven methods already in the public domain. The absence of such a rationale for private contracting diminishes the plausibility of the claim that business firms can simultaneously manage schools successfully, reduce public costs, and turn a profit.

- An important source of appeal for contractors has been offers to advance funds to their potential customers for such things as upgrades in physical plant and computer facilities. The lure of investments, however, reflects the frailties of local government finance more than any inherent advantage in contracting. Contractors are not the bankers of choice for local governments.

- One of the best-known exponents of contracting out management is Education Alternatives Inc. (EAI). However, EAI has failed to establish a reputation for corporate responsibility, to take effective control of the schools under its purview, to produce improvements in educational outcomes (despite the advantage of additional resources), or to demonstrate that it can make money managing public schools. To date the bulk of the company's cash flow has been derived from stock offerings and financial speculation.

2

- Using competition to advance education reform remains an interesting idea that deserves fair and rigorous trials. In Chapter 4, we offer recommendations on ways to approach contracting without forgetting that other pathways to reform are available as well. In any case, we do not take vouchers, contracting, or other market devices to be suitable substitutes for public policies that push schools to meet higher standards of accomplishment. Leadership and support from state and national government will be crucial to the success of education reform.

The chapters in this book adopt different approaches to the evaluation of business management of public schools. Chapter 1, by Rima Shore, is a comprehensive survey of the practice of contracting out in public education, and provides a broad historical background for the U.S. education system as a whole. Chapter 2, by Craig Richards, conducts a close financial analysis of the current industry leader in the field of educational contracting, Education Alternatives Inc., and an in-depth budgetary analysis of EAI's arrangement with the city of Baltimore, Md. Chapter 3, by Max Sawicky, draws from Shore and Richards to consider how economic theory and practical experience inform the concept of contracting out the management of public schools. The final chapter, by Sawicky, Richards, and Shore, focuses on the policy implications of the authors' findings.

The Birth and Reformation of American Education

Public support for education in the United States took root and developed in tandem with the birth and growth of the nation. As Rima Shore observes in the next chapter, the purpose of education went beyond the imparting of knowledge; it aimed to instill the value of citizenship. Such values as equity and inclusiveness became associated with the promotion of universal education. Horace Mann saw a salutary social outcome stemming from his belief that "if education be equably diffused, it will draw property after it."

Although contracting out to business concerns is older than the Republic, education developed in the United States as a service produced by government, not merely financed by it. In the earliest years of the

20th century, interest grew in the possibility of improving education by applying the methods of scientific management used in private industry. John Dewey, among others, took a dim view of such trends, fearing "there is danger that the concentrated interests of business men and their influential activity in public matters will segregate training for industry to the damage of both democracy and education." In other words, it was feared that business interests would propagate a form of education that was strictly limited to enabling students to function as employees.

The concept of accountability in education, which originated in the Taylorist, mass-production model of industrial organization,[1] began as a premise that the educational "product" could be accurately quantified, and that those responsible for producing the product could be provided with material incentives to provide more at less cost. This concept of accountability, under which responsibility is specified in terms of productivity, rewards, and sanctions, is distinct from the truism that public officials and employees must be held responsible for their performance. The tension between the demands for accountability on one side and democracy, equality, and citizenship on the other has been fought and refought many times throughout American history, Shore points out, and this push for accountability came to little.

In the decades following World War II, the central developments in education were the expansion of the educational system and the enlargement of the federal role. Both were fueled by the civil rights revolution and, after the launch of the Soviet satellite Sputnik in 1957, the promotion of educational progress as a dimension of national security. A renewed interest in accountability ensued, this time leading to a program of experimentation, sponsored by the federal Office of Economic Opportunity in the 1970s, known as "performance contracting." As with current initiatives, those experiments contemplated explicit measurement of and compensation for results, which would be defined chiefly in terms of test scores. Additional parallels include the focus on school districts with disproportionate numbers of low-income families; the grasp for technological fixes in the form of teaching machines that would supplant, to some extent, the need for human instruction; boosterism by business interests, which gave rise to grandiose, unredeemed claims and fatal haste in implementation; charges of contractor malfeasance, in the form of cheating in the administration or reporting of student tests; and the exclusion of educators' organizations from participation in the for-

4

mulation or governance of the arrangement, with predictable ensuing political turmoil.

Today's reconsideration of previously discredited initiatives stems in part from dissatisfaction with educational productivity. There is a widespread perception of a great infusion of resources into the public education system with no commensurate improvement in results. Even if the infusion has been overstated, as a recent Economic Policy Institute report (Rothstein and Miles 1995) shows, the demand for better results, by one means or another, will remain strong.

Current Efforts to Contract Out Management

There is to date little experience with hiring business firms to manage public schools or school systems. The industry leader, EAI, has run only nine public schools, and the arrangement was terminated as this study was being completed. EAI's role in Dade County, Fla., entailed only management consulting, and it was terminated as well. In Hartford, Conn., what began as a plan to run the entire system evolved into a tumultuous consulting relationship and unrealized plans for EAI to run five schools. Subsequently, the school board voted to "dissolve" its arrangement with EAI.

As of the beginning of 1996, the exhaustive list of private management efforts was also a short one. The Whittle/Edison Project began to run three schools in September 1995, a firm in Tennessee had a contract to run a single school, and a firm in Minneapolis held a contract to act as the school system's superintendent.[2]

The only track record thus far belongs to EAI in Dade County, Baltimore, and Hartford. Evaluations of the company's educational impacts in Dade County and Baltimore showed no gains relative to schools outside its purview. No evaluations of their usefulness in Hartford have been conducted, except for the city's summary judgment that the firm had to go. Similarly, its management outcomes (with respect to education, facilities, security, etc.) in Baltimore were no better than those in other schools used as benchmarks. For such little return, as Craig Richards shows, EAI had the benefit of significantly greater resources in Baltimore. If we accept the customers' judgments as final, EAI failed in all three locales.

To be fair, some latitude is called for in evaluating the efforts of EAI and other school-management firms, as the industry is in its infancy.

New firms in emerging markets might naturally be associated with above-average financial and investment risk. Also, their educational methods might be expected to evolve, in view of the firms' limited experience with implementation. Shore reports that, indeed, some advocates of contracting make the reasonable claim that a new program might need a decade before it can begin working to best advantage. But this likely time lag raises a risk: educational reform efforts are subject to influence by parents and public officials who want reforms to yield quick results. The implied political frustration could block viable reforms, encourage unrealistic demands by reformers and unrealizable claims by prospective contractors, or force a fatal haste in implementing the program.

Another key concern about the viability of contracting out school management is whether business firms can deliver the expected service and still make a profit. Richards shows that EAI has failed to profit from any of its efforts. (The company has reported earnings, but they can be attributed to interest on assets and capital gains from financial speculation, not to operations.) The bottom line, from the school or school system's point of view, is that it may be exposed to the contractor's financial risk. Indeed, Richards shows that EAI's investment operations are more risky than those of the typical local government. Public officials in Hartford and Baltimore have been wise in resisting EAI's demands for greater control over public revenues.

A related issue is the contractor's responsibility and integrity, qualities that are important in business relationships where trust, informal agreements, and continuous refining of the arrangement are crucial supplements to formal, written contracts. What may be tolerable or customary in some industries should be unacceptable in education contracting. Richards finds EAI's accounting practices legal but misleading, and news reports have noted EAI's inaccuracies and recalcitrance in reporting on its educational operations.

Finally, as to EAI's budgetary practices in Baltimore, Richards provides a detailed analysis showing that EAI enjoyed a substantial financial advantage in the schools under its control. On this account, other things being equal, it ought to have done better than similar schools outside its control, even if its own educational methods were no better than theirs. But EAI schools gave no clear sign of relative accomplishment, either in test scores or according to the independent evaluation arranged by Baltimore City. Rather than do more for less or for the same resource outlay, it did the same with more dollars. Again, given the short life of the Baltimore experience, the conclusion should not be overstated, but it remains the only real result in this entire field thus far.

Had EAI done better than comparable schools with the same money, the ways in which it used resources differently would be worth investigating. Richards shows that EAI shifted funds away from instructional expenditures and toward facilities, teacher training, and technology consulting. The latter two, not incidentally, were provided by EAI on the advice of EAI in its dual roles of manager and subcontractor. Its lack of success throws cold water on the thesis that deficiencies in these areas are at the root of school productivity shortfalls. It suggests that the problems with Baltimore's schools are not necessarily a matter of insufficient spending on technology or misguided efforts to reduce class size or to hire teachers with better credentials.

Contracting and Economic Theory

Is contracting a logical solution to the perceived problems of high education spending and poor educational outcomes? It is, after all, widely accepted by the public that competition and profit-seeking drive firms to greater levels of efficiency in the twin goals of minimizing costs and pleasing customers.

But as Max Sawicky points out, these two goals are not necessarily consistent. A firm might seek advantage over its rival by offering the same product at a lower price, but it might instead offer a different product that made a simple price comparison difficult. A Ford Taurus for $16,000 is better than an identical Taurus for $17,000, but it is not necessarily better than a Mercury for $17,000. In other words, cutthroat price competition might be softened by the availability of products with diverse characteristics. Education contracting clearly falls into this category. Contractors do not bid against each other for the job of delivering a particular average test score at the lowest price; rather, they emphasize the uniqueness of their educational methods. In fact, school management contracts typically do not specify educational performance criteria as the basis for the contractor's compensation.

The basic features of education itself widen the gap between education management services and traditional products supplied by firms in more competitive markets:

- *The education "contract" is not just between parents and school authorities.* The public interest in educating each child can outstrip the motivations of parents in two respects: universal education provides both societywide economic benefits and citizenship/values benefits that may be of little immediate concern to parents.

- *Defining the nature of education for purposes of contracting is difficult.* The nature of the educational product is inherently complex and difficult to define in terms useful in writing contracts or formulating productivity incentives.

- *Necessary regulation of the educational process undermines the rationale for contracting out.* Because its outcome is difficult to define, the manner in which education is provided becomes a point of interest and implies some degree of regulatory oversight. Insofar as the contractor must be regulated (that is, managed from without by public officials), there is less distinction between the contractor and a public agency and less rationale for using an outside organization.

The difficulty in defining and measuring "output" is common to all managers of the educational enterprise, whether public or private. Such difficulty challenges the manager's ability to specify productivity incentives for workers. In the absence of such incentives, the manager is reduced to stipulating and enforcing rules for how a job is to be done. This is precisely the way public agencies operate now.

The model of labor-management relations as it applies to management contracting in education is vulnerable to criticism. In general, firms may be thought to be competitive because they can use sanctions against workers for unsatisfactory performance. The implication is that labor turnover abets productivity. But long-term job tenure has been found to improve productivity. Moreover, the educational mission itself is built on long-term relationships between school employees and students. High turnover reduces the effectiveness of teachers, counselors, or disciplinarians whose job it is to deal with the same students over a sustained period. Those features make education contracting more difficult than contracting for things like highway construction or food service.

Accepting teachers and other professionals as partners in the governance of education, rather than as inputs with costs to be minimized, requires communication in a mutually acceptable manner and employment based on agreed-upon rules. Most public employees support the institution of civil service standards or collective bargaining as the medium for the employee-employer relationship. If only for its own sake, education management and reform must engage the institutions cooperatively.

Sawicky considers how basic competitive forces might work in a "market" for the management of public schools. Two important problems have been noted: there are few sellers, and they offer diverse products. Competition is best served by many sellers offering the same product so that the customer can comparison shop for the product with the lowest price. Industry failures recounted earlier will discourage investors and dampen expectations for a wave of new sellers. By 1996, EAI's share price had plummeted from its peak of $48 in 1993 to less than a tenth as much ($3.25 as of March 8, 1996). On two occasions, trading in the company's stock was suspended.

The number of sellers in a market depends on barriers to entry. In the case of education management, school districts may expect the contractor to advance them funds for upgrades to physical plant and computer facilities, as EAI and the Edison Project have done. That obligation limits the ability of firms or organizations with little capital to compete for contracts. One possible outcome is that some nonprofit organizations, which have a better record of achievement in education than do the well-capitalized business firms in this field, may be eliminated from contention.

The success of sellers in finding customers also depends on the flexibility, particularly the freedom to exit, that is possible for the customer. Some costs of reorganization are entailed in terminating a contract. There could also be a political penalty for public officials associated with the arrangement. Those factors reduce the willingness of potential customers to come forward.

It could be argued that public school authorities and parents are less interested in saving money and reducing expenditures than in getting better results. In this light, price competition recedes in importance in comparison to a contractor's perceived capacity to offer an innovative approach and to risk capital for investments in the customer's schools. But contractors' claims that they possess uniquely effective educational methods are questionable. Much research on educational effectiveness is in the public domain. Moreover, the use of an improved educational method or the incorporation of new technology or facility upgrades does not require contracting out the entire management of a school. In fact, the bundling of assorted functions (instruction, security, food service, maintenance, accounting) into a single management contract can obscure the savings that might be gained or lost in particular areas.

A special inducement to school districts has been contractors' offers of "investments," typically computer hardware, instructional software, and improvements in physical plant. Of course, any for-profit organization seeks to recover the costs of any such investments, with interest. In effect, the contractor could be said to be offering banking services by virtue of such arrangements. Given the financial records of some contractors, public school officials ought to look elsewhere for lenders. If such funds are not available through public borrowing, then it may be more advisable to reform the process of public investment than to reform the education system.

Implications for Public Policy

In the final chapter, the authors argue that, if local authorities are inclined to experiment with contracting, then they need to consider ways to exploit market forces to achieve better results. A key prerequisite for any reform is the availability of data on the workings of the school system and the performance of its students, so that the effects of reforms can be analyzed.

A basic operating principle is that local governments must understand that the obligation to organize a competitive market lies with them as the customer. Such markets will not necessarily take shape on their own, as previous experience with education contracting has shown. Organizing the market means, among other things, that the contracting initiative should be contingent on attracting a reasonable number of bidders, bidders should be required to conform to some set of specifications as to their obligations under the contract, the specifications should include measures of educational "output" on which the contractor's compensation will be based, and contractor performance should be subject to independent review. Average districtwide spending per pupil is a particularly poor criterion on which to base the contractor's fee, because the contractor's actual costs will depend on the specific characteristics of the schools under its jurisdiction. Contracts should be separated by logical function (e.g., instruction, security, food service) so that progress or problems in particular areas can be pinpointed.

Given the special nature of public education, some regulation of contractors will be called for. In addition to setting goals for instruction, a local government will need to consider the contractor's financial practices, its information reporting, its adherence to locally preferred labor standards, and its role in local politics.

Although contracting out has captured the imaginations of many school officials and local governments, it should be remembered that some alternative reform strategies, such as charter schools, public school choice, and school-based incentives, are no less promising. Furthermore, local reform efforts should be linked with statewide and national standards of educational accomplishment.

Hiring of business firms to manage schools may indeed represent the promised land, but first we need properly equipped expeditions to inform us of that. The terrain of education reform remains rugged, but it is not entirely unmapped. We hope this report illuminates previously uncharted territory and provides constructive directions for future exploration.

CHAPTER 1

A History and Survey of Contracting for Management Services in Public Education

BY RIMA SHORE

INTRODUCTION

"No more prizes for predicting rain. Prizes only for building arks." With this statement, IBM Chief Executive Louis Gerstner proclaimed the Noah principal—the tenet that as a nation we must now respond to the crisis of public education not with studies or strategies but with action. Gerstner was expressing the impatience, even exasperation, that many Americans feel as political and educational leaders continue to debate the best course for school reform and calculate the cost of inaction a full decade after the publication of *A Nation at Risk*—the 1983 document that alerted Americans to the dangers of widespread, inadequate schooling.

In the aftermath of that report, education was hoisted high on the national agenda. But according to the National Assessment of Educational Progress, a decade of school reform has failed to produce substantial improvement nationwide. Overall student achievement has fallen far short of citizens' expectations and employers' needs. International comparisons showing substantial gaps between American students and those in other developed countries (particularly in math and science) have been particularly demoralizing (Stevenson and Stigler 1992).

To be sure, the American educational system has made huge strides over the last century. In recent decades, our schools have provided access to public education to many children who had been unable to participate fully due to poverty, race, ethnicity, religion, gender, age, or physical or mental disabilities. Over the last quarter century, African American and Hispanic students have made gradual but steady progress. These are important achievements, but today the public discourse about American education tends to be preoccupied with failure (Graham 1993; Sizer 1992).

New Interest in Privatization

The desire for bold, comprehensive solutions has led numerous school districts to consider privatization as a route to dramatic school improvement. This study focuses on the practice of hiring private businesses to manage day-to-day operations, including instruction, at one or more public schools or for an entire local school system.

School districts have long sought outside help from the private and public sectors as they carried out the complex business of educating children. Hundreds of vendors provide a wide array of services and products to public schools—ranging from garbage collection to curricula, from bus service to instruction for Title I reading programs. These limited contracts and arrangements are not within the scope of this study. Rather, we are focusing on the practice of contracting out for comprehensive management services. In the 1990s, this practice has resurfaced, bolstered by wider interest and more resources. Until recently, Education Alternatives Inc. (EAI) was the market leader. A second company, the Edison Project, began managing four schools in the 1995-96 school year. Based on a strong first year, Edison has plans to operate an additional eight schools in 1996-97.

Substantial Investments, Scarce Evidence

Dozens of people in school systems, universities, professional associations, think tanks, and businesses were interviewed as background for this chapter.[3] Some argued vehemently that old governance structures have become obsolete, and that contracting out is one of a range of new mechanisms that will transform education as we know it. Others argued, just as forcefully, that privatization is simply the most recent, and potentially the most tarnished, of the silver bullets now being aimed at the public schools. Still others declared themselves agnostics, arguing that contracting out is fine when it is done well and disastrous when it is done badly.

Many of those interviewed agreed on one point: *rarely in the history of education have so many been willing to stake so much on the basis of so little evidence.* The handful of providers now competing for major contracts offer little hard data on the impact of their methods on students, teachers, schools, or communities. School districts are being asked to make large investments in contracts with private companies without benefit of systematic, rigorously designed evaluations of existing efforts. Some school boards and community groups therefore have rejected proposals from these firms. Parents—even those displeased with school performance—remain widely skeptical about market-based education; only 10% of parents surveyed recently by *Public Agenda* supported privatization efforts.

Despite such setbacks, the privatization trend appears to be putting down sturdy roots. Many school boards and communities seem to be judging prospective contractors not on the basis of outputs but on the basis of inputs—the educational credentials and experience of their executives, the research and development that underlies their approach, or the upfront investments they offer to make in a school district's facilities.

As the major players line up contracts, numerous other companies—ranging from start-up firms to Fortune 500 corporations—are poised to enter the marketplace. Some, like EAI and Edison, are systems changers, dedicated to transforming the operation of schools or school districts. Others are niche operators, serving particular populations or filling specific functions. Still others are curriculum and technology providers, furnishing schools and school districts with curricula and learning systems. The focus of this study is on those offering to run schools in their entirety as opposed to providing specific services, products, or management consulting to publicly managed schools. The latter is more in the tradition of public education, while the former is a more radical departure from existing arrangements.

A variety of indicators suggests that the markets are expanding. In 1994, when Portsmouth, Va., issued a request for proposals for educational management services, 22 firms—both national and local—showed up at the bidders' conference. A newsletter, *The Education Industry Report* (formerly known as *The Education Investor*), tracks development in the market; it has a subscription base of several thousand. The publisher, John McLaughlin, estimates that hundreds of players are positioning themselves to enter the field. McLaughlin also was commissioned by the National School Boards Association to prepare a handbook, which will be distributed initially to 15,000 school boards around the nation, explaining the advantages and mechanisms of contracting.

Overview of This Chapter

This chapter presents the history of contracting in public education and surveys developments on the national scene. It begins by placing the issue of contracting in political, legal, and historical perspectives, and then describes the factors that have swelled the demand for private management services in the 1990s. The chapter then surveys today's marketplace, summarizes what we know about recent educational outcomes of contracting, and discusses what we have yet to learn about its impact on students, schools and school districts, and communities. Finally, it offers conclusions and suggests some directions that privatization might take in coming years.

Summary of Major Findings

This chapter reaches several major conclusions:

- None of the current experiments in privatization has achieved the results that were predicted or promoted by its advocates. Despite higher levels of per-pupil spending and significant investments in program enhancements, none of the recent privatization efforts has, thus far, produced clear-cut gains in student achievement. There have been very few independent evaluations of significant scope, and neither venders nor consumers have pushed forcefully for closer scrutiny of outcomes.

- Despite mixed results, the practice of contracting for management seems to be here to stay, at least for the foreseeable future. In coming years, the market may be driven by the interest and resources of investors who see vast potential in the education marketplace. Second, the challenges of public schooling are so daunting that few educators will reject, out of hand, proposals that promise an infusion of resources into the system. The question surrounding privatization initiatives in public schooling is not whether interest in them will persist, but what forms they will take and how they might be shaped to serve the public interest.

- For the moment, the supply of companies that have the capacity and the will to enter this risky market remains limited, and the demand, while growing, is not huge. If privatization is to serve the public interest, in education as in other fields, it requires a lively marketplace where organizations of different kinds can compete, goading or inspiring each other to boost both quality and efficiency. In today's educational marketplace, those conditions do not yet exist. However, the contracts won by for-profit companies may encourage a variety of other organizations to join the fray, including research centers, school-university collaboratives, cultural institutions, trade unions, groups of teachers from successful neighborhood schools, parent groups, or community-based organizations.

- The history of private management of public schools is rooted in the history of performance contracting, a practice that was found to carry some risks. Venders—especially publicly owned companies—might reap profits without assuring quality or improving achievement, by creating conditions in which the value of their stock will rise. Privatization may allow or encourage some communities to relinquish direct responsibility for public schools, especially those that enroll large numbers of low-income and minority children. Finally, when privatization entails an increase in the use of technology that is associated with the use of fewer full-time teachers, it may weaken crucial bonds between teachers and students.

• At the end of the day, the failure of privatization experiments may indirectly benefit schools and school districts. If a corporation cannot raise student achievement, despite expenditures that exceed those of the public school district, then the American public may begin to come to terms with the fact that schools are not always the wasteful, inefficient institutions they are thought to be, and that adequate public school funding and equity are absolutely crucial to our children's achievement and well-being.

PUBLIC AND PRIVATE

On January 25, 1994, a Senate appropriations subcommittee met to hear testimony on the private management of public schools. Executives from EAI and Edison—the two leading private contractors for instructional services—presented the case for privatization, emphasizing accountability and efficiency. Opponents of privatization, including a leader of the American Federation of Teachers, emphasized the shaky record and considerable risks of contracting out. A fundamental, underlying question is why government ought to provide education directly to begin with, rather than merely finance it.

Why public education? What do we mean by public? How did the idea evolve that public officials ought to be responsible for planning and delivering instruction to America's children, as well as be accountable for their achievement? And what is likely to happen if that assumption is abandoned?

Schools and the Public

In the United States, education is a state responsibility. Today, all states have legislation authorizing local education agencies to establish and run public schools. The result is a national public school system consisting of some 15,000 local school districts. Governments in the local districts own, finance, and operate their public schools. Public ownership has long been considered an essential attribute of public education in the United States—but advocates of "contracting out" point out that that is not the case in many other nations. In Britain, Australia, France, and Canada, local public school agencies typically fund schools, but they do not always own or operate them. In those countries, publicly funded schools may be run by independent organizations, including religious organizations. Indeed, the United States is one of the few industrialized countries where it is assumed that public schools will be operated by a government agency (Hill 1994).

Some policy analysts offer models from abroad as evidence that our nation can and should maintain a public school system without relying exclusively on government employees to carry out the day-to-day tasks of educating children. Paul T. Hill argues that education is "public" when it is funded by the public, when admissions policies are set by the public, and when goals are, at least to some extent, shaped by the public. He believes that schools must be publicly regulated to avoid racial discrimination, and must be accountable for performance to elected public bodies. "The difference between my definition and the common definition," he says, "is that public education does not have to be run by civil servants in a public bureaucracy." In that model, government is a provider, but not necessarily a producer, of educational services.

Others argue that public operation of schools is the best way to ensure inclusivity and equity, and that the goals of democratic education—including college preparation for anyone who wants it—do indeed set American schooling apart from education in other nations.

They contend that once a function is privatized, government tends to relinquish responsibility for controlling that function (Hunter 1995). They point out, moreover, that when education is public, the district's instructional leader generally comes to office by way of parent and community advocacy. Superintendents may not be elected, but they generally have strong ties to the community and are accountable to it. When superintendents delegate key decisions about curriculum, instruction, and staffing to corporate executives, they are in effect abdicating the leadership responsibility invested in them by their core constituencies, and weakening their commitment to equity.

Who Is in Control?

There have always been stretches along the border between public and private education where the line is blurred. For example, federal law mandates that when public schools cannot provide an appropriate education to a student with an educational disability, it must pay a private institution to provide those services. Public funds now support tuition at private schools for about 60,000 children with disabilities (Payzant 1994).

Over the last five years, the privatization movement obscured an already fuzzy line. It sometimes strained the ability of spokespeople for schools and private companies to describe the new reality. The media routinely announced, for example, that a company like EAI or Edison would be "managing" or "operating" a school or a school district. The companies themselves generally said in their public relations materials that they were entering a "partnership" with the public school district, but they did little to dispel the notion that they were, in essence, managing the school or a district. School officials acknowledged that they were, in some cases, turning over tax dollars to the contractors, and that in those instances the company would be paying all the bills and making day-to-day decisions about curriculum, instruction, staffing, and budgeting. In that sense, school officials were literally "passing the bucks," but they bristled at the notion that they were abdicating responsibility for the children entrusted to their care.

Case in point: EAI's original contract to manage the entire Hartford, Conn., school district. EAI's promotional literature fudged the issue of who would be in control; it stated that Hartford would be the first district in the nation to "manage all of its 32 schools through a public-private partnership." But the company's position was clear. EAI described its mission as the "private management of public schools." The basic stump speech of EAI Chairman John T. Golle is entitled, "Operating Public Schools: A Private Sector Perspective" (Golle 1994).

According to Hartford school officials, EAI was not engaged to "run" the schools, but rather to help the Board of Education put in place a long-term plan that the board devised but was unable to implement. They claimed that this arrangement would free the superintendent, Dr. Eddie Davis, to focus on academic issues, especially in area of standards and curriculum (Judson 1995).

Phyllis Cohen is adamant on that point. She is deputy superintendent for instructional leadership in Dade County, Fla., where EAI had a five-year contract to provide services to South Pointe Elementary School—the deal that put EAI on the map in 1990. The contract ended in June 1995, and Dade County school officials opted not to renew, saying the relationship with EAI had always been viewed as experimental and short-term.

Cohen denies that EAI ran South Pointe. "We use the Tesseract model [EAI's instructional system] as far as the teaching is concerned, but EAI does not have anything to do with any part of the school administration," she said in an interview, shortly before the decision was made not to continue the experiment. "It's *our* principal, *our* support staff, *our* teachers...."

Legal Implications

Understandably, all of those individuals are eager to position themselves, in the public eye, as responsible and accountable. But the question of who is in control reaches well beyond public relations or local politics. The issue of the delegation of authority has crucial legal implications.

"One of the barriers to [school] reform is an issue called the delegation of authority," says Dean Millot, an attorney and social scientist associated with the Rand Corporation. "Different states have different attitudes about the extent to which local government agencies can delegate decisions and authority which were granted to them by the legislature." He notes that American public schools have always contracted for equipment and supplies, as well as for auxiliary services like trash removal or cafeteria management. But from a legal standpoint, there are important distinctions between those kinds of services and the provision and management of instruction. "When you contract out food services, the school board establishes who will participate and what they will eat, and there are a lot of specifications that can be included, such as nutritional content," Millot says. "So the board seems to be making the decisions. But when you're talking about an educational program and saying to a contractor, in effect, 'you determine how to best meet state requirements,' you may arguably be delegating authorities which are beyond the power and authority of the school board to delegate...."

In that sense, the definition of "public education" becomes a legal problem, and will inevitably be taken up by the courts as individuals and groups, such as parent associations or teachers unions, challenge the right of local school boards to contract out educational services to private vendors. Says Millot, "It comes down to some very basic philosophical points about the role of government and government agencies, and the extent to which the legislature is the dominant factor in the political process."

Public and Private in Historical Perspective

The practice of contracting out school management to private companies throws into question the role of government in preparing children to become productive adults. This is hardly a new challenge. Battles about who should control schools and who should attend them have often been fought in our nation's political arena. In colonial New England, where many communities established schools, taxpayers were often unwilling to support public education, and records from town meetings reflect their insistence that parents should take responsibility for educating their own children (Vinovskis 1987). In tracing the history of U.S. public education from its earliest beginnings, we can also follow the thread leading to today's debate over privatization and gain some insight in the process.

In the first years of nationhood, some Americans argued that the public had a stake in the education of future citizens. Stressing the intellectual demands of citizenry, Thomas Jefferson advocated three years of compulsory public education for the sons of free citizens. Public education was a key element in the programs of the Working Men's parties founded in the early 19th century. In the late 1820s and early 1830s, many labor leaders called for free, equal, and universal education. One 1829 paper called for "a national education calculated to make republicans and banish aristocrats" (Cohen and Barnes 1995).

But the notion of public schools continued to meet considerable resistance. As Horace Mann reportedly acknowledged to the audience at a Waltham, Mass., school convention in 1836, "Many are unwilling to send their children to the public schools because they are subject so much to the town.—They ask: why is all this interference in schools, the choice of books, times of attendance? They consider the school committee as an obtrusion.—They say: are not the children our own?" (cited in Grumet 1988).

Mann made the case that the public has a stake in the development of the children who "will soon have the rights of citizenship" and will become "blessings or curses" to society. Echoing Jefferson's views, he argued that political participation requires considerable intellectual capacity, and that only universal education, fostering critical thought, would provide the social glue needed to hold the nation together. He also associated public education with equity and social justice, arguing optimistically that "if education be equably diffused, it will draw property after it" (cited in Cohen and Barnes 1995, 5)

Mann was instrumental in the enactment, in 1852, of the nation's first compulsory attendance statute by the Massachusetts legislature. However, resistance to public education remained strong, and compulsory schooling was not universal nationwide until it was mandated by Mississippi in 1918 (Russo et al. 1995). Even after compulsory attendance laws were passed, they were frequently evaded and did not have a decisive impact on public education until the turn of the century (Vinovskis 1987).

"The Concentrated Interests of Business Men"

As compulsory public schooling finally took hold in the early years of this century, the dramatic enrollment boom posed daunting organizational, logistical, and financial challenges, shaking public confidence in public education. In the early decades of this century, a reform movement sprang up that demanded more efficient governance and management of public schools. Stirred by the views of Frederick W. Taylor, an early proponent of "scientific management," critics argued that schools were deplorably inefficient and desperately in need of the kinds of economic tools used by well-run businesses. In 1913, Frank Spaulding, superintendent of the Newton, Mass., public schools, addressed the national convention of the National Education Association, and described his successful introduction of scientific management to the Newton schools. In the same year, Franklin Bobbitt published *The Supervision of the City Schools*, recasting the school administrator in the role of Taylor's plant manager (Guttenberg 1971a).

The scientific management movement took hold over the next several years, as superintendents all over the nation bowed to demands by businessmen on their school boards and tax rolls to boost efficiency. Among the innovations brought about by scientific management in the century's early decades was the introduction of efficiency experts, who won high-priced consulting contracts to revamp school management— an early instance of "contracting out" to private-sector vendors. Many educators welcomed this development. George Strayer of Columbia Teachers College, for example, made the case that professional managers would bring more efficient administration to public education, and that men with experience in business and higher education would move school boards away from the self-interest and corruption of ward politics toward disinterested professionalism (Cohen and Barnes 1995).

Other educators, notably John Dewey and his colleagues in the left wing of the Progressive movement, had a very different notion of school reform. Dewey warned against the influence of corporate leaders on education, observing in 1915 that "...there is danger that the concentrated interests of business men and their influential activity in public matters will segregate training for industry to the damage of both democracy and education...." (Dewey and Dewey 1915). Inefficiency, he argued, was far less perilous for a democratic society, and far less injurious to children, than inequality and social fragmentation. Like Horace

Mann, he saw public schooling as a kind of social glue, a source of coherence and community. In his view, school reform was nothing less than an effort to repair a social and moral fabric frayed by the divisive force of capitalist industrialism (Cohen and Barnes 1995).

By 1920, scientific management had alienated many teachers, but most were not protected by tenure; only in cities where teachers unions had already formed were they able to fight successfully against this trend. By 1930, a reaction set in against scientific management, and the movement lost its hold on American education. But over two decades the "cult of efficiency" had left its mark, recasting school organizations in the industrial mold; burdening classroom teachers with scores of clerical tasks; and creating a demand for school leaders who were bottom-line-oriented managers rather than inspiring scholars or curriculum developers (see Callahan 1962).

This extremely compressed account of two centuries of public schooling is meant to suggest that today's controversy over contracting reflects a tension that has persisted through the entire history of American education. The public has long been divided over the rationale for public schooling, the goals of public education, and the role of the private sector in educating its future workforce.

The Federal Role Expands

The decades after World War II saw a dramatic expansion of the federal role in education. Two major events of the 1950s catalyzed this movement. *Brown v. Board of Education of Topeka*, the landmark 1954 Supreme Court ruling, challenged the traditional autonomy of state and local school authorities by prohibiting legally mandated racial segregation in public schools. *Brown* strengthened the civil rights movement and over the next decade lifted racial discrimination, poverty, and ineffective schools to the top of the national agenda. The launch of the Sputnik satellite by the Soviet Union in 1957 undermined Americans' confidence in their public schools. In response, Congress passed the National Defense Education Act—setting a legislative precedent by providing federal assistance to local schools (Jost 1994).

During the 1960s, education was considered a crucial weapon in the War on Poverty and a key element in the legislation passed to wage that war. The programs that resulted, such as the Elementary and Secondary Education Act (ESEA) Title I programs, the Job Corps, and Head

Start, did have a significant impact on student achievement and access to higher education, although their funding increasingly was cut to meet the demands of the conflict in Vietnam.

With an expanded federal role came increasing demands for accountability. Today, these calls are so frequent and insistent that accountability sometimes seems like an old, enduring feature of American education. In fact, it is a relatively recent phenomenon. "In the old days," Robert Havighurst has written, "a teacher's responsibility was limited to maintaining an orderly classroom in which pupils could concentrate on their schoolwork and 'recite' what they had learned. It was understood that some pupils would fail, perhaps because they were 'lazy' or 'not bright,' but that was their fault, or their nature, and they or their parents were responsible for their failure. The teacher was accountable for *teaching* and the pupil was accountable for *learning*" (Havighurst 1972, original emphasis).

The passage of ESEA in 1965 changed all that. In 1970, Leon M. Lessinger wrote, "A growing number of people are becoming convinced that we can hold a school—as we hold other agencies of government— to account for the results of their activity." He noted that "educators are put in the position of reporting results for funds expended," and called this demand for accountability "a most radical departure from present-day practices" (cited in Mickler 1984, 92). The new and intense demands for accountability led directly to a phenomenon known as performance contracting.

Performance Contracting

In the late 1960s, a number of officials left positions at the U.S. Department of Defense and formed the Institute for Politics and Planning (IPP). Arthur Barber headed the group. Barber had earned a physics degree at Harvard University and had developed electronics systems for the Air Force before joining the Defense Department as assistant deputy secretary for East-West relations, under Paul Nitze. IPP's vice president, responsible for educational programs, was Frank Sloan, who also worked under Nitze as deputy assistant secretary for Southeast Asia, with responsibility for Vietnam. Barber and Sloan were joined by Charles L. Blaschke, who, as an army lieutenant, had served on Barber's staff at the Defense Department.

Those officials left the Pentagon during the Johnson Administration and set up IPP, a Washington-based group determined to apply state-of-the-art planning and management technologies, developed for the military, to public policy. Barber recalls that their board included Harvard University Professor Henry Kissinger.

"We came out of the Kennedy administration," Barber says. "We had a we-can-lick-the-world attitude." Public schools were a prime focus of their efforts, despite the fact that they had virtually no formal training in educational policy or administration. They were aware of the work of the education researchers, like James Coleman, who were applying analytic methods to education policy and planning. Numerous works on that topic had appeared in the late 1950s and early 1960s, beginning with a monograph called *Systems Analysis and Education* by two Rand Corporation researchers, J.A. Kershaw and R.N. McKean (1959). They were also aware of the accountability movement in education (see, for example, Lessinger 1970). But for the most part, they were skeptical about the education establishment. "The professional education people and the technology people coming out of [the Defense Department] were in different worlds," Barber recalls. "We were operating on a separate track. I don't ever remember going to a professional education meeting."

Their views on public education were shaped in the Pentagon, where Defense Secretary Robert McNamara's "whiz kids" were refining the management tools that McNamara had introduced so successfully at Ford Motor Co. Barber recalls considerable discussion—including several conversations initiated by McNamara—about why the military was so much more effective in training young people than the public schools were. His understanding was that the "training gap" was also a subject of conversation between Secretary McNamara and President Kennedy.

"Our idea," says Barber, "was to do some thinking about [education] policy and then go and do it. We didn't want to just write papers." At the Defense Department, Barber and his associates—particularly Blaschke—had been involved in contracting out the design and manufacture of complex weapons systems. Indeed, the practice of contracting was so prevalent in the Pentagon that Peter Schenck of Raytheon Corporation commented, in 1969, that "there are highly placed military men who sincerely feel that industry is currently setting the pace in the research and development of new weapons systems" (cited in Carson 1980).

Convinced that the same reliance on industry would yield results in education, the men who formed IPP introduced into the educational sphere the concept of "performance contracting"—the process of issuing a request for proposals (RFP) and getting private, for-profit companies to say how they would raise achievement and for what cost. In designing the new educational strategy, they adapted the methods described by Frederick M. Scherer in a 1964 study entitled *The Weapons Acquisition Process: Economic Incentives* (cited in Guttenberg 1971b). Richard Guttenberg, who joined IPP as a Columbia Teachers College graduate student intern and then spent a year on staff, described the ethos of the organization this way: "Their attitude was: if it can be thought of, it can be planned, and if it can be planned, it can be done. Kids can't read? No problem. If we can contract out for a complex weapons system, a reading system is a piece of cake."

While they were operating on a "separate track," as Barber recalls, there were parallel developments in the field of education. The notion of accountability was, during this period, being refined and applied to all levels of public schooling. But by all accounts, the former Defense Department officials were the first to put theory systematically into practice. They looked for funding, and found that the Model Cities Agency was willing, in principle, to use antipoverty funds to support their initiative, particularly if potential dropouts could be targeted for services. So IPP set about looking for a school district that would try it out.

The Texarkana Experiment

Initially, there were few takers. Over time, a small number of districts, mostly in the South, expressed some interest. Stymied by their students' consistently poor showings on standardized tests, their school boards were willing to take a chance on an untested intervention. The first site— Texarkana—became the most visible and, ultimately, the most notorious experiment in performance contracting.

IPP entered into a technical assistance contract with Texarkana (Arkansas District Number 7 and the Liberty Eylau District in Texas) and brokered the deal. Model Cities Agency funding was secured, and an RFP was sent to more than 100 firms, including numerous defense contractors. As policy analysts noted in 1969, "Corporations traditionally engaged in personnel training and the development of complex defense systems were expected to have little trouble in developing new ap-

proaches and techniques for educating and training the disadvantaged"
(Levitan and Mangum 1969). Although the dollar value of the contract
was small, an impressive array of private companies took notice: approximately 40 firms sent representatives to the bidders' conference,
and 10 submitted written proposals. Bidders included subsidiaries of
Westinghouse (Westinghouse Learning Corporation) and McGraw-Hill
(Educational Development Laboratories). Several defense contractors
submitted bids, including Raytheon Corporation. General Learning Systems, Dorsett Education Systems, and a small company called Quality
Educational Development (QED) also submitted proposals. Guttenberg
recalls that most of the companies had names that included "systems"
or "laboratory," signifying their scientific approach to educational issues. Most touted some form of educational technology. Educational
Development Laboratories, for example, proposed to introduce the
"Tachtistiscope"—a machine that projected slides and filmstrips on large
or small screens, offering individuals or groups of students self-paced
reading exercises.

In September 1969, Dorsett Education Systems, run by Lloyd Dorsett
of Norman, Okla., won the contract. Dorsett agreed to provide two hours
per day of reading and mathematics instruction to 300 "potential dropouts," and set up "Rapid Learning Centers" in existing schools—some
in mobile facilities, others in remodeled classrooms. The centers were
refurbished, offering air conditioning, carpeting, and upholstered furni-
ture. Dorsett's instructional design relied on technology, including audiovisual units of the company's own design, programmed instructional
materials, and a method known as "contingency management"—an instructional strategy based on stimulus-response theory in psychology
(Guttenberg 1971b). Paraprofessionals were hired to assist in the centers. According to the contract, the company would be paid only if students reached agreed-upon achievement levels. The level of compensation was tied to the extent of the gains (Jost 1994).

Dorsett extended the performance contracting principle to students
and employees: he introduced a system of rewards for meeting specific
performance goals. The company offered students green stamps, tran-
sistor radios, and a portable television. Teachers apparently were offered stock options in the firm. But the incentive system—touted as one
of the program's "revolutionary" features—became bogged down in
management difficulties and was never carried out to any great extent

(Guttenberg 1971b). During the first year of operation, the system was plagued by technical problems. For example, day-to-day rewards (green stamps) were awarded on the basis of successful completion of certain machine-programmed material; when the machines were inoperative (as often happened), the incentive system broke down as well, causing intense frustration among participants (Garms and Guttenberg 1970).

Guttenberg, who later became the director of evaluation and assessment for New York City's public schools, recalls that the evaluation plan for Texarkana was primitive and included few controls. Early reports suggested astonishing gains for 59 students tested after only five months of instruction: on the average, scores went up 1.4 grade levels in math and 2.2 grade levels in reading. Those outcomes were reported by the media, including a prominent story in the *Wall Street Journal*. Based on the preliminary results, early in 1970 the Office of Economic Opportunity (OEO), headed by Donald Rumsfeld, decided to expand the experiment. "The idea that OEO had was a very simplistic one," says Paul Hill, who worked for OEO at the time. "You just give people cash incentives for student performance and they will deliver."

Expanding the Experiment

Thomas K. Glennan Jr., who was OEO's director of research at the time, recalls that "OEO was attempting to position itself as the analytic arm [of federal government] that would test new, programmatic, social interventions. What we rapidly decided to do was to create a good experimental design and to test this intervention, and that's how the thing came into being...." The key word was "rapidly." The decision to proceed was made in April 1970. Determined to get performance contracting up and running at multiple sites by the time schools opened in September, OEO rushed headlong into the planning and bidding processes.

By this time, Charles Blaschke had left IPP and had spun off his own three-person consulting firm, Education Turnkey Systems. OEO hired Blaschke's firm to implement and oversee performance contracting projects at sites across the nation—from Anchorage, Alaska, to the Bronx, N.Y. By July 1971, 20 school boards in 17 states had negotiated performance contracts with six companies, supported by $6.5 million of OEO funding. Each site served 600 disadvantaged students in grades 1-3 and 7-9 (Guttenberg 1971b).

"Send the Salesmen..."

OEO's rapid action was, in part, politically motivated. Richard Nixon had recently taken office as president, and White House staffers were eager to put a Republican spin on poverty and education programs. Thomas Glennan notes that the White House liked the idea of a "more rational approach to making social policy." Peter Briggs recalls that the point man for performance contracting in the White House was Chester Finn, an aide to White House Counsel Daniel Patrick Moynihan.

Inside-the-beltway politics was not the sole consideration. The project also reflected keen interest in contracting among school board members across the nation, who were intrigued by the notion of guaranteed results. A survey conducted in 1970 found that two out of three board members supported the idea of performance contracting—although half of those favoring the idea expressed some reservations. Respondents gave two major reasons for their support: a drop in their confidence in teachers, who seemed more interested in negotiating better deals for themselves than in accepting responsibility for outcomes; and growing awareness that boards were being held accountable for student achievement. Opponents said that performance contracting would dehumanize schools, and argued that the notion that learning could be "guaranteed" was naive (Webb 1970).

In the early months of 1971, the National School Boards Association sponsored a series of five conferences across the nation to familiarize board members and administrators with performance contracting. Announcements of the conferences that appeared in the *American School Board Journal* in January 1971, called performance contracting "a concept that may change the face of education in the 1970s."

At the same time, teacher groups, including the American Federation of Teachers, staunchly resisted performance contracting. AFT President David Selden called it "hucksterism." ("He had a point," says Richard Guttenberg, who was decidedly unimpressed by some of the entrepreneurs bidding on early contracts.) AFT statements charged that school districts were being captured by the "Industrial-Educational Complex"—a term they abbreviated as IEC. The union announced that it was setting up three "IEC monitoring posts" to evaluate proposed contracts and alert communities to the implications of performance contracting.[4] The terms were not merely echoes of the political rhetoric of the day; they apparently were meant to draw attention to the roots of

OEO-FUNDED PERFORMANCE CONTRACTORS
Alpha Systems
Association of Teachers
Learning Foundations
Plan Education Centers
Quality Education Development
SingerGraflex

OTHER PERFORMANCE CONTRACTORS
Behavioral Research Laboratories
Combined Motivation Education Systems
Dorsett Educational Systems
Educational Solutions
Larabee and Associates
Learning Research Associates
New Century/Communications Patterns
Thiakol Chemical Corp.
Westinghouse Learning

SUBCONTRACTORS
Audio-Visual Supply Company
Open Court Publishing

performance contracting in the Pentagon.

Despite union opposition, the movement took hold. "Just send the salesmen in to see us," board members from seven states reportedly chorused when surveyed by the *American School Board Journal*. Between 1970 and 1972, performance contracting spread well beyond the bounds of the OEO experiment. In addition to the six companies funded by OEO, at least nine other contractors and two subcontractors entered the market, winning bids from more than 25 communities (see list).[5] Dorsett Educational Systems won additional contracts to set up reading programs in several Colorado schools. Among the new contractors was Thiakol Chemical Corporation, which secured a contract to run a program for 875 high school students in Dallas, Texas. Peter Briggs, Blaschke's second-in-command at Education Turnkey Systems, recalls that a number of the bidders, including Thiakol, had already made forays into public-sector education by running Job Corps camps in the late 1960s and were eager to leverage this experience in the education market.

Compared to the lucrative deals some of the companies were accustomed to making, the contracts were slight. But, as Peter Briggs points out, "businesses saw these early contracts as a foothold into a growing and potentially huge market. The Feds alone were pouring three to four billion a year into education, and this in itself was an incentive to go after some of those contracts."

The Case of Gary, Indiana

In one of the best-known cases of performance contracting, the Gary, Ind., Board of Education engaged the services of a California-based company, Behavioral Research Laboratories, to manage all aspects of Banneker Elementary School. That model, which the literature of the time referred to as "total prime contracting," was a departure from most performance contracts of the early 1970s, which involved "limited subcontracting." That is, they provided a limited array of services to a specific population within a school or school system (Guttenberg 1971b).

In contrast, Gary's contract called for the company to receive $800 for each of the school's 800 students—the total cost of educating a Gary pupil at that time. In return, the company agreed to bring achievement scores up to or above national grade levels in basic curriculum areas. The company promised to use innovative methods, emphasizing individualized instruction, to achieve its goals. There was a money-back guarantee: at the end of three years, the company would refund the fee paid for any child who did not achieve this goal, and independent evaluators would be engaged to make this determination.[6]

The AFT expressed severe reservations about the Gary project. Teachers were transferred from the school to accommodate the staffing patterns introduced by the company. Critics also noted that class size had increased: one teacher and two paraprofessionals worked with groups of 40 children, relying heavily on self-paced materials.

The Experiment Unravels

The experiment did not survive long enough to allow longitudinal study. The heady enthusiasm that had greeted performance contracting early in 1970 evaporated when the news broke that in Texarkana, Dorsett had been letting some students preview items from the tests that were used to measure their progress. Results at other sites appeared to be uncontaminated, but a negative program evaluation issued in 1972 sealed the fate of performance contracting. The evaluation found "very little evidence that performance incentive contracting...had a beneficial effect on the reading and mathematics achievement of students participating in the experiment" (Battelle Columbus Laboratories 1972).

Why was the experiment shut down so fast? Most accounts of performance contracting suggest that the Texarkana testing scandal effectively ended the experiment. Embarrassing revelations were especially unwelcome at a time when the Nixon administration was struggling with Watergate damage control. Moreover, inter- and intra-agency rivalry may have been on the minds of the project's supporters. OEO had stepped on some influential toes when it wandered into territory usually controlled by the Department of Health, Education, and Welfare (HEW) (predecessor of the Department of Education and the Department of Health and Human Services). In testimony before a Senate appropriations subcommittee, moreover, OEO had been taken to task for encroaching on the turf of the United States Office of Education. For all those reasons—and doubtless others—the experiment had become a political liability. Charles Blaschke says, "We know the [evaluation] report came out six months premature, right before the appropriations hearings for OEO's continuation."

But Thomas Glennan insists that OEO's performance contracting experiment began and ended on schedule, and that it had been set up, from the start, as a one-year test. He acknowledges that the whole thing was "done too fast," adding that the companies involved "vastly underestimated what it would take to get results in schools." They failed to realize that, as Keith Geiger, president of the National Education Association, recently wrote, "Pupil progress is hard won, and even the best of schools have only limited leverage on pupil performance" (Geiger 1995).

"It was a measure of our hubris," says Peter Briggs, "that even though we knew there would be implementation problems, we thought we could get it up and running in a year."

Looking back on the performance contracting experiment, a number of observers argue that the concept had not gotten a fair test: start-up schedules left too little time for program design, and evaluation was undertaken too soon. Peter Briggs charges that in the assessment process, there was foul play on both sides. He contends that teachers at OEO's Bronx site created such adverse conditions for the post-test that, for example, the children were moved to a rented movie theater on the Grand Concourse to take the test, and were escorted there by city police.

Moreover, union opposition had been immediate and relentless, especially because teachers were rarely if ever consulted or involved in program design. The American Federation of Teachers called for the abolition of performance contracting, and adopted a resolution urging all AFT locals to "educate their members and boards of education, as well as parent and community groups, as to the educationally negative aspects of performance contracting." In particular, the AFT opposed the incentive schemes associated with the model, arguing that it would not be possible to develop the appropriate criteria or unbiased measurements needed to implement such plans. The National Education Association also opposed performance contracting, and an NEA representative appeared before the Senate appropriations subcommittee hearings on the OEO budget to register objections to the experiment. Many local teachers organizations, such as the San Diego Teachers Association and the Washington Teachers Union, actively opposed performance contracting in their cities. It was no coincidence that performance contracting took hold first in Texarkana, where the local teachers association was weak (Garms and Guttenberg 1970).

All those factors undoubtedly contributed to the demise of performance contracting. However, the major reason for its failure was the fact that upholstery, carpeting, and teaching machines could not, by themselves, meet schools' and parents' expectations of immediate and substantial academic progress. Stanford Professor Henry Levin points out that the project's failure stemmed from glib, flawed analysis of the problem it was meant to solve. "...The contractors and [the] OEO people bought the view that schools aren't doing well because they don't have bright people, or they're not trying....They had thought that teaching kids...to read or to do math is push-button stuff....They overstated the possibilities."

The performance contracting experiment began and ended quickly, but there is little reason to believe that more time would have yielded better results. After all, the experiment was sold as an inexpensive, cost-effective solution to educational problems—a boon to taxpayers— and made no provision for research and development. As Guttenberg

notes, contractors were expected to have fully developed "learning systems" on hand; the companies, not the school system or the funder, were
expected to absorb the cost of making any adjustments or further developments in the systems. It became quickly evident that the contractors'
off-the-shelf teaching machines and teacher-proof materials would not
produce the hoped-for results. Realizing that, in the absence of R&D,
time would not solve the problem, OEO was apparently eager to cut its
losses.

Once federal support was withdrawn, performance contracting became history. As Alex Molnar of the University of Wisconsin comments,
"It disappeared without a blip on the radar screen" (cited in Jost 1994,
276).

WHY NOW?

Twenty years after performance contracting vanished, the idea of contracting out instructional services reappeared on the scene.[7] A few of the individuals who had been involved in performance contracting were at the forefront of privatization efforts in the late 1980s and early 1990s. Chester Finn, who has been described as the "go-between" linking the OEO experiment to the Nixon White House, was one of the early principals in the Edison Project, a market leader in educational contracting. Thomas K. Glennan Jr., who was the OEO director of research, is now senior education advisor at the Rand Corporation, and is deeply involved in the effort by the New American Schools Development Corporation (NASDC) to get nine private (mostly nonprofit) design teams involved with public schools on a contract basis.[8] Paul T. Hill, who worked at OEO, is now among academia's most eloquent advocates of contracting out.

Hill draws lessons from performance contracting, calling it "a sobering experience that you have to look at, and something that could be repeated [today]....Some [contractors] didn't have a clue, and others cheated." He concludes that contracting out must involve much more than performance incentives, and cannot work without serious oversight by a public agency.

In contrast, most supporters of privatization interviewed for this study were eager to disassociate today's developments from the failed experiments of the early 1970s, asserting that they have nothing to do with each other. "Performance contracting was no big deal," one person advised. "It shouldn't be a big part of your story."

Now and Then
The parallels with performance contracting are striking, however:

- *Once again, the phenomenon responds to insistent calls for accountability.* The 1983 publication of *A Nation at Risk: The Imperative for Educational Reform* sharpened the focus on accountability and moved legislatures and state boards of education to issue mandates for competency and proficiency. Competency testing, required by only four states in 1977, became the rule rather than the exception and, as one study noted, "seems to have taken its place in America along with baseball and grandmother's apple pie" (Amundson, Trent, and Gilman 1988).

- *Once again, the interest in contracting out public services to private companies has coincided with a shift in the status of defense industries—this time due to the end of the Cold War.* Investors are shifting their focus from defense industries to service industries, with an emphasis on industries involved in rebuilding the nation's infrastructure—including education.[9] At the same time, defense contractors are once again looking for new areas of activity, and are once again eager to apply their expertise in planning, management, and data processing to civilian problems. Case in point: in 1994, the Lockheed Corp., the California-based company known for manufacturing fighter-bombers, was seeking contracts in the field of youth services. Lockheed recently won a contract to help the state of Virginia step up collections of parents' child support payments to families on welfare (Behr 1995).

- *Once again, the experiment encompasses both total school management and more limited consulting contracts.* The Gary, Ind., project was a direct forerunner of the kinds of contracts that EAI and Edison have negotiated. The school district turned over the total per-pupil funding to the private company, in return for promises of greater efficiency and higher achievement. Other (more limited) performance contracts were forerunners of the consulting arrangement negotiated in recent years between the Public Strategies Group and the Minneapolis Public Schools.

- *Once again, technologists have been at the forefront of the educational contracting movement, with proposals to use self-paced, individualized instruction.* As primitive audiovisual equipment gave way to personal computers, the Tachtistiscope gave way to Tesseract— an EAI educational strategy that also emphasizes technology. The "teacher-proof curricula" of the 1970s gave way to the integrated, self-paced courseware of the 1990s. As its name implies, the Edison Project stresses technology. Founded by Christopher Whittle, the communications mogul who launched Channel One (news programming for schools with commercial sponsorship), Edison has favorably impressed some parent groups, and many prominent educators, by promising a computer in every student's home, as well as networked technology in the classroom. Today's technology is certainly more sophisticated, but judging by the business plans and marketing strategies of instructional software companies like Academic Systems Corp., the premise remains the same: by making use of educational technology, it is possible to meet the needs of individual students while holding down personnel costs. The possibility of independent study appears to be crucial to the economic viability of contracting, since most contractors commit themselves to producing better results than public schools with the same dollars. Without controlling labor costs, they cannot hope to meet basic expenses, fulfill their sometimes extravagant promises to customers, and squeeze enough savings out of the system to turn a profit.

- *Once again, disputes over testing have been covered by the media, and have placed a cloud over the first privatization experiments.* EAI has acknowledged errors in test reports that magnified student gains in Baltimore. And in Dade County, tests administered by the school district's own assessment office did not confirm the gains documented by EAI's own evaluators. Observers have questioned EAI's claims regarding test results in its private schools (Rigert 1994). Those disputes are discussed further in Chapter 3.

- *Once again, public interest in contracting coincides with wider acceptance of material incentives for students.* On March 1, 1995, Speaker of the House Newt Gingrich launched a national program called "Learning by Earning." The green stamps offered by Dorsett a quarter century ago are gone; today, the preferred method of payment is cash—$2 for reading a book and answering questions about it. Speaker Gingrich defends the program as a way to "change the culture." Opponents, such as Sara Freedman of the University of California at Berkeley, saw it as "a return to behavioral reinforcement kinds of experiments, and that's not the way we think about learning any more" (Seelye 1995). It is common wisdom among most educators that extrinsic motivation may boost short-term results but cannot sustain achievement over time; the teacher's role is to help students find their own (intrinsic) motivation to succeed.

- *And finally, once again, school boards in desperate straits have provided the first contracting opportunities.* The early performance contracts used dropout prevention funds. Today, private contractors are targeting marketing efforts in districts with high numbers of dropouts and low achievement, particularly urban districts or schools with large minority enrollments. In fact, some of the same communities that took part in performance contracting are again looking to the private sector for solutions. In 1970-71, Hartford, Wichita, and Boston were among the sites of the OEO experiment. Hartford awarded a contract to Alpha Systems; Wichita contracted out to Plan Education Centers; Boston contracted out to Educational Solutions (Guttenberg 1971b). In the current period, EAI won a contract to manage the Hartford school system, and the Edison Project won contracts to operate a school in Wichita and a school in Boston.

Beyond Performance Contracting

There are also sharp differences between the performance contracting of the 1970s and more recent privatization efforts. Some of those differences have been tied specifically to education and the school reform efforts of the 1980s and early 1990s. But more general changes in the economic and political environment also came into play. Several key economic and political factors made the early 1990s far more conducive to contracting out public school management:

The privatization of government assets and services. The 1960s and 1970s had been decades of public-sector expansion, during which the federal government supported and regulated activity in many areas, including research and education. In the 1980s and 1990s, beginning with the election of Ronald Reagan, that trend reversed. As John B. Goodman and Gary W. Loveman have written, the Reagan Administration issued new marching orders: "Don't just stand there, *undo* something. A central tenet of the 'undoing' has been the privatization of government assets and services" (Goodman and Loveman 1991).

The concept of privatization—transferring public services and public assets to private ownership—is certainly not an invention of the 1990s. Nor is it limited to the United States. Indeed, it is more common in countries that have been, historically, more amenable to enlarging the public sector (Sclar 1995). By the end of the 1980s, sales of state enterprises around the world had climbed to over $185 billion; they were increasing by at least $25 billion a year (Goodman and Loveman 1991). Privatization is a key element in the economic agendas of industrialized countries, developing countries, and the newly independent countries of

Eastern Europe and the former Soviet Union.

The concept itself is not new, but the claims now being made for privatization as a comprehensive approach to the problems of modern government are unprecedented. Paul Starr has written, "In the United States, advocates have called for privatizing such widely accepted forms of public provision as public schools, national parks, waterworks, fire departments, public transportation infrastructure (including airports, bridges, and turnpikes) and prisons, Social Security pensions, Medicare, the post office, public hospitals, and social services" (Starr 1987).

Underpinning the movement is the conviction that government is incompetent and that its inefficiency is a key factor behind the chronic fiscal crisis that plagues the public sector. In the 1980s and 1990s, that position has been rehearsed so often, in so many settings, that it is practically an article of faith in our nation today. Recently, however, critics of privatization have begun to challenge the view. For example, early in 1995 economist Elliott D. Sclar presented testimony to a task force convened by the U.S. Secretary of Labor, asserting that "the major source of contemporary public sector fiscal problems is financial. It is not a result of an upsurge in public sector inefficiency. Rather it is caused by complex politics and economics which have caused a significant falloff in public revenues relative to expenses" (Sclar 1995).

The corollary assumption—that private-sector service providers can operate more efficiently and thus generate savings—also bears scrutiny. Sclar notes that, in fact, after two decades of effort to shrink the public sector, advocates of privatization can point to relatively few cases in which the privatization of critical services has actually generated substantial savings through greater efficiency.

In contrast, advocates of contracting continue to emphasize the efficiency of private management, drawing parallels with other forms of privatization that have proven to be cost-effective. In his testimony to the Senate subcommittee, for example, Denis Doyle offered "the example of St. Paul Mayor George Latimore, who 'privatized' garbage and trash collection, converting public employees into private operators, saving money, and increasing performance. For the same reason schools frequently 'contract out' for such services. Does not the logic extend to instructional services? It does" (Doyle 1994a).[10] Doyle's analogy between the transfer of garbage and the transfer of knowledge went unchallenged.

Bipartisan political support. While privatization is certainly a key plank of the Republican agenda, government officials of both parties appear to be concluding that privatization is inevitable—the only way to deal with fiscal shortfalls and cut costs in a fiercely antitax environment. Case in point: the city of Washington, D.C. In Washington, where Democratic politics dominate, the City Council had opposed privatization and adopted one of the nation's most stringent laws regarding privatization, requiring the city to show that outside contractors could provide services for at least 10% less than could city employees. In February 1995, not without some unsubtle pressure from the new Republican congressional majorities, Mayor Marion Barry reversed that stance, announcing through his spokesperson that "privatization cuts across everything we're looking at," particularly youth services (Behr 1995). (Despite this policy, Washington, D.C., has yet to privatize any public schools. On July 19, 1995, its Board of Education voted down a proposal to let a private firm, most likely EAI, manage several schools. Community opposition was fierce.)

In the realm of education, most public figures express, if not outright support, at least polite interest in contracting. The Clinton Administration has taken the position that it is worth a try. At the congressional subcommittee hearings on private educational management, Thomas W. Payzant, of the U.S. Department of Education, acknowledged that there are virtually no data confirming the wisdom of contracting, but concluded blandly that "if communities want to hire companies to come in and help their schools, they ought to be able to do so" (Payzant 1994).

Advances in information technology. The information revolution has transformed the ways people think about governance in a range of fields. Traditional management structures were based on central concentration and control of assets, including information and ideas; a great achievement of the 19th century was the ability to move people where the work was. Now, new possibilities for the cheap and rapid transfer of knowledge—the most critical asset of today's organization—have broken down the command-and-control model and have encouraged devolved decision making in many areas. Management strategist Peter Drucker observes two key trends, rooted in technological advances, that are reshaping today's corporations: (1) it is now more feasible to move the work to where the people are, rather than the other way around; and (2) it is now possible, and highly desirable, to "unbundle" organizations of all kinds, farming out more and more functions to outside contractors (Drucker 1992). Those trends also are transforming long-held assumptions about management in the public sector. To a greater extent than ever before, a large organization, such as a school district, now can consider contracting out either some management functions or the total management of some schools. At the same time, a company based in Minnesota or Tennessee now can contemplate running schools anywhere in the world.

Awareness of organizational dynamics. The idea that organizations have "cultures"—shared values and norms of behavior that persist over time, even when group membership changes—today is accepted so widely and is observed so commonly that it is easy to forget how recently it entered public consciousness. Researchers have considered the possibility for decades, but outside academia it enjoyed little attention until the late 1970s, when a highly visible group of professors from Harvard and Stanford universities and the Massachusetts Institute of Technology, as well as consultants from McKinsey & Co., turned a spotlight on corporate culture as a key factor in building a competitive organization (Kotter and Heskett 1992). They focused attention on a tough challenge faced by collaborating organizations: getting a firm grasp of each other's cultures.

As a result, today's contractors and school administrators are far more sophisticated about organizational dynamics. The performance contracting experiments of the 1970s rested on the assumption that a school district could bring in contractors and graft them to the existing organization. Today's contractors know that they have to make a difficult transition from the culture of the corporation to the culture of the school; they understand that there has to be acceptance on the part of community members, administrators, teachers, and students. And they understand that they have to work the media.

The search for a new growth industry. Technology has aged out of the "emerging industry" category, and health care and biotechnology stocks are caught in the uncertainty of health care reform. Defense industries are in transition, reeling from the shrinkage of the military budget. Investors, including venture capital firms, are on the lookout for a new growth industry. In 1992, *The Venture Capital Journal* heralded a new era with an article entitled "Education Opens Its Doors: A Huge, Un-wieldy Market May at Last Be Ready for Private Equity Initiatives." Stock analyst G. William Bavin recently wrote, "Drive by an increasingly complex economy and rapidly changing technologies, demand for highly trained people—the knowledge workers who can harness these changes—is exploding." As a result, he continued, "the education industry is in the early stages of a significant growth cycle, to be powered by the private sector" (Hinden 1995).

Education has a decided appeal to many investors, particularly as it is an industry with which everyone has had personal experience. The potential for growth is enormous. As EAI's John Golle emphasizes, "...Education is a business, a very large business, about $384 billion a year in the United States. It has grown uninterrupted since 1940 at a compounded rate of 4.7% through recessions and wars. It is a very, very large business" (Golle 1994). Education is also a capital-starved industry, as John McLaughlin, publisher of *The Education Investor,* has commented (cited in Jost 1994).

The Appeal of Private Management

A number of private, for-profit firms have, for decades, been offering educational services to specific public school populations such as those eligible for Title I (formerly Chapter I) or special education services. Those companies have established solid track records. But the companies that are positioned to take on the management of entire schools and school districts either have shown mixed results or have yet to open a school. Many communities therefore have rejected contracts with the companies or deferred decisions. At the time EAI secured the Hartford contract, at least 16 school districts had turned down or delayed the company's proposals to manage additional schools (Rigert 1994). The Edison Project made numerous unsuccessful bids before winning its first contract in 1994. And a number of recent entries into the market, such as Public School Services Inc., have responded to RFPs to manage public schools but have yet to land a contract.

And yet, the concept of contracting out shows few signs of fading. Board members and business leaders across the country seem eager to consider engaging for-profit companies to provide instructional services. As in the 1970s, many school boards seem to be saying, "Bring on the salesmen." Even communities that have rejected proposals by the market leaders often leave the door open, postponing final votes rather than ending negotiations. This occurred recently in Colorado Springs, Colo., and in San Diego, Calif.

Other school districts are engaging private contractors for specific services, but appear to be open to the possibility of more extensive partnerships. In New York City, former chancellor Ramon Cortines announced, in 1995, that a private contractor would be engaged to provide janitorial services to his school system. In an interview held in February 1995, he said that he had held discussions with EAI and Edison, and had not ruled out limited partnerships with for-profit companies. "If I were looking for a technology program, for example, I would certainly talk to Edison," he commented. "There's nothing wrong with competition. But I would never relinquish responsibility for my schools."

Many other government officials and chief school officers, including those known for progressive views, speak enthusiastically about the potential of contracting out to private organizations, including for-profit companies: Governor Roy Roemer of Colorado supports it; New York State Education Commissioner Richard Mills says that he would "welcome the catalyzing effect that competition from private contractors might have on the public schools."

Does a Track Record Matter?

Robert Crosby, president of Public Education Services (a subsidiary of NonPublic Education Services) is positioning his 15-year-old company to compete with EAI and Edison. Crosby expressed frustration that those companies have been winning contracts, sometimes without competition, despite "nonexistent track records." He adds pointedly that the Baltimore contract won by EAI was "never competed—it was a sole-source contract, which was absolutely unbelievable for people in the field, that they would give an unproven company $30 million a year for five years with no competition."

Why would school boards and superintendents be willing to take a chance on those companies? "It's the theory of the bottom of the barrel," Crosby says, offering a succinct explanation that goes to the heart of privatization's appeal: "Performance in a school district has gotten so bad that there is no alternative other than 'someone else.' If you bring in 'someone else,' you can beat him up. But you can't beat yourself up."

Thomas Glennan of the Rand Corporation is not surprised by school boards' willingness to forgo proven effectiveness. He says that when school people consider adopting a new design, they want to know whether it works. "But that doesn't normally mean, has it produced clearly identifiable outcome results that are surely attributable to the intervention?" If that were the standard, he points out, schools would have to wait eight to 10 years, until the program "settles down." A key difference between the cultures of public and private organizations is the time frame in which they typically operate: profit-making companies cannot afford to wait that long before they go into the field to market their product. Glennan observes, "People make decisions on the basis of something besides proven performance—usually on some sense of the design, what people say they're doing, the process that's being used. That's how most of these designs are actually chosen."

Nothing to Lose

Kay Davis, executive director of the San Diego Business Roundtable for Education, acknowledges that the bidders who have made proposals to the San Diego Unified School District have yet to demonstrate their expertise, but she argues that some kind of change is essential. "[Edison] isn't up and running. And EAI has mixed results, depending on who you're talking to. But on the other side, there's a track record of failure. There's not enough incentive and support from inside the system to make changes. So why not give it a try? We have nothing to lose. And it's not hair-brained, cult stuff. They will match the California curriculum; they'll work with local districts on textbook adoption. They want to improve on the core curriculum."

Davis contends that one additional enticement is irresistible to many public school advocates, especially those in the business community. "They're coming in with a pot of money. You never seem to be able to get a chunk of money in education that doesn't go to teachers' salaries. So we can use it to make the school look like an important place to be. We can upgrade the technology. We can use it for staff development." School boards are keenly aware that school safety is among parents' top concerns; the desire to repair and improve the school environment is a powerful incentive. A recent national survey by the General Accounting Office found that more than a third of the country's 80,000 school buildings are now in need of major repairs or replacement, and that it would cost $112 billion to bring them up to standard.

In calls to administrators and school advocates around the nation, the refrain was constantly heard: we have nothing to lose. Mayor Kurt Schmoke of Baltimore reportedly once said to EAI's president, "Golle, I don't know if you are as good as some people tell me you are, or not. But this I do know. You can't be any worse" (cited in the American Federation of Teachers 1994).

All those elements certainly affect the willingness of school boards to put their faith in unproven contractors—even ones with uncertain track records and tarnished reputations. But the overriding factor may be school board members' sense that they are held personally responsible for poor or declining achievement, and the consequent appeal of a contract that not only appears to infuse capital into the system at the outset, but also seems to "guarantee" results.

The decision to contract out may be driven not only by fear of a muddied reputation, but also by the hope of making a name for oneself as a daring reformer. As Richard Hunter has observed, the public is often more concerned with symbols that convey success than with data that demonstrate actual achievement gains. In an analysis of EAI's Baltimore contract, Hunter writes, "It seems that privatization is a convenient symbol that holds symbolic meaning for many politicians and educators alike. This is true for both the mayor of Baltimore, Kurt Schmoke, and his superintendent of public instruction, Walter Amprey. They have received considerable local and national publicity for using EAI to operate several schools" (Hunter 1995). In the highly publicized 1995 search for a New York City schools chancellor, Amprey appeared on the list of individuals under consideration for the job, as did Edison executive Deborah McGriff, suggesting that involvement in privatization does not limit—and may enhance—career opportunities. Hunter suggests that the high-profile nature of their privatization experiment may explain Superintendent Amprey's decision to enlarge EAI's role in Baltimore, despite questionable results and strong opposition from the teachers union, as well as the fact that Amprey received an early four-year contract over the strong opposition of the union and others in the Baltimore community.

Relevant Developments in Education
A number of interrelated developments in the sphere of education appear to be helping the contractors' cause:

The conviction that reform efforts have failed. Public interest in contracting clearly reflects Americans' desperation about fixing schools now. Many are demoralized that the rash of school reform efforts launched over the last decade has failed to turn the tide. Business leaders are expressing increasing concern about the quality of the workforce. Parents are not content with small, incremental change. Elected officials, especially urban mayors, are preoccupied with the sense that they are losing middle-class families as public schools deteriorate. And educational decision makers are convinced that, in the current fiscal climate, legislatures may make radical, short-term reform a condition of substantial financial support.

"No more pouring money down the rat hole of education," said Kay Davis of the San Diego Business Roundtable, expressing a widely held conviction that money has not made and will not make a difference in the public schools. Recent property tax cutting in several states, including Colorado, Michigan, Oregon, and Wisconsin, reflects growing resistance to increasing the local support of education (Odden 1994).

Those perceptions persist, despite some real progress in addressing the problems of American education. Over the last 20 years, major school reform efforts have sought to define school readiness and expand preschool opportunities for disadvantaged children; improve teacher education and review certification requirements; set achievement standards in critical subject areas and design curricula that can help students reach those standards; and implement school-based management. None of those efforts has proved to be the "silver bullet" that will cure all educational woes, but strides have been made in all of those areas.

During the same period, researchers and practitioners have amassed a large body of evidence about what works: which strategies, programs, and practices can help students achieve at significantly higher levels and which are likely to fail. Some of the programs are already in wide use and have strong track records; others have yet to be disseminated. The Effective Schools movement launched in the 1970s has generated a substantial knowledge base about the characteristics of schools that succeed where most schools fail (Odden and Odden 1995). More recently, independent evaluations of particular research-based instructional strategies, such as Reading Recovery, Success for All, and Reciprocal Teaching, have shown that they can dramatically boost student achievement. A great deal is known, moreover, about the kinds of curricula that engage children in the act of constructing meaning, rather than merely absorbing new information. Scores of organizations across the nation, including many based in colleges and universities, are helping public schools integrate the curricula into their classrooms.

Those and other exemplary programs and strategies have been created primarily by university-based researchers in collaboration with public schools; they have been shown to result in achievement gains for virtually all children, including those who must overcome steep economic, social, linguistic, or developmental hurdles. However, none of the strategies is yet sufficiently widespread to improve the academic performance of many students. Many educators who are familiar with these strategies and the research that supports them believe that school boards should be seeking ways to incorporate best practices into their own systems, rather than starting over with private management companies.

Disgust with turf battles. There is growing consensus that new governance structures are the key to strengthening schools. A 1994 report by the Committee for Educational Development stated: "CED believes that there can be no significant progress in educational reform—and no lasting improvement in educational achievement—until those who govern the system change the way schools are organized and managed" (Hamburg 1994).

A 1993 report by the Public Agenda Foundation compared a typical American school district to "a giant dysfunctional family" and reported that turf battles paralyze most reform efforts. In many districts, battles are raging between the board of education and city hall; among multiple labor unions; and among school board members. The report said that taxpayers are fed up with the extent to which political maneuvering is invading educational policy, and with the resulting gridlock (Farkas and Johnson 1993). The widely publicized confrontations involving New York City's former chancellor Ramon Cortines, Mayor Rudolph Giuliani, and the board of education only intensified that perception.

Privatizers have capitalized on public disgust with turf battles by stressing their ability to break the gridlock of public education. Former EAI president David A. Bennett, for example, argued in a 1992 article that privatization is the only means of doing so (Hunter 1995). However, in recent years, EAI found itself embroiled, both in Baltimore and

Hartford, in the kinds of turf battles, with community groups, teachers unions, and board members, that it sought to eliminate.

Those calling for new governance structures note numerous options, including not only site-based management but also voucher systems and charter schools. Increasingly, the range of options they present includes contracting to private companies. The discussions tend to be ideological, rather than substantive. But at least one policy analyst, Paul T. Hill, has presented a thorough account of how a contracting system could work, replacing the entire system of public education governance (Hill 1994).

Wider acceptance of educational technology. The role of computer courseware in public school curricula is widely accepted—though still poorly understood—and a contractor's promise of more equipment, more emphasis on educational technology, and more computer training for teachers is more likely than ever before to have wide appeal.

Twenty years ago, the Tachtistiscope struck many observers as a Rube Goldberg device. Today, most parents are eager for their children to use personal computers in school (and at home), and accept the notion that the classroom teacher may sometimes function as a direct provider of instruction and sometimes as a coach or guide to students who are exploring a subject on their own.

In higher education, start-up companies like Academic Systems Corp. are marketing courseware designed to take the place of professors in some curricular areas, such as remedial math. Strapped for funds, university administrators are taking notice. No one is talking about replacing teachers altogether in K-12 classrooms, but in general there is wider acceptance of the concept of integrated learning systems that reduce reliance on teachers for direct instructional services.

Hands-on involvement by business leaders. A national survey of employers produced for the U.S. Department of Education late in 1994 found widespread skepticism about the ability of schools and colleges to prepare young people for the workplace. Employers reported that one-fifth of American workers are not fully proficient in their jobs (Appelbome 1995a).

Fed up with an industry that is producing flawed products, corporate managers have been trying their hand at education. Throughout the

1980s and 1990s, a number of corporations have established or expanded their own instructional programs to address shortages of qualified employees. Some have organized substantial educational and training units, calling them "Motorola University" or "Disney University."

In addition, some corporations have adopted, sponsored, or even established schools in the communities where their employees live. Computer firms, including Apple, IBM, and Compaq, all have programs in schools, but so does Burger King. Some companies are going beyond program support. The Walt Disney Corporation, for example, has formed a partnership with the Osceola, Fla., school board and Stetson University to open a new school in 1996, called the Celebration School and Teaching Academy. The school, which is expected to cost $36 million, will serve a planned community of 20,000 residents that is being developed near Walt Disney World. Disney rejected a bid from EAI to run the school, turning instead to the local school district. The school will be run by a three-person board of trustees reporting to the district; Disney will appoint one of those trustees.

Disney spokespeople say that they have no plans to get into the business of school management; however, the experience they are gaining in Osceola certainly positions the company to enter the market in the future. The Disney organization is, for example, involved in curriculum planning for the new school, and has brought in as consultants prominent school reformers like Harvard University psychologist Howard Gardner. Disney's consumer products division is developing new multimedia curricular materials for the school; it intends to market the products nationally in two years (Toch 1994).

The charter school movement. The legal structure of public education presents numerous stumbling blocks to schools that want to consider private management. Because individual schools have no independent legal status, they cannot enter into contracts with private companies for management services, nor can they be a focal point for collective bargaining. Charter school legislation removes some obstacles to more diverse participation in managing publicly financed schools.

Charter schools, as defined by the U.S. Department of Education, are "publicly sponsored autonomous schools, substantially deregulated and free of direct administrative control by the government." Freed from thousands of rules and regulations, such public schools are given authority over most school decisions, from budgets to hiring, and have wide discretion over the use of per-pupil funding. In exchange for this freedom, they are held accountable for students results.

Formally, a charter school is sponsored by a public entity—such as a government body, university, or local school board—but may actually be established and operated by teachers, administrators, parents, not-for-profit organizations, or for-profit companies. Since the concept was introduced in 1991, at least 11 states have enacted legislation that allows for charter schools, introducing changes in state law that make it theoretically possible for publicly funded charter schools to opt for private management. In fact, charter schools in Massachusetts and Michigan already have decided to contract management services to private companies, and the charter school movement is likely to open the door to private management in other states as well.

THE MAJOR PLAYERS AND THEIR WORK

All these factors—political, social, economic, legal, and educational—have converged to create a setting that makes the privatization of public school management very attractive, particularly in districts whose schools have large enrollments and significant numbers of disadvantaged students. Attracted by a potentially vast education market, the leading competitors have made hefty investments to bolster their educational management capacity; others are now reorienting their businesses to enter the market.

EAI and Edison have been marketing their services nationwide. Two additional companies have won contracts to manage a single public school or school district. Other contractors are serving niche markets.

- By October 1995, EAI had won contracts to act as a consultant in Dade County, Fla.; to manage 12 schools in Baltimore, Md.; and to manage five schools in Hartford, Conn. EAI's original contract with the Hartford school district was to manage the entire school district. Almost a year into the contract, in June 1995, EAI scaled back its plan, electing to manage only five of the district's 32 schools. That same month, Dade County opted not to renew its contract with EAI. In Baltimore, despite the publication in August 1995 of an evaluation report that found little improvement on several key indicators of achievement, the school district decided to extend EAI's contract for an additional year. By the end of 1995, however, Baltimore City elected to terminate its contract with EAI. The following month, January 1996, Hartford did likewise. (EAI also operates two private schools in Minnesota and Arizona.)

- Edison won contracts for the 1995-96 school year to operate four elementary schools in Boston, Mass.; Mount Clemens, Mich.; Sherman, Texas; and Wichita, Kan. As of June 1996, the company had plans to operate middle schools in all four cities. In addition, Edison had lined up contracts to open elementary schools in Colorado Springs, Colo.; Dade County, Fla.; Lansing, Mich.; and Worcester, Mass.

- The Public Strategies Group was acting as a consultant to the Minneapolis, Minn., public schools, in an arrangement that linked the company's revenues with student achievement. The president, Peter Hutchinson, had become superintendent of the school system.

- Alternative Public Schools Inc. had entered into an option agreement with the Wilkinsburg, Pa., school district to manage Turner Elementary School. A series of lawsuits brought by the school board and teachers union delayed a final decision for several months, but a contract worth more than $2 million a year was signed in July 1995.

- Numerous companies had contracts to provide services to special populations. Those companies include Sylvan Learning Systems, Ombudsman, NonPublic School Services Inc., and Educational Clinics.

As the privatization drama unfolds, the cast of characters remains remarkably small. The following descriptions offer an overview of some of the most important players. Brief descriptions of their projects are provided below.

The Edison Project

The company is formally known as Whittle Schools L.P. and known popularly as the Edison Project. Founder and Chairman Chris Whittle gained attention for returning *Esquire* magazine to profitability in the 1980s and for establishing Channel One, a company that produces commercially sponsored news for classroom use. Whittle later faced considerable financial losses. The collapse of his Knoxville-based media company, Whittle Communications, left Edison adrift and in need of an additional $50 million in financing to stay in business and open its first three schools in September 1995. In March 1995, Edison completed a $30 million financing package, which provided the capital needed to open the three schools. Under the terms of the financing, however, Whittle was required to share the job of chairman with Janet Hickey, a representative of the Sprout investment group. Though Edison is an independent company, several of Whittle Communications' general partners are funding Edison; Whittle was expected to post losses of $30 million for 1994.

In 1992, Whittle hired Benno C. Schmidt, then president of Yale University, to head the Edison Project. The original plan was to establish 1,000 private schools. That plan was reduced to 200 public schools, and 15 were slated to open in 1995. A subsequent strategy called for opening a third that many in 1995 and operating public school partnerships that used the same per-pupil spending as other schools but that realized savings (i.e., profits) from cuts in administrative costs and other operating expenses. In other words, Edison would be functionally identical to EAI.

55

However, Schmidt points to major differences between the two market leaders, and many educators are quick to agree that Edison's model draws on a richer research base, a group of more able and thoughtful educators, and a more enlightened view of the role of technology in education. Philosophically, the Edison model is quite different from EAI. Rather than implementing a new system of teaching, Edison proposes sweeping changes in every part of the school and school day. The model calls for an extended school day and school year. Edison's plan also calls for students to speak two languages by the end of the fifth grade, and to pass six advanced placement exams before graduating from high school. It calls for a curriculum rich in the liberal arts and technology, supported by networked computers in the classroom as well as computers in every home.

According to the company's literature, every student in an Edison school will be required to meet the company's explicit minimum standards to graduate from each of the five sequential "academies"—blocks of two or three grades across 13 years of education. The last of the academies is expected to operate at a level now expected of students at the nation's finest colleges and universities. Because students will remain with the same team of teachers over several years, the company believes that current student-teacher ratios are flexible enough to meet the needs of virtually all students.

Edison also hopes, over time, to do away with tenure for teachers and to abandon union pay scales and work rules. The company plans to give teachers wide discretion in how they teach, but will hold them to the rules of the marketplace. It has committed itself to pay the best teachers far more than the average and to get rid of the worst. Finally, Edison promises to meet objectively measurable goals for student achievement.

By mid-1996, Edison had spent some $75 million developing its program, which has won the respect of many educators. It draws heavily upon the educational research of the last decade and incorporates some of the best practices now in use in public schools. In some cases, Edison's curriculum designers have collaborated with the developers of existing programs, such as Success for All, the reading program designed by Robert Slavin and his associates at Johns Hopkins University.

Edison did not begin implementing its first contracts until September 1995. At all four initial sites, public officials, teachers, and parents were reportedly enthusiastic about Edison's efforts in the first year. As of June 1996, the company had plans to expand to a total of 12 elementary and middle schools in 1996-97. Edison's supporters and detractors agree that it is premature to draw firm conclusions about the company's future, however. Solid evaluation results will not be available for several years, and it is unclear whether, over time, the company will be able to sustain intensive, high-quality services and still turn an adequate profit.

Education Alternatives Inc.

Until January 1996, Education Alternatives Inc. was the market leader in the for-profit education business, reporting as much as $32 million in annual revenues. At one point, EAI had contracts to manage or advise 12 public schools in Baltimore and five public schools in Hartford, Conn. As of February 1996, EAI had no contracts.

Based in Eagan, Minn., EAI was founded in 1986 by John Golle, a former Xerox salesman and founder/partner of Golle & Holmes, a provider of corporate training programs. Golle left Golle & Holmes a multimillionaire and dabbled in civic and educational projects for several years before hearing about a company being sold by a debt-ridden computer giant, Control Data Corporation. The company, known as USA Schools, had been formed by Control Data in the early 1980s to study the possible role of business in school reform efforts. Golle acquired the company in 1986 for less than $100,000 in assumed debt. Five years later, Golle took the company public: its first public stock was offered in 1991.

When Golle acquired the company, he received the rights to the philosophy and teaching system developed by Control Data researchers. Known as the Tesseract Way, the system was named for a magical pathway in the children's classic *A Wrinkle in Time*. The Tesseract model requires teachers and parents to work together to create a Personal Education Plan (PEP) for each student. The plan calls for students to take part in the PEP process, helping to set their own goals. Teachers would facilitate rather than teach, encourage rather than praise, and provide progress reports rather than grades. Children work at their own pace, with the help of a computer learning system called SuccessMaker, developed by Computer Control Corp. (CCC). To the greatest extent possible, students would work in groups and learn by doing. The Tesseract Way is based on well-known techniques in the public domain that have been widely and successfully applied in schools across the nation. EAI claims to have assembled these proven components in a new, more effective way. Once again, the value of the model is one issue and the company's capacity to implement it another.

Golle opened two private schools based on the Tesseract system—one in Eagan, Minn. (1987), and a second in Paradise Valley, Ariz. (1988). He planned to open a chain of 20 for-profit private schools, but establishing new schools proved to be far too expensive. In 1990, he shifted his strategy and landed a five-year contract to implement the Tesseract model in a public elementary school in Dade County, Fla. In 1992, EAI secured a five-year, $125 million contract to manage nine Baltimore schools (eight elementary schools and one middle school). The Baltimore contract was later enlarged to encompass a total of 12 schools.

EAI's biggest coup was to be the management of the entire Hartford school district. However, almost a year into the contract, the company opted to scale back its plan to managing five of the district's 32 schools. The same month, the five-year Dade County contract expired and the school district did not renew. As noted above, between December 1995 and January 1996, EAI's other customers terminated their contracts.

The company has been embroiled in controversy practically since its inception. It has reported consistently impressive gains at its two private schools, but has achieved those gains, in part, with testing practices that tend to inflate gains. Pretests were given in the fall, when children are returning from long vacations and tend to score low on achievement tests; posttests were given in the spring, when students generally do their best. Comparing fall scores with spring scores therefore overestimates actual gains; most testing experts insist on fall-to-fall or spring-to-spring comparisons.

EAI has been widely criticized for misrepresenting test results in its own progress reports. As we note in the next section, the company's own reports of test scores, both in Baltimore and in Dade County, have been questioned by outside evaluators. Critics also charge that the company misled investors by reporting the budgets of the schools it manages as revenues. Some argue that publicly held companies, such as EAI, hold special risks for public education since they do not actually have to succeed in schools to reap profits; they merely have to persuade investors of their potential profitability by landing high-profile contracts or reporting impressive (even if inflated) revenue streams.

Too Few Venders

The case for market-based education rests on the premise that competition improves quality and productivity; it assumes that, without lively competition, markets do not work well for consumers. While numerous companies, with varied profiles, are poised to enter the market, at this point there are too few qualified venders to create a fair and effective competitive bidding process (Brown 1995). Indeed, the contract that EAI won to manage several public schools in Baltimore was not put out to bid, and there was no competition whatsoever.[11] The future of private management of public schools rests, at least in part, on the quantity, quality, and variety of entrepreneurs entering the marketplace, so that school districts can make reasonable and appropriate choices of venders and services.

Providing Districtwide Management Services

Can a private company successfully manage an entire public school district? In Minneapolis, a small private consulting firm, the Public Strategies Group, provides "leadership services" to the school district as a whole; and in Duluth, Minn., EAI briefly provided interim management services on a districtwide basis. But the only full-scale, long-term arrangement of this kind was aborted, so the question remains unanswered.

EAI came close to setting a precedent. In July 1994, Hartford became the first school district in the nation to entrust the management of an entire school district to a private company over an extended period. The contract, which was signed in October 1994 but was retroactive to July 1994, authorized EAI to manage the city's 32 public schools, serving 25,000 students. The contract committed EAI to improving schools within the district's current budget—$8,450 per pupil (Innerst 1994). After a year under contract, the company faced fierce opposition from parents, teachers, and the school board, which voted down EAI's districtwide reform proposals. In June 1995, EAI proposed to scale back its plan from managing the entire district to overhauling five "sympathetic" schools (Schmidt 1995).

Duluth: Providing interim management. In 1992, Education Alternatives was providing services to two private schools, and had racked up some public school experience in one Dade County school and two Salt Lake City schools. But after six years in business, it had not yet found a school board willing to turn over an entire district to a private company. On March 4, 1992, company officials arrived in Duluth.

Duluth's school system was in crisis. There had been four superintendents in four years, and the board was divided on numerous issues. The interim superintendent, who had been given a two-year contract, had resigned with only two weeks notice. By the end of the day, a deal was struck: EAI would come into Duluth for a four-month period to manage the school system through the end of the term, and would also evaluate the district's finances and operations. EAI's fee for the services was $40,000. At the end of four months, the contract was not renewed. Because the contract was so short-lived, no meaningful evaluation data are available.

Minneapolis: Performance contracting revisited. In mid-1993, the Minneapolis public schools were in trouble. Faced with charges of fiscal mismanagement, the superintendent had turned in his resignation. In November 1993, the Board voted, by a 4-3 margin, to hire a small consulting firm called Public Strategies Group to provide "leadership services" to the school district, which encompasses 79 schools, serves 44,000 students, and has an annual budget of $350 million. The three-person company was given a three-year contract. For purposes of state law, its president, Peter C. Hutchinson, was named superintendent. That was an unusual step, as the company and its president had virtually no experience in public education. However, the group received an early endorsement from the Minneapolis Federation of Teachers, and Hutchinson made clear his intention to lean heavily on the expertise he found within the system.

The contract is structured to ensure performance-based accountability. According to the contract for the 1994-95 school year, the board paid Public Strategies Group $60,000 per year, plus reimbursement for reasonable expenses. In addition, the company received payment for satisfactory completion of specific tasks on the District Improvement Agenda. The October 1994 contract listed assignments valued at $470,000. That total includes the superintendent's base salary of $60,000. The contract also lists "Items from previous work agenda" valued at $21,000.

Each major item in the District Improvement Agenda, the school system's strategic plan for improving education, was assigned a dollar value. For example, in 1994-95, the district was obliged to pay the company $65,000 for meeting student achievement targets; $20,000 for implementing a family involvement initiative; $30,000 for developing assessment tools; and $30,000 for work on the core curriculum.[12]

Managing a Group of Schools Within a District

Hartford: Managing five schools. According to the EAI's original contract—involving management of the entire school district—EAI would not receive a management fee. The company and the school district worked out a complicated arrangement that authorized EAI to retain half the savings it generated at the end of each school year after recouping its own expenses. The other half was supposed to go to the school district. EAI also agreed to invest $20 million for capital improvements, including $15.6 million in the first year of the contract for building repairs and new computers. EAI further pledged that by September 1995 every Hartford school would have computer labs providing one computer for every 10 students (Judson 1995). In light of those commitments, school officials predicted that the company would not be able to find enough savings in the budget to recoup its investments, much less make a profit. Critics wondered how EAI would meet its commitments, in view of the district's $2.6 million budget gap.

The award of the contract had followed months of controversy. Some expressed concern that EAI had sold the contract on the basis of its experience in Baltimore, where test scores were tainted; they pointed out that Baltimore's Superintendent Amprey, who had heartily endorsed the firm, was hardly a disinterested party. The Hartford Federation of Teachers argued that the way to improve schooling is to attract and retain good teachers, by offering favorable contracts and working conditions. Stock analysts who follow EAI insisted that its success in Hartford would depend on its ability to hold the line on teacher salaries. Parents of Hispanic students, who make up roughly half the district's population, expressed concern over EAI's limited experience with bilingual education.

Despite those doubts, EAI maintained a steady 6-3 margin of support on the Hartford School Board and won its contract. However, as the September 1995 start-up date approached, the project ran into increasingly steep obstacles. Many community groups continued to oppose the contract, and the board proved to be reluctant to cut teachers' jobs to pay for EAI's proposals. Toward the end of the 1994-95 fiscal year, the board projected a $145,000 deficit. At the same time, controversy erupted over invoices submitted by EAI for extensive employee air travel and accommodations.

In June 1995, the board proposed a plan to turn over five schools to the company, and EAI Chairman Golle pledged to "transform [the five schools] from top to bottom over the summer" (Green 1995). He declared that his company preferred to bring about thoroughgoing reform at five schools rather than incremental change across the district. Golle expressed confidence that the successful reform of these pilot schools would encourage others to implement EAI reform efforts. At the outset of the 1995-96 school year, the board and the company were entangled in disputes over payment for past services; EAI's role at the five sites remained unclear. The city claimed that EAI had failed to document most of the savings it claimed, whether legitimate or not. EAI claimed the city was not living up to its obligations under the contract. In January 1996, the city decided to end its relationship with EAI (Judson 1996).

Baltimore: Managing 12 schools. In 1992, EAI landed a five-year contract to manage nine schools in Baltimore, despite the protests of many parents and the city's teachers union. The company also had a consulting contract covering three additional Baltimore schools. EAI spent $1.1 million up front to improve the school facilities and buy computers and other supplies. It moved quickly to clean and repair the schools and take charge of security. Maintenance and financial management services were contracted to EAI's partners in a group that EAI calls the Alliance for Schools That Work—Johnson World Controls and KPMG Peat Marwick.

In Baltimore, EAI received popular approval for repairing buildings and streamlining ordering procedures, and for boosting parent participation and faculty morale in some schools. At the same time, the company undermined its own credibility (and, consequently, the value of its stock) by issuing erroneous test results that inflated student achievement; cutting teaching positions and replacing experienced paraprofessionals with low-paid interns; and failing to comply with state special education mandates. In May 1995, the Baltimore City Council subpoenaed the company's records and launched a review of its finances, legal fees, and lobbying activities.

Dissatisfaction with the arrangement grew in the city. The mayor's opponent for election, City Council President Mary Pat Clark, made the

EAI contract a central campaign issue. Despite the controversy, Mayor Schmoke won reelection by a comfortable margin. Notwithstanding his victory, the mayor went on to criticize EAI and seek a reformulated contract. Agreement could not be reached and EAI was dismissed in December 1995.

Managing an Individual School

Dade County: Consulting contract to implement instructional model. In 1990, Education Alternatives Inc. was awarded its first public school contract by the Dade County, Fla., school district. EAI entered into a five-year contract with South Pointe Elementary School—a school of approximately 720 students with a large "at-risk" population. Two-thirds of the students are Latino; 11% are African American.

The terms of the contract stipulated that Dade County would continue to operate the school and control most of its $2.3 million budget. EAI would cover the additional costs incurred to implement its instructional model, including computers, teacher training, and the salaries of 24 student teachers from the University of Miami. Those expenses, along with EAI's $1.2 million fee, would be financed through fundraising. The goal was to raise $2.2 million from private donations over the five years of the contract.

At the end of the five-year contract, Dade County school officials opted not to renew the contract with EAI, saying that the partnership had always been viewed as an experiment rather than a long-term relationship. Other reports contend that the partnership soured because EAI wanted the school district to absorb some of its operating costs, and district leaders did not want to spend more money on a program that was not delivering the desired results. Test scores at South Pointe did increase during the five-year contract period, but they were not significantly higher than those from a nearby school with a comparable student body, which had functioned without the program enhancements provided by EAI.

Superintendent Octavio Visiedo has said that EAI underestimated the challenges of public education and failed to deliver the dramatic improvements they had predicted; but he has also said that the program overall was "very successful," and praised the relationships it forged between teachers, students, and parents. The Dade County School Board apparently has not soured on the idea of private management: at the same time that it ended its relationship with EAI, it signed a letter of intent to negotiate with the Edison Project to manage three elementary schools (Lim 1995).

Wilkinsburg: Controlling staffing. When the Wilkinsburg, Pa., Board of Education announced interest in contracting out management of Turner Elementary School, arguably the most troubled school in a district plagued by low achievement, 16 groups responded, including corporations, nonprofit agencies, and universities; five eventually submitted proposals. In July 1995, the board signed a contract with Alternative Public Schools Inc. (APS) to run the 400-pupil school. While the town's population of approximately 21,800 is 53% African American and 47% white, most whites have taken their children out of the public schools, and as a result the district (and the students who attend Turner) are virtually all African American.

This contract is the first in the nation that permits a private company to replace teachers in a public school. Of the school's 24 teachers, 15 were laid off and nine were reassigned. In this way, APS has won more authority than other for-profit companies, including EAI and Edison, which function primarily with existing teachers. In this sense, Wilkinsburg is one of the most crucial test cases of the private management of public schools (Appelbome 1995b).

The Nashville-based company, which has never before run a school, is receiving the $5,400 per student that the district now pays to run the school. In return, APS has pledged to raise student achievement by extending the school day and year, using the school as a hub of social services, linking teacher compensation to achievement, and grouping students into grade "families" that stay together as a cohort, with the same teacher, for at least two years. The Wilkinsburg contract is worth more than $2 million a year.

Wilkinsburg's negotiations with APS were controversial from the start. The town has strong union loyalties, and opponents of the board's decision were very active. A series of lawsuits and countersuits brought by the school board and the teachers union in the months prior to the opening of school in September 1995 first blocked and then permitted the company to open the school (Zlatos 1995).

Wichita: Redesigning an existing school. In January 1995, the Board of Education of Wichita, Kan., voted to conclude a contract with Edison to manage one school, Dodge Elementary School, beginning in 1995-96. The school, which serves grades kindergarten through five, is being redesigned. According to Terry Boswell, assistant to the superintendent responsible for partnerships, "Edison has said they can do a better job with the same dollars [by introducing] a different kind of instructional delivery system and a different type of curriculum." The board will evaluate their success based on student achievement, as measured by pre- and posttest scores.

According to Boswell, this is "sort of an open magnet school." The enrollment is drawn from the neighborhood, and children who already attend Dodge are able to opt for the redesigned school. School officials anticipated that an additional 150 to 200 children would be drawn from other neighborhoods; as with other magnet programs, a lottery system determines eligibility.

Edison receives $3,600 for each student via the flow-through from the state to the district to them. From those funds, the company must hire a principal, pay the teachers, and pay all of the bills. Edison also must finance its program enhancements, including a longer school day, a longer school year, and a computer in the home of every student. The company is contracting back to the district for auxiliary services, such as garbage removal and auxiliary services.

The Board of Education required financial guarantees, and Edison has deposited $1 million in escrow in a Wichita bank. According to Terry Boswell, "In case Edison goes belly up or something doesn't work, $50,000 of this money goes back to the district as transition money, so we can go back to the school building and get things set up the way we need them to be."

The contract calls for Edison to hire a principal and teachers from the district's current base of employees. Edison can fire employees, and employees can quit. All employees, including both teaching and non-teaching personnel, are guaranteed safe passage back to the district, with no loss of benefits or seniority.

Boston: Creating a charter school. In March 1994, the state of Massachusetts designated 15 schools as charter schools. The Edison Project won contracts to manage three of the schools. However, Edison subsequently decided to run only one—the Renaissance School, in partnership with the Horace Mann Foundation. It is a new elementary school serving 700 students and located in the Fenway neighborhood. The enrollment will grow each year, topping out at 1,100—making it the largest charter school in the state.

Impacts

Contracting in public education holds out the promise of schools and school systems that take full responsibility for raising achievement. As John Golle likes to say, private contractors are "termination-friendly." If results are disappointing, a school district can simply cancel its contract. That, he says, is true accountability. The theory is neat. It turns out, however, that in practice people with different vested interests do not readily agree about how results have been, or ought to be, measured and interpreted.

To date, private management of public schools has not substantially boosted achievement. The schools run by EAI in Dade County and Baltimore did not outperform comparison schools, despite significant investments in program enhancements. In Minneapolis, students districtwide did not meet the achievement goals set by the management company.

Termination has not been swift in any of the situations. In Dade County, the contract was not terminated in its five-year duration, but it was not renewed at the end of the contract period. In Baltimore, the contract was renewed for two years despite disappointing outcomes and a critical evaluation by independent evaluators, but was eventually terminated. In Minneapolis, the management company appears to enjoy the confidence of school officials, parents, and students despite disappointing results.

This section offers further detail on the impact of recent privatization projects. Generally speaking, the data are thin—especially when one considers the millions of dollars that have been invested in these efforts. There is a clear and urgent need for ongoing, systematic evaluation of privatization initiatives.

Student achievement. In Baltimore, test results have been controversial. In August 1993, the company reported that the 4,800 students attending the nine Baltimore schools it managed had, over a three-month period, advanced an average of 0.88 grade levels (compared with a benchmark of 0.30 grade levels that would be expected in that period). In June

1994, EAI admitted that the results were erroneous and that the gains held only for 954 underachieving students in five of the nine schools. EAI blamed its technology partner, CCC, for the error. CCC blamed EAI. Following EAI's admission, the company's stock plummeted.

Moreover, achievement data released in late October 1994 showed that reading and math scores actually dropped slightly in the eight Tesseract elementary schools but rose slightly in the rest of the system. Reading scores at EAI's schools dropped by four percentiles and math scores by eight percentiles. During the same period, students in a control group of eight elementary schools similar to the EAI schools gained five percentiles in both reading and math. A report by the American Federation of Teachers notes that "scores in the EAI schools were going up before EAI took over, so the current scores represent a reversal of a positive upward trend—not the continuation of a decline" (American Federation of Teachers 1994).[13]

The city's official evaluation, conducted by the Center for Educational Research at the University of Maryland Baltimore County (UMBC), was published in August 1995. It found that, overall, EAI schools in Baltimore did not do significantly better than seven comparison elementary schools operated by the city, despite the fact that EAI schools received more money per student. (The comparison schools were chosen by school officials to represent similar size, poverty level, and pre-1992 achievement. The evaluators note that school district officials had changed the comparison group and that making such a change once an experiment is underway is "irregular.")

The UMBC evaluation found EAI schools to be funded at a higher level than other district schools. They were said to receive 11.2% more per pupil funding than the control schools during the 1995-96 school year. In the next chapter, Richards presents evidence that this differential was much higher. The UMBC team reached the following overall conclusions about instruction and student achievement:

- *Test scores:* Standardized test scores at EAI schools did not change significantly from 1992, the year before EAI took over. The same was true for the study's control schools and the city overall.

- *Teaching style:* Teachers at EAI schools spent less time teaching their classes as a whole and more time teaching small groups of students.

- *Test readiness*: Test preparation was a major focus of the instrumental day for at least three months of the academic year in both EAI schools and control schools. The evaluation team found too much instructional time devoted to testing and particularly to test preparation.

- *Technology*: The evaluators found that "there is little about the computer-using experience [at EAI schools] that can be considered preparation for the 'age of technology.'"

Overall, the evaluators concluded that EAI's claim that it could boost achievement without spending more than the district already was spending "has been discredited." Despite EAI's failure to translate additional funding into achievement gains, Baltimore moved to extend the contract for two years. The city wanted to reduce, if not eliminate, the financial advantage afforded EAI schools and include performance criteria in a new contract. As noted above, renegotiations ultimately proved unsuccessful.

In Dade County, EAI's assessment data also were challenged. EAI reports that 1994 unedited test scores for South Pointe elementary students in grades four to six, compared with all grade four to six students in Dade County, "showed that South Pointe students performed well." But according to Phyllis Cohen, Dade County's deputy superintendent for instructional leadership, "There is some question as to whether they do any better than they would do if [EAI's] model wasn't there. There is a discrepancy between the testing done by our Office of Educational Accountability and the testing that the EAI people sponsored....They brought in their own outside evaluator, who disagreed with ours." She says that the school district's evaluation office and EAI have agreed to disagree. "They were two different kinds of studies, and maybe each in its own right had validity."

In Minneapolis, the student achievement goal of the public schools is: "Increase the achievement of all children. Eliminate the gap in achievement between students of color and other students, and between female and male students." A report on citywide performance, the February 17, 1995 "District Improvement Agenda," shows that reading performance (measured on the *California Achievement Test*) went down from the 1992-93 to the 1993-94 school year. Math achievement held steady, but showed no improvement. Moreover, the gap in reading performance between students of color and other students has increased slightly but steadily over the last three years. Despite those disappointing outcomes, both parents and students believed that the schools' instructional effectiveness had increased, compared with the previous year's (Minneapolis Public Schools 1994). Students report high levels of learning when asked if they learned a lot; no significant difference was reported between racial/ethnic groups.

In summary, there is no reason based on the data to believe that private management enhances student achievement, at least over a period of one to three years.

Attendance. Although EAI claimed that attendance improved dramatically at nine EAI schools in Baltimore, Md., state education officials report that attendance actually declined slightly after the first school year. In Dade County, Cohen noted that attendance at the school was better than average.

In Minneapolis, student attendance held steady from 1992-93 to 1993-94, at 87% for elementary schools and 77% for secondary schools.

School climate. The 1995 UMBC evaluation of EAI schools in Baltimore reported that EAI schools and the control schools were "similarly clean." However, there was a wide perception among many parents and community members that EAI was effective in the area of facilities management; many said that school buildings were improved and were well maintained, setting a higher standard for the rest of the system. Ralph Smith, now of the Casey Foundation, recalls the pleasure of parents who went to the Harlem Park Middle School in Baltimore, where he was working as a consultant: "They couldn't believe their eyes," he says. "The tile in the bathroom was not merely white; it sparkled. That September, when they went into the schools attended by their other children, parents took a look at the bathrooms that had been recently cleaned by the district in preparation for the school's opening, and they said, "these bathrooms are not clean." The district was forced to contend with a higher standard.

Some teachers have commented to the press that the equipment supplied by the company was geared to public relations efforts rather than to teachers' actual needs. One elementary school teacher noted that EAI had supplied her with a rocking chair, intended to give her classroom a cozy feel. She was promptly photographed seated in the rocker. But what she really needed, she said, were coat hooks, and they were given lower priority.

Despite scattered complaints, teachers at EAI schools reported, for the most part, that the supplies they requisition were delivered efficiently and quickly—a phenomenon that many view as nothing short of miraculous. Those factors appear to have had a positive impact on the morale of teachers, other employees, and students.

In Dade County, Phyllis Cohen noted early in 1995 that EAI's presence positively affected school climate. In a telephone interview, she described greater student enthusiasm, as well as high parent participation and parent satisfaction, and student enthusiasm. She characterized teachers as "feeling very committed to the model." That commitment was apparently not strong enough to persuade the board to renew EAI's contract.

Special education programs. The UMBC evaluation of EAI's efforts in Baltimore concluded that the company's most significant accomplishment was in the area of special education. According to the company, a major goal in Baltimore was the broad application of the inclusion model of special education, which provides instruction (with appropriate support and modifications) for all students in regular classrooms. In Baltimore, EAI reduced the number of special education staff. The company also received a waiver from the Maryland State Department of Education to use interim Individual Education Plans (IEPs) for all students with disabilities in Tesseract schools. In its request for the waiver, EAI made a commitment to depart from an existing IEP only with the consent of the student's parents.

Compliance with special education mandates proved to be problematic for EAI. In accordance with the 1992 consent decree that governs special education delivery in Baltimore's public schools, eligible students who are denied special education services must receive compensatory hours of service. In an evaluation on the early implementation of Tesseract by the school district, relatively minor problems were documented at three of the eight Tesseract elementary schools; however, far more serious violations were found at Harlem Park Middle School. This school was required to provide 136,893 compensatory hours of special education to Harlem Park students—more than 250 times the number of hours required before EAI came on the scene. In fact, the Harlem Park School accounted for 89% of the compensatory hours awarded for the entire district during the 1991-92 school year (Ruffini, Howe, and Borders 1994). In March 1994, the Baltimore school system reached an out-of-court agreement in which the schools admitted substantial noncompliance with the special education consent decree.

Despite all these problems, the UMBC evaluation of EAI schools in Baltimore found that the company did succeed in mainstreaming large numbers of special education students, and considered this to be a positive outcome.

The community. Some critics of privatization have worried aloud, and in print, about the impact of contracting in public education on community life. They note, for example, that EAI has cut most paraprofessional positions, replacing experienced personnel with low-wage interns who tend to stay on the job for one year or less. They point out that unlike the interns—mostly recent college graduates—the paraprofessionals generally come from children's neighborhoods and provide stability and continuity in their lives. Taking away their jobs not only impoverishes the classroom experience; it also adds to the economic hardship of the community.

Other critics, like Alex Molnar, Walter Farrell, and Michael Apple, go a step further, by stressing the word "out" in contracting out. "By signing a contract with EAI or Edison," Molnar has written, "a school district is in effect assuring a transfer of wealth from minority workers in its community to white investors somewhere else" (Molnar 1994).

Michael Apple (1993), in the book *Official Knowledge: Democratic Education in a Conservative Age*, goes even further, arguing that the private management of public schools is the outcome of a scenario in which private industry first impoverishes urban public schools, assuring their failure, and then proposes to rescue them—for a price. He suggests that companies bully municipalities into offering tax breaks, thereby draining the tax base upon which school systems depend, and then blame those impoverished schools for students' poor achievement. They then arrange to take over management of schools or school districts, profiting from the failure that they helped to create.

All those critics stress that contracting to profit-making companies may have devastating effects, both direct and indirect, on the community.

The companies have made some efforts to reach out to parents and community members. In Wilkinsburg, Alternative Public Schools Inc. has committed itself to making Turner School a hub of community services. Both EAI and Edison place a great deal of emphasis on parent involvement. The UMBC Baltimore evaluation notes that EAI introduced four new parent involvement activities at its schools. However, they found little difference in the level of parent involvement between EAI and comparison schools.

PROSPECTS

None of the current experiments in privatization has achieved the results that were predicted or promoted by its advocates. The early results have been mixed, at best. Despite higher levels of per-pupil spending and significant investments in program enhancements, none of the recent privatization efforts has produced clearcut gains in student achievement. There have been few independent evaluations of significant scope, and neither venders nor consumers have pushed forcefully for closer scrutiny of outcomes.

School boards have reason to regard bidders' proposals with skepticism. And, indeed, many school boards have rejected proposals from for-profit educational management companies. For the moment, elected officials are wandering warily onto this rough terrain, unsure how voters will respond to the idea of public schools as sites of profit. For the moment, the supply of companies that have the capacity and the will to enter this risky market remains limited, and the demand, while growing, is not huge.

The "Cart of Supply"

Despite disappointing results, the practice of contracting out seems to be here to stay, at least for the foreseeable future. In coming years, it will continue to be driven by two forces.

First, the cart of supply may pull the horse of demand. The market may be driven by the interest and resources of investors who have taken the measure of their neighbors' disgust with public management of education and see vast potential in the education marketplace. As investment dollars flow into this market, many kinds of companies are likely to enter the arena, armed with powerful marketing tools and political allies, whose social philosophies support the companies' aims.

Second, the needs of our children are so compelling, the challenges of public schooling so daunting, and public resources so scarce, that few educators harbor the illusion that they can do it alone. Few will turn their backs on offers of help, even if those offers carry a price tag. More and more schools are forming alliances with each other, with colleges and universities, community-based organizations, business groups, and civic organizations. The partnerships do not necessarily stem from a surge in civic pride or a swell of sociability; rather, they reflect the fact that many of our youngsters are in desperate need, and the adults who staff our schools are overwhelmed. Even those who have compunctions about the profit motive are unlikely to reject, out of hand, proposals that promise to relieve schools of crushing burdens—such as meeting the intense needs of children living in poverty, ensuring school safety in gang-dominated neighborhoods, or keeping up with repairs on decrepit buildings.

The question, therefore, is not whether privatization initiatives in public schooling will continue, but rather what forms they will take, and how they can be shaped to serve the public interest.

Schools will continue to form new relationships with outside organizations—but what kind of organizations? Will profit-making corporations maintain the lead, or will they fade as not-for-profits gain expertise and confidence and make the most of their privileged position in the American economy?

Will the Profit Motive Prevail?

Two vocal advocates of market-based educational strategies, John McLaughlin and Denis Doyle, argue that competition will invigorate the nation's educational enterprise. McLaughlin is firmly convinced that for-profit companies will play a leading role in education over the next decade. "When you look at what [today's entrepreneurs] can do," he says, "you realize how fundamentally schools can change. It's really not necessary any more to bring kids in five days a week for seven or eight hours a day to be taught in pods of 30 kids. We have to open our eyes and our pocketbooks and open our minds to what private industry can offer that will kick education into the 21st century. There's no money in the public till to do some of the things a private company can do privately, if they can make some money on it." McLaughlin says that the only thing that will slow the momentum of privatization is "a lot of protectionism driven by misinformation, and driven by a lack of knowledge on the part of school people about how the information age has reshaped the way we work."

McLaughlin acknowledges the potential for abuse. "We have a tremendous responsibility to protect kids from shysters and hucksters and snake oil salesmen who want to misuse the latest technologies in school," he says. But he is persuaded that contracting out can be done with full citizen input and an open and truly competitive bidding process. He calls the Baltimore case "a terrible example" of privatization, and urges more attention to less visible efforts, like the model developed by Alternative Public Schools Inc., which features a project-oriented curriculum organized around instructional blocks, a strong community orientation, an extended school day and year, and the opportunity for students to stay with the same team of teachers for two years.

Or Will Not-For-Profits Take the Lead?

Other observers are equally convinced that not-for-profits will sooner or later take the lead, and probably sooner. Denis Doyle has written, for example, that for-profit companies "may be the entering wedge, not for privatization, but for an enlarged role for not-for-profit providers of education. They may set the stage for their less burdened compatriots" (Doyle 1994b). He envisions a marketplace dominated by contractors like Robert Slavin (who has pioneered a program called "Success for All"), Theodore Sizer (who has created the model known as "Essential Schools"), Henry Levin ("Accelerated Schools") or James Comer ("Effective Schools"). Doyle points out that for-profit companies are burdened with costs that exceed those of not-for-profits by margins of 30% to 50%, and will be hard pressed to compete with those reformers.

Doyle admits that "Chicago School" economists would argue that for-profits operate so much more efficiently than not-for-profits that the 30% margin is illusory. But he believes that in tax treatment, ease of operating, and licensing—"all the red tape issues in education"—the advantages of not-for-profits are indeed significant. "That, in fact, is the reason that out of roughly 25,000 private schools [in this country], only 50 or so are for-profit."

He notes one more factor that favors not-for-profit—a strong streak of irrationality in economic activity that can have a major impact on markets. Doyle believes that the typical American parent is disinclined to thrust her children into a for-profit setting if a reasonable alternative is available. "I believe in profit very strongly," he says, "but given a choice between a Sizer school and a Whittle school, I'll take Sizer any day, and I think most parents would."

Polls confirm Doyle's suspicions. A recent survey by *Public Agenda* showed that only 10% of parents nationwide favor private management of public schools. An earlier *Public Agenda* survey conducted in Connecticut—where the nation's most ambitious privatization initiative was under consideration—found little support for contracting out. Only 24% of respondents thought that the state should "rely on private companies to run the most troubled school districts because these districts have had long histories of poor performance." Most people (57%) believed that private companies will "care more about profits than about the education of children." Educators and the public at large—including both white and minority parents—were in agreement on that point (*Public Agenda* 1994).

If privatization is to serve the public interest, in education as in other fields, it requires a lively marketplace where organizations of different kinds can compete, goading or inspiring each other to boost both quality and efficiency. In today's educational marketplace, those conditions do not yet exist. However, for-profit companies may inspire a variety of other organizations to join the fray. As Paul Hill notes, the core purpose of contracting is to "create schools that have clear missions and definite strategies for motivating students and delivering instruction" (Hill 1994, 9). He imagines that in the near future, local school boards may build upon the charter schools movement, granting every school that wants one a charter. The school system would maintain a portfolio of contractors that might include trade unions, groups of teachers from successful neighborhood schools, school-university cooperatives, community-based organizations, as well as for-profit companies. It would manage many contracts at once. Public officials would retain ultimate responsibility for school quality, and would assure a diversity and a liveliness that would enrich teachers' and students' lives, and help to animate communities.

Potential Dangers of Privatization

Students may indeed benefit, in time, from their school districts' access to many kinds of instructional and noninstructional services, offered at competitive prices from a variety of organizations. The current experiments with the private management of public schools may help to move us toward a more flexible, entrepreneurial approach to securing educational resources and reaching educational goals.

However, the experiments carry risks, both for the students entrusted to private companies and to the school systems that hire them.

First, the premise of privatization is that venders have a clear stake in the success of the students they serve. However, publicly traded companies such as EAI may not have as much incentive to assure quality or improve achievement as school boards or parents or other taxpayers might assume. After all, they need not follow through on their promises to earn a profit; they need only to create the impression of sufficient success (by winning contracts and headlines) to raise the value of their stock and enrich their shareholders. The public officials who support them also benefit from the contracts, gaining wide media exposure and reputations as innovators—even when the innovations fail to help students.

Second, when communities contract out to private companies, they risk undermining community members' sense of personal, active responsibility for their public schools. That prospect worries many educational reformers, who are increasingly convinced that schools alone—even the most efficiently run schools—cannot meet the needs of the nation's children, and that school reform, as an isolated enterprise, is the wrong goal. Communities and families, as well as schools, hold the key to promoting the healthy development and learning of America's children. All the stakeholders in a community must be accountable for improving achievement (see Shore 1995).

We are not moving in that direction; indeed, the American public's commitment to its schools appears to be weakening. For most of American history, Americans have been ready and willing to open their wallets to support public education, especially in good economic times. This is no longer the case. Now, when the economy ticks up, the impulse is generally to cut taxes and cut services, including education.

In part, this may reflect a dramatic demographic shift. At the turn of the century, about half of all adults in the nation had children in the public schools; today, the percentage has dropped to 22%. Public schooling has become the project of educating children who are not our own. As Madeleine Grumet has written, "...if ethics and the common culture could gather together the concern and attention that we devote to our own children and extend this nurture to other people's children, then we might indeed find in the school the model for a just society that [John] Dewey envisioned." But instead, most school policy is shaped with other people's children in mind: "They are other people's children, and so it makes perfect sense that to guide our decisions we shall rely on the rules we use to tell us how to treat people we don't know" (Grumet 1988).

The private companies that come into a community to manage one or more schools are typically headquartered in a distant place. Their leaders do not come from the community. Their strategies have not emerged from the strengths, needs, cultures, or textures of that community. Their solutions may in fact bypass local institutions and reject local residents (for example, by replacing paraprofessionals who come from the neighborhood with transient college students who are willing to serve as interns for low hourly wages). Their profits are not likely to be reinvested in the community. This fact is particularly worrisome in view of the fact that virtually all the venders now in the marketplace have targeted school districts with large enrollments of low-income and minority students.

Finally, privatization threatens to interrupt and diminish the crucial bonds between teachers and students. Education takes place, after all, in the context of relationships. It is a labor-intensive activity. To make a profit, most privatizers must, sooner or later, come to terms with the need to cut the instructional staff—no matter what program or methods they promote. That is why technology is at the heart of virtually all the privatizers' promises. From the standpoint of the industrial model, it makes sense: instructional courseware may prove to be more cost-effective in some cases than small-group or individual instruction by caring teachers; and in some cases, technology can help to strengthen some skills. But at the heart of public schooling is an irreplaceable phenomenon—the words and looks and gestures exchanged between children and teachers, as they construct meaning together.

A Final Paradox

Even the staunchest proponents of market-based strategies acknowledge that to date none of the experiments in privatization has succeeded in substantially or consistently improving student achievement. Paradoxically, their failure may, over time, benefit the communities that have entrusted students to them. If a corporation cannot raise student achievement despite expenditures that exceed those of the public school district, then the American public may begin to come to terms with the fact that schools are not always the wasteful, inefficient institutions they are thought to be, and that adequate public school funding and equity are absolutely crucial to our children's achievement and well-being.

In these ways, school districts and the children and communities they serve may ultimately profit the most from the early forays of corporations into the educational marketplace.

CHAPTER 2

Is Privatization in Public Education More Efficient?

The Case of Education Alternatives Inc.
in the Baltimore Public Schools

BY CRAIG E. RICHARDS

INTRODUCTION

This chapter offers an in-depth view of Education Alternatives Inc. (EAI) in two basic dimensions: it discusses financial practices and it analyzes the company's economic relationship with the Baltimore City Public Schools (BCPS). The purposes are to uncover financial motives of the company beyond the expected goal of earning profits, and to understand how the company obtained and used resources under its Baltimore contract.

As noted elsewhere in this study, Baltimore's experience with EAI is the leading case to date for considering the use of private business firms to manage public schools. When this study was begun, EAI could have been considered the industry leader in this field. Over the following 12 months, however, EAI lost most of its public school contracts. That is quite a commentary on the fragility, volatility, or perhaps dynamism of the industry. The Baltimore episode should be useful in gaining insight into the future of the particular model of education privatization under consideration in this study.

When any public or private company or institution contracts with another organization for services, the customer typically seeks some combination of lower costs, increased quantity, and improved quality. Researchers who try to account for variations in efficiency and productivity in education typically focus on three aspects of schooling: (1) the quantity and quality of inputs to the school, such as teachers, students, materials, and facilities; (2) the quantity and quality of educational processes in school, which means things like curriculum, governance, school climate, and safety; and (3) the level or quality of school outcomes, such as student achievement, graduation rates, and post-secondary transitions to work or college (Good and Brophy 1986; Richards 1991). A comprehensive analysis of a public-private contract would examine each of these aspects before making final judgment about whether the contract is good for schoolchildren.

By way of illustration, a private contractor might save the school district money but fail to improve student achievement. The contractor might improve student achievement in reading and mathematics, but accomplish that by using class time formerly devoted to science, history, or fine arts. To evaluate a contracting arrangement, one must stipulate performance criteria and determine how the contractor fared in meeting such requirements. If the contract specifies criteria explicitly, one could take the customer's requirements as a baseline from which to evaluate performance. This study makes a partial contribution to such a comprehensive analysis by examining as carefully as possible, given available information, whether or not the contract between EAI and the Baltimore City Public Schools has been profitable for EAI and "efficient" for Baltimore. By efficient, we mean the improved combination of cost, quantity, and quality noted.

In the public mind, there are two broad categories of schools in the United States: public schools paid for with tax dollars, and private institutions financed by tuition. Most associate private schools with religious organizations subject to constitutional requirements for the strict separation of church and state. This public-private distinction is an oversimplification of a complex web of entanglements. Indeed, even the constitutional injunction against state and church entanglements is not absolute: urban schoolchildren in parochial schools are often eligible for Chapter 1 funds and other sources of state and federal funding (Richards and Encarnation 1986).

One particularly difficult kind of public-private entanglement to which the Constitution does not speak is the role of private, for-profit corporate interests in providing publicly financed education for children. Some believe that for-profit firms, enamored of penetrating a $250 billion educational market, are incapable of serving children's interests while pursuing profits. Proponents of privatization counter that for-profit firms would have a higher self-interest in providing the kind of education parents want for their children, because the failure to provide quality at a competitive price will result in a loss of customers, profits, and ultimately the business itself as other firms enter the market.

Of course, for many years public schools have been contracting for services with private for-profit companies. Examples include the busing of school children, cafeteria services, building maintenance, legal services, accounting, security, and educational testing.[14] In addition, desks, textbooks, computers, office equipment, and construction are invariably obtained through purchases or leases from private sector organizations (business firms or nonprofit organizations).

Public schools contracted out for educational services prior to EAI. In New Jersey, for example, a network of private schools of special education has contracted with individual school districts to teach educationally challenged children for more than two decades (Richards and White 1989). Some of those schools are organized as for-profit institutions and some as nonprofit.

Because there is some experience with private management, the question whether a private provider can provide equivalent or superior services for equal or reduced cost can be subjected to empirical investigation. Whether a private company will manage a public school better than the public school itself depends, among other things, on the comparative quality of the current public management, the quality and experience of the private firm, and the accountability and enforcement provisions in the contract.

This chapter is organized into five sections. Following this introductory section, in section 2, we describe EAI, the source of its profits, and the transparency of its accounting procedures. The purpose is to provide background for school districts contemplating contracting with private providers of educational services by illustrating some complexities involved in knowing the contractor.

Section 3 examines the contract between EAI and the Baltimore public schools. In particular, it addresses how the contract's budget allocations were determined. Next, it compares actual per pupil expenditures by elementary, middle, and secondary school type with EAI schools and with a comparison group of schools with similar student profiles. The section concludes with an analysis showing how Baltimore public schools could have saved money by using alternative methods for calculating EAI's per pupil allocation.

Section 4 compares spending patterns in the nine EAI schools with nine other Baltimore public schools. It examines expenditure trends in the total budget, instruction, personnel, and maintenance and operations. Section 5 summarizes the major findings and policy recommendations for districts considering contracts with private providers. The findings are elaborated in the final chapter of this study.

WHAT IS EAI?

In this section we show that EAI has a sophisticated corporate structure with financial, reputational, and managerial support from highly respected corporations. EAI was originally part of a Control Data Corporation subsidiary, USSA Private Schools Inc. Control Data Corporation (CDC) created USSA Private Schools in an attempt to penetrate the primary and secondary education markets for computers. To that end, CDC studied education practices worldwide and incorporated its findings into a computer-based education product called "Plato." In addition to product marketing, CDC planned to build a chain of private schools across the United States. Financial problems in the mid-1980s forced CDC to divest 22 successful businesses, including USSA Private Schools, which was sold to John Golle and Capital Dimensions.

According to its 1994 Annual Report, EAI provided three types of services: schools management, consulting services, and proprietary products. By June 30, 1994, the company provided services to more than 8,800 students in 13 public and two private schools in four states. When this study began, EAI had management contracts with the public school systems of Hartford, Conn., and Baltimore, Md.; management agreements with the public school systems of Eagan, Minn., and Paradise Valley, Ariz.; and consulting contracts with the public school systems of Baltimore and Dade County, Fla.

EAI organized a group of business firms into what it calls "The Alliance for Schools That Work." The Alliance includes KMPG Peat Marwick, the largest accounting and consulting firm in the world; Johnson Controls-Facility Management Services, a firm that specializes in facilities maintenance, energy use, transportation, and other noninstructional services for schools; and Computer Curriculum Corporation (CCC), a unit of Simon and Schuster that developed an early lead in computer instruction. CCC says that its multimedia courseware is used by more than 1 million students in K-12 schools around the world. Simon and Schuster is a publishing unit of Viacom Inc. A subcontractor to EAI, Gladenia Inc., furnished instructional interns to EAI for employment in the Baltimore Tesseract schools. Gladenia's responsibilities included recruitment and screening, employment agreements, payroll and required withholding(s), general supervision, and administration. Interns were drawn primarily from local colleges and universities.

John T. Golle is chief executive officer and chairman of the board of directors. As CEO and board chairman, Golle was paid $134,017 in 1994. In addition, he owned 9.3% of the company's stock as of October 12, 1994, which made him the largest insider stockholder. Some of the other major players at the corporate level included the following:

- David Bennett, EAI president, was superintendent of schools in St. Paul, Minn., for seven years and past president of the Large City Schools Superintendents' Organization.

- Mabel Gaskins, vice president for marketing, was assistant commissioner for the Minnesota Department of Education.

- Kathryn Thomas, vice president for staff development, was employed by CDC, where she originated the Tesseract prototype.

- Frank Kuhar worked at Ernst and Young for 14 years.

- Richard Burke, vice chairman of the board, created and founded United Healthcare.

John T. Walton is the second largest stockholder and also has donated millions to the New School Design Foundation. The New York State Teachers Retirement Fund happens to be the 13th largest of 30 institutional stockholders in the firm. The Hartford-based Travelers Inc. and Prudential Insurance Company of America are the 18th and 24th largest, respectively, of 30 institutional stockholders. Those positions were held before Hartford hired EAI, according to the 1994 13F Report filed by EAI with the Securities and Exchange Commission. The funds are controlled by professional fund management teams, and it is unlikely that executives of the American Federation of Teachers, Travelers, or Prudential were even aware of their companies' investments in EAI.

How Does EAI Make Its Profit?
This section demonstrates that EAI has yet to show that it can make a profit by managing schools. To the extent that it does make a profit, the profit comes from interest earnings and speculation on the price of EAI stock.

In attempting to determine how EAI makes a profit, it was necessary to analyze the relative contributions of three sources of income: (1) operations; (2) investment of cash; and (3) stock sales. Net earnings (losses) were separated into operating profit (loss) and interest income (loss). Before-tax numbers were used, because tax payments can skew net figures. **Table 1** describes in detail EAI's sources of income.

As Table 1 indicates, in 1993 EAI posted net income per share of 32 cents. Of that, EAI posted net earnings of 21 cents per share. That year, interest income (12 cents) boosted the per share figure by another half. In 1994, an operating loss of 5 cents a share was offset by interest income of 49 cents a share, netting approximately 43 cents per share. In the first quarter of 1995, ended September 30, EAI posted a loss of 3 cents per share. EAI's reliance on interest income may simply reflect a startup company's strategic use of reserves to sustain the company while it seeks to nurture its core business. On the other hand, EAI has been using such funds to float the company for five years. Nonetheless, EAI is an early industry entrant and, as such, assumes great risk. Lehman Brothers' influential Mike Moe makes a similar point but cautions the risk-averse investor:

> We believe education is the next "health care" and use the analogy of Education Alternatives becoming the next Columbia/HCA, whereby that firm became a huge company by being the low cost/ high [quality] provider of an essential service. We believe that same model can work for Education Alternatives' operating a national network of schools and being the low cost/high quality provider. Given the inherent hurdles Education Alternatives faces as a pioneer in its industry, the shares of Education Alternatives are very speculative, and appropriate only for the investor who can tolerate a high degree of risk. However, our confidence in the company's ultimate success, its leadership position in a potentially huge market, and relatively low valuation in relationship to our projected growth forecast, makes the shares of Education Alternatives, in our view, a compelling 1-S buy for speculative, growth investors (Moe 1994).

We next assess EAI from the point of view of a potential investor. We disaggregate EAI's return on common equity into return on assets (ROA) and leverage. ROA is a measure of income generated by the profitability of the service provided, while *leverage* is a measure of income generated through debt and stock financing (e.g., interest on bor-

TABLE I

EAI Income Statement, 1990-94
(Dollars in 000s Except Per Share Amounts)

	Year Ended June 30					Qtr. Ended September 30	
	1990	1991	1992	1993	1994	1993	1994
Revenues							
Tuition and Fees	2,181	1,534	2,820	29,628	34,104	5,363.00	6,095.00
School Management	25	765	94	381	299	18.00	67.00
Consulting and Other		46	30				
Proprietary Products							
Other				46			
Total Revenues	2,206	2,345	2,944	30,055	34,403	5,381.00	6,162.00
Direct Expenses							
School Costs	2,972	1,940	2,646	26,746	30,281	4,896.00	5,616.00
School Management		715	140				
Consulting and Other		27	46				
Proprietary Products							
Provision for Doubtful Accounts	6	55	179	167	183	63.00	56.00
Other				159	63	14.00	25.00
Total Direct Expenses	2,978	2,737	3,011	27,072	30,527	4,973.00	5,697.00
Gross Profit (Loss)							
(Revenues Less Direct Expenses)	(772)	(392)	(67)	2,983	3,876	408.00	465.00
Selling, General, Administrative	909	1,059	1,660	2,248	4,177	791.00	1,319.00

TABLE I (cont.)

EAI Income Statement, 1990-94
(Dollars in 000s Except Per Share Amounts)

	Year Ended June 30					Qtr. Ended September 30	
	1990	1991	1992	1993	1994	1993	1994
Operating Profit (Loss) (Gross Profit Less SGA)	(1,681)	(1,451)	(1,727)	735	(301)	(383.00)	(854.00)
Other Income (Expense)							
Interest Income	50	57	187	442	2,883		
Interest Expense	(41)	(104)	(11)	(8)	(2)		
Other Income, Net	9	(47)	176	434	2,881	728.00	618.00
Earnings (Loss) **Before Tax** (Operating Profit Plus Other Income)	(1,672)	(1,498)	(1,551)	1,169	2,580	(345.00)	(236.00)
Income Tax Expense				50	46	15.00	
Net Earnings (Loss)	(1,672)	(1,498)	(1,551)	1,119	2,534	330.00	(236.00)
Net Income (Loss) Per Share	(1.39)	(0.95)	(0.44)	0.32	0.43	0.04	(0.03)
Common Shares Outstanding, Weighted Average	1,203,123	1,582,133	3,499,759	3,498,595	5,923,913	7,986,480.00	7,505,874.00

Source: 1994 Annual Report and April 30, 1993 Prospectus.

rowed money and sale of stock). The results appear in **Table 2** below.

With a low of -37.6% in 1991 and a high of 7.3% in 1994, EAI's return on assets over the period has never topped the performance of a Treasury bond. Historically, EAI has been highly leveraged, peaking in 1993 at 1.092. This is not particularly unusual for a startup company. In 1994, EAI's leverage dropped off to 1.188. During 1994, EAI only raised $730,000 by exercising options and warrants and issued no new stock. *Barron's* characterized EAI's financing as follows:

> Education Alternatives has been more successful at issuing stock than at any of its other competencies: It raised $5.6 million in an initial public offering in May 1991 at $4 a share; it raised $1.9 million in June 1992 at $7 a share; and it raised $31.1 million in May 1993 at $22.25 a share....(Donlan 1994)

There is no evidence yet that EAI can make a profit running schools. The company cleared 11 cents a share in the six months ended December 31, 1994, but thanks only to $1.6 million in interest income on the invested proceeds of last year's stock issue. EAI sustained a loss of 8 cents a share on the business of operating schools. Because EAI stock is highly speculative, investors have to wonder if EAI can find ways to reinvest their equity that produce a better return than T-bills.

TABLE 2

Disaggregation of EAI's Return on Common Equity

| | Percent Common | on | Leverage | | |
Year	Equity	Assets	Leverage	Common Earnings	Capital Structure
1991	-0.588	-0.376	1.564	0.935	1.672
1992	-0.519	-0.322	1.612	0.993	1.624
1993	0.031	0.028	1.092	1.007	1.085
1994	0.087	0.073	1.188	1.001	1.187

Source: 1994 Annual Report, and April 30, 1993 Prospectus.

Was EAI Invested in High-Risk Funds?[15]

To begin this section, it is important to understand that EAI has two different kinds of cash on hand for investment purposes. The first is based on proceeds from the sale of its stock, borrowed funds, and other revenues not directly committed in contracts. The second consists of unspent funds that have been transferred to EAI under contracts with school districts; those funds have been earmarked for use in schools. Standards of investment risk for the two kinds of assets are quite different. This section discusses the importance of the two kinds of investment risk for school districts.

How private companies invest their cash should matter to their customers insofar as the transactions in question take place over an extended period. Contractors can encounter financial difficulties that hamper their ability to fulfill contractual commitments. Even worse, the contractor might commingle funds advanced by the customer with internal funds used in risky financial investments. In California, Orange County's disastrous experience in financial speculation illustrates how taxpayers can wind up footing the bill for investment misadventures of their own local government. As of June 30, 1994 EAI had invested in six funds holding high-risk instruments called derivatives.[16] Such investments accounted for $6,195,000 of $36,746,000 invested in marketable securities, or 16.86%. The remaining securities were U.S. Treasury notes and mortgage-backed securities issued by federal agencies such as the Federal Mortgage Association, known as Fannie Mae. Generally, the derivatives are structured in a way that they rise in value as interest rates decline and decline in value as interest rates rise. When interest rates rose in 1994 the value of EAI's investments fell. EAI invested $2,181,000 in Worth Bruntjen's mutual fund at Piper Jaffray. By December 17, 1994 the investment had lost two-thirds of its original value.

Piper Jaffray is a holding company with subsidiaries that provide broker/dealer services, asset management, investment advisory services, and trust services. The company has a strong reputation, particularly in the Midwest. Recently Piper's reputation was tarnished by aggressive, unsuccessful investments in mortgage derivatives; losses probably exceeded $800 million.

Worth Bruntjen, a senior vice president at Piper Jaffray with 27 years' investment experience, managed assets totaling $3.5 billion in December 1995, including $827 million in the Piper Jaffray Institutional Government Income Portfolio. Investors in the portfolio, which topped government bond performance charts in 1993 with a five-year average annual return of 13.5%, have since lost 23.5%. As Bruntjen runs all his portfolios in similar fashion, the implied damage would be $822 million. According to Susan Kuhn, writing for *Fortune*:

> Last year over half of the fund's assets were invested in leveraged derivative securities, including 15% in principal-only U.S. agency bonds [strips], 20% in so-called inverse floaters, and 8% in Z-bonds, CMOs akin to zero-coupon Treasuries. Crazily, the fund claimed to be short-term in nature, with an implied duration of three years—but, says John Rekenthaler, editor of *Morningstar Mutual Funds*, "the fund had to be a hell of a lot longer," exposing investors more harshly to losses when interest rates rose (Kuhn 1994).

The effect of the loss is far-reaching. Many local governments in the Midwest who put operating cash balances in Bruntjen's fund took losses. Moreover, from 1991 to 1993 Piper Jaffray's Worth Bruntjen ran a $3 billion investment for the state of Florida for three-and-a-half years, aggressively using mortgage derivatives. Florida State Treasurer Tom Gallagher had also put the state's operating cash balance in Bruntjen's fund. In 1993, the Florida money managed by Bruntjen had gained 13%, but in 1994's first quarter it fell 18% (Bary 1994). As part of Piper's $70 million good faith compensation to Bruntjen's investors, EAI was to receive reimbursement of 50 cents on the dollar from Piper.

EAI also invested "several million dollars" in mortgage-backed securities, including some derivatives known as "inverse floaters." For example, EAI put $691,000 into a derivative packaged by Prudential Home Mortgage Securities Co. Backed by 20-year home mortgages, the instrument promised to pay higher profits whenever interest rates fell. When interest rates rose, the value of the investment fell. As of September 30, EAI's first fiscal quarter, the investment was worth $449,000, reflecting a decrease of 35%.

EAI funds invested in derivatives were not public funds but rather proceeds from the sale of stock. Nonetheless, EAI's losses—from whatever source—adversely affect its ability to do business and could threaten its ability to deliver on contracts. EAI's losses have been substantial. In FY 1994, the total value of EAI's investments dropped by more than $10 million. In the first quarter of FY 1995, the value dropped another

$3 million.

EAI's CEO John Golle publicly defended the derivatives investments. Quoted in the *Baltimore Sun*, Golle said EAI has "plenty of cash to operate schools, and the investments—in Treasury notes and mortgage-backed derivatives—eventually will bring EAI between 7% and 8% on its investments....What were we supposed to do, put [our money] in a shoe box?" Golle also said, "In retrospect...maybe we shouldn't have [made the investments] because of the decline of the market value." He added, "We do not own the exotic derivatives like Orange County."

As a private company, EAI has the right to invest any way it likes. Many established companies like Bankers Trust, for example, invested heavily and, for a while, quite successfully in derivatives. As customers, however, local governments can demand that caretakers of public funds adhere to any standard of financial prudence desired. In fairness, governments such as the aforementioned Orange County, Calif., Florida, and several in the Midwest have also invested in derivatives. The private sector has no monopoly on financial misjudgment.

Maryland has been generally conservative in its investments of public funds. It is appropriate to ask whether EAI's investment strategy was too risky for Baltimore. Louise Green, the head of Baltimore's Bureau of Treasury Management, is satisfied with a 5.5% return on the city's $540 million investment portfolio. Maryland municipalities and counties are generally satisfied with yields of 3% to 6%. Baltimore City limits Green to placing all but $100 million of the city's money in investments that will mature within 12 months.

Maryland state law limits government treasurers to investing in "blue chip" securities, such as federally backed securities. Baltimore is authorized by state law to invest in direct or indirect obligations of the U.S. government, certificates of deposit, and repurchase agreements. City policy requires that securities underlying repurchase agreements must have a market value of at least 100% of the cost of the repurchase agreement, and the city takes possession of the securities when the repurchase agreement's maturity is over five days.

There is little doubt that Piper Jaffray's Institutional Government Income Portfolio, with its 13% annual yield, would breach Baltimore's investment risk standards. Nevertheless, Baltimore Mayor Kurt Schmoke said, "My concern about EAI's financial condition is simply whether they have the resources to carry out commitments they made to our school system....So far, it doesn't make me nervous."

Did EAI invest cash from contracts in derivatives? We found no evidence to support that possibility. EAI's cash and cash equivalent balance or its long-term securities (which were written down $10 million in FY 1994) might have been part of Bruntjen's fund, but nothing in public documents supports such a charge. In the absence of any public disclosure requirement, it behooves school districts contemplating contracts with private providers to ensure that the contract stipulates acceptable levels of risk for any funds held by a private contractor. It would be preferable for the district to release funds on a quarterly basis and invest them itself in the interim.

Are EAI's Accounting Practices Misleading?

In this section, we show that while EAI did not break the law or generally accepted accounting practices, it did represent its cash flow and income projections in a highly optimistic manner that served to promote speculative interest in EAI's stock and produce millions in revenues for EAI. The negative press that followed coincided with a sharp drop in the price of EAI's stock.

On February 23, 1994 two EAI shareholders filed suit in federal district court in Minneapolis against EAI, some of its officers (Golle, Mellum, Kuhar, and Bennett) and its accountants (Arthur Andersen and Co.), claiming that they used irregular accounting methods and made unfulfilled promises to inflate EAI's stock price from September 30, 1993 to February 8, 1995 for personal gain. The suit claimed that EAI's John Golle publicly stated in October 1993 that EAI would have $100 million in revenues by June 1994, because it would sign on new schools. In fact, EAI was able to add only two more Baltimore public schools by June 1994. Shareholders also claimed that EAI and Arthur Andersen used "unusual or fraudulent" accounting methods to calculate revenue from the original Baltimore schools. Most of the money Baltimore paid EAI, about $30 million a year, was returned to the city to pay teachers' salaries and administrative expenses—expenses over which EAI had no control. EAI booked the sum as revenue, citing full responsibility for it.

The suit further charged that company officers deliberately inflated revenues to boost stock prices so they could sell their stock for huge capital gains. On January 31, 1995, Federal District Court Judge Richard Kyle dismissed the suit, Case No. 3-94 Civil 101, because both parties agreed to settle out of court. Our analysis of stock offerings by EAI indicates that, over the period in question, the company officers named in the suit sold large blocks of stock for substantial returns.

After the shareholder controversy, EAI said it would count only fees under the latest Baltimore contract—essentially a consulting contract for two elementary schools—under which EAI can make only recommendations. EAI did not change the way it booked revenue on the nine elementary schools under the previous, five-year contract, which gave EAI authority over operations.

Howard M. Schilit, accounting professor at American University and author of *Financial Shenanigans: How to Detect Accounting Gimmicks and Fraud in Financial Reports*, has made a bit of a reputation by tracking EAI's performance. He has been cited in *Barron's*, the *Wall Street Journal*, *Business Week*, and the *Baltimore Sun*. Schilit does not dispute that EAI's accounting practices fully conformed to generally accepted accounting principles (GAAP). In a telephone conversation, Schilit explained that EAI did not break any rules, because there are no relevant rules. However, he said, if "it strikes you as being wrong, there is probably something wrong."

Schilit says that EAI gave investors the impression that its business was much larger than it really was by booking as revenue the entire sum it got from Baltimore for managing the nine schools in its initial contract. Most of this money, per the contract, was returned to the city immediately to cover such costs as teacher salaries, over which EAI had no control. Schilit says EAI should have booked only its fees as revenue—the small percentage of school expenditures it kept. Such practice is more in line with the way consultants (e.g., accountants, investment bankers, lawyers) recognize revenue. Such consultants normally earn an hourly rate, fixed fee, or percentage of a deal.

If the business had been booked in a way that more closely reflected reality, EAI would have reported only a third of the revenue that it did—about $10 million a year. Schilit claims that prior to his seminal October 1993 report, EAI stock traded at $41 per share and, after his report, it dropped to $10 per share, which suggests that speculative interest was based at least in part on a misreading of the size of EAI's business. Schilit is paid to track EAI and other companies by Stan Trilling, a Los Angeles-based Paine Webber Inc. stockbroker who has sold EAI shares short for clients. Trilling hired Schilit after reading his 1993 report. The report was one of a series of white papers provided to subscribing investors.

Some countervailing sentiment was expressed by Lehman Brothers' Michael Moe, who remained bullish in the fall of 1994. In a company report published on October 24, 1994, Moe said:

> Our view is that it is generally more useful for investors to have more information as opposed to less. Education Alternatives receives its fee not based on a fixed percentage but on cost savings and if they spend more than they receive, the company is liable for it....Regardless of whether Education Alternatives "grosses up" revenue or not, net income, earnings per share and cash flow are unaffected, and ultimately these are what investors value a company on.

> While there are not any companies in Education Alternatives' own industry to compare it to, a number of management and outsourcing companies such as Marietta, Service Master, and EDS use similar accounting policies.

While all the experts agree that EAI's accounting practices met GAAP guidelines, it is also the case that investors and perhaps less sophisticated school districts may have overestimated the size and growth rate of EAI's business. Again, that kind of perceptual problem speaks to the high cost of information school boards may face in determining their relative risk in signing contracts with private, for-profit firms.

EAI'S CONTRACT IN BALTIMORE

EAI assumed responsibility for the management of nine of Baltimore's Public Schools. The objective of the administration of the Baltimore City Public Schools was to stimulate improved performance in some of the city's most troubled schools and improve economic efficiency in school management. Key to evaluating the efficiency of Education Alternatives is determining the *average per pupil cost of education* in Baltimore, particularly as applicable to schools of the type given over to management by EAI. We now address the following five issues:

- How are allocations made within the Baltimore City Public Schools budget?

- How was the per pupil allowance determined in the original contract between Baltimore and EAI?

- What are the costs of educating students in each of the different types of public schools (elementary, middle, and secondary) in Baltimore?

- How well do the selected "Comparison Schools" compare with EAI schools in per pupil expenditures?

- What savings might the Baltimore City public school district have achieved by using alternative methods for calculating the EAI allowance?

Why are these five questions important? First, we need to understand something about the size and structure of the Baltimore City public school district's budget to understand the scope and significance of EAI's contract. Second, we need to understand how the district and EAI arrived at their per pupil figures as specified in the contract. Third, we need to see if other legitimate methods of estimating per pupil expenditures might have resulting in significant savings for the Baltimore public schools.

Troubled urban school districts throughout the country continue to seek alternatives that promise to provide economic efficiency. Due to the relative newness of privatized management in education, cost comparisons between private management corporations are not yet available. As a result, districts must rely on their own cost history to determine fair contract value. The following pages present a series of analyses of the cost of education in Baltimore that suggest alternative means of determining fair contract value. Finally, if we determine that Baltimore paid significantly more than it is currently spending for other similar schools in the district, then any conclusions about student achievement gains will necessarily require cost-effectiveness comparisons rather than simply cost comparisons (Levin 1978).

Overview of the BCPS Budget Allocations

This section provides a descriptive overview of the BCPS budget. For FY 1993 the total budget for the Baltimore City Public Schools equaled $587 million. A 5.1% increase was requested for FY 1994 to bring the total budget to $617 million. Total FTE (full time equivalent) enrollment for the district was 101,009 in the fall of 1992. FTE enrollment was projected to equal 101,809 by the fall of 1993. Resulting per pupil expenditures (PPE) are displayed in **Table 3**. Considering the total budget for the BCPS and the full-time enrollment for FY 1993, per pupil expenditures were $5,768. With the budget increase of 5.1%, per pupil expenditures increased to $6,061.

Instructional expenditures totaled $435.5 million in 1993. A breakout of the major budget areas (FY 1993) is displayed in **Figure 1**. The FY

TABLE 3

Summary of BCPS Budget Totals and Enrollments, 1993 and 1994

	Enrollment	Total Budget	Per Pupil Expenditures
FY 1993 (Actual)	101,809	$587,229,678	$5,768
FY 1994 (Projected)	101,809*	617,083,208	6,061

* Previous year FTE used in absence of projected data for FY 1994.

Source: 1993-94 site-based budgets.

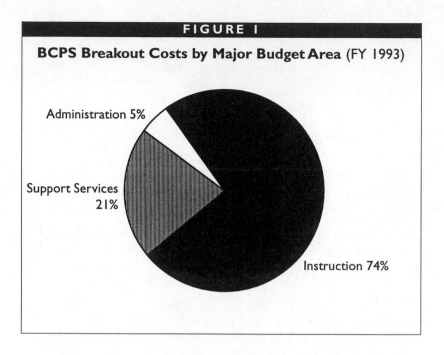

FIGURE 1

BCPS Breakout Costs by Major Budget Area (FY 1993)

Administration 5%

Support Services 21%

Instruction 74%

1994 requested budget included a 4.7% increase in allocations to instruction, as **Table 4** demonstrates. In both FY 1993 and FY 1994 administrative costs composed approximately 5% of the total district budget. Interestingly, summation of the district's site-based budgets for FY 1994, which include instructional as well as noninstructional costs, produces a total of $432,676,607, only slightly exceeding 70% of the projected budget for that year. That would suggest that either additional instructional support is provided by the district's central administration, or that inconsistencies exist in the reported data. In addition, the total number of FTE pupils included in site-based budgets equals 99,744, indicating either a significant number of out-of-district placements or other inconsistencies in the reported data.

The BCPS budget is distributed among 178 school units including special facilities and the eight elementary schools and one middle school privately managed by Education Alternatives Inc.[17] Among the district's 178 schools are 113 elementary schools with an average FTE population of 479; 25 middle schools with an average FTE population of 888; and 18[18] high schools with an average FTE population of 1,079. Four schools

TABLE 4

BCPS Total Budget Breakout Costs
FY 1993 and FY 1994

	Instruction	Support Services	Administration
FY 1993 (Actual)	$435,448,663	$120,633,952	$31,147,063
	(74%)	(21%)	(5%)
FY 1994 (Projected)	455,700,571	126,996,091	34,386,556
	(74%)	(21%)	(5%)

Source: 1993-94 site-based budgets.

in the district serve as elementary/middle schools. In addition, the district houses 11 special education facilities with a total of 2,608 FTE pupils.

In the current BCPS budget, schools are allocated what are called "site-based budgets." Site-based budgeting is a trend which was only recently adopted by the BCPS to provide building administrators with greater freedom to prioritize spending according to the needs of their individual schools. Within the BCPS site-based budgets, funds are subdivided into *nonrestricted* and *restricted* categories. The fund categories are determined according to the source of the funds. *Nonrestricted* funds are generally those generated by local revenues and allocated through the district's "Education Fund." *Restricted* funds are funds received by the district in the form of federal or state aid. Among the restricted funds are funds allocated to individual schools through the district's "Chapter 1 Fund" and "Child Nutrition Fund."

Site-based allocations include general instruction (salaries, wages, etc.), other instructional services, special education, and transportation (contractual services). Since implementing site-based budgeting, the BCPS central administration has continued to provide some services to individual schools. School-based costs that are not allocated directly to schools include food services, instructional resource, facilities—fuel costs, facilities—operations staff, facilities—repairs, security, and cleaning. For the 1993-94 school year, the average site-based allocation for elementary schools equaled just over $2 million. Site-based budgets for middle schools averaged just over $3.5 million and for high schools just over $4.7 million.

The EAI/Tesseract Contract

This section shows that the source of the original $5,918 per pupil allocation to EAI by BCPS seems to have been based on the calculated per pupil expenditure levels of $5,768 (FY 1993) and $6,061 (FY 1994). How the 15% administrative payback in the original contract was established and why it was reduced to 7.5% in the modified contract for 1994 could not be determined.

Overview of the financial agreement. In 1994 Education Alternatives Inc. managed nine of Baltimore's public schools and retained limited contracts with three additional schools. Of the nine schools fully managed by EAI, eight were elementary schools and one was a middle school. Schools included in EAI's Tesseract project were:

Dr. Raynor Browne Elementary School	#25
Edgewood Elementary School	67
Malcolm X Elementary School	38
Sarah M. Roach Elementary School	73
Graceland Park-O'Donnell Heights Elementary School	240
Harlem Park Elementary School	35
Mildred D. Monroe Elementary School	32
Mary E. Rodman Elementary School	204
Harlem Park Middle School	78

At the outset of the Tesseract project EAI was allocated a total budget for the nine schools according to the guidelines in **Table 5**. A per pupil allowance was determined relative to the district's total budget and FTE population. A 15% payback was included to cover administrative and support costs provided by the district's central administration. How this figure was determined and what specific services were actually provided remains unclear. The resulting per pupil allowance was allocated to EAI to generate a total budget of $23,937,770.

TABLE 5
Original EAI/Tesseract Contract

$5,918	Per Pupil Allowance
- $888	(15% "Payback")
$5,030	Net Per Pupil Allowance
x 4,759	Number of Pupils at Nine EAI-run Schools
$23,937,770	Total Funds to EAI, 1993-94

Source: Clarke, Mary Pat (1994).

In March 1994, the BCPS and EAI modified the contract (see **Table 6** for a summary) to reduce the administrative payback to 7.5%; the result was an 8.8% increase in EAI's total allocation after payback.

A comparison of the changes in the contract (**Table 7**) shows that EAI's contract was improved by approximately $2.1 million over the first-year contract. It remains a complete puzzle why the Baltimore City public school district increased EAI's allocation by $2.1 million.

The original contract for the Tesseract project was awarded to EAI through a noncompetitive bidding process. Economic theory suggests that in the absence of competitive bidding, the only basis for determining cost is the cost history of the organization itself. Given the data just presented in the budget overview, the source of the original $5,918 per pupil allowance is not readily apparent. It does seem, however, to fall between the calculated per pupil expenditure levels of $5,768 (FY 1993) and $6,061 (FY 1994) in Table 6. Rationales for the 15% payback in the original contract and the 7.5% payback in the modified contract are even more elusive. According to the breakout of costs in Figure 1, the payback figures may represent a composite of administrative and support service costs. Although the payback figures in both cases exceed district administrative costs as a percentage of the total budget (5%), they fall well short of the combined total of administrative costs and support services (26%).

TABLE 6

EAI Formula Modified March 23, 1994

$5,918	Per Pupil Allowance
- $444	(7.5% "Payback")
$5,474	Net Per Pupil Allowance
x 4,759	Number of Pupils at Nine EAI-run Schools
$26,050,766	ADJUSTED Total Funds to EAI

Source: Clarke, Mary Pat (1994).

TABLE 7

Comparison of EAI Contracts

$26,050,766	March 23, 1994 Contract
-23,937,770	Original EAI Contract
$2,112,996	**Refunded to EAI**

Profile of the Nine EAI Schools

This subsection depicts a general decline in full-time equivalent (FTE) pupils among the nine EAI schools before and after EAI's management of the schools. As we have seen from the analysis of EAI's contract with the Baltimore City Public Schools, pupil enrollments determined the dollar amount of the contract. Growing or declining enrollment in the nine EAI schools could have a significant impact on EAI's expected revenues. A demographic profile tells us something about how representative the students in these nine schools were of the children in the rest of the school system. **Table 8** presents the enrollments and **Table 9** the demographic profile of students among the schools currently man-

TABLE 8

Enrollments in EAI Schools

School	1991-92	1992-93	Net Change	
Dr. Raynor Browne Elementary	249	288	39	(16.0%)
Edgewood Elementary	449	426	-23	(-5.0)
Graceland Park -				
O'Donnell Heights Elementary	354	348	-6	(-1.7)
Harlem Park Elementary	558	534	-24	(-4.3)
Mary E. Rodman Elementary	636	620	-16	(-2.5)
Sarah M. Roach Elementary	393	391	-2	(-0.5)
Mildred D. Monroe Elementary	246	220	-26	(-10.6)
Malcolm X Elementary	286	296	10	(3.5)
Harlem Park Elementary	1,298	1,251	-44	(-3.4)
Total	**4,464**	**4,373**	**-92**	**(-2.1%)**

Source: Nelson, Howard. 1994. *The Private Management of Public Schools.* American Federation of Teachers.

TABLE 9

1993-94 Demographics of EAI Schools

School	Total Enrollment	Mobility Percentage	Chapter 1 Percentage	Free/ Reduced Lunch Percentage
Dr. Raynor Browne Elementary	387	54.5	75.0	96.2
Mildred D. Monroe Elementary	272	41.5	50.6	85.8
Harlem Park Elementary	619	49.4	73.1	95.0
Malcolm X Elementary	388	37.4	67.7	93.4
Edgewood Elementary	526	37.5	35.3	80.3
Sarah M. Roach Elementary	439	29.2	28.4	75.0
Mary E. Rodman Elementary	731	18.1	38.9	76.6
Graceland Park -				
O'Donnell Heights Elementary	381	37.6	70.8	86.1

Source: Golle (1995).

aged by Education Alternatives.

Table 8 indicates a general decline in FTE pupils among the nine EAI schools before and after EAI's management of the schools. Figures presented in the table were published in a report entitled "The Private Management of Public Schools" that was released in May 1994 by the American Federation of Teachers. The figures clearly present a trend apparent in the BCPS data used in later analyses as well. The figures are, however, significantly lower than those presented by either the BCPS or EAI. That fact represents one example of the difficulties that exist in providing a reliable profile of the EAI-managed schools, particularly as each child generated a payment of $5,474.[19]

There appears to be little debate that the student population of the nine schools managed by EAI consisted largely of disadvantaged students; in fact, EAI was assigned some of the most troubled schools in the district. Discrepancies again exist regarding the FTE pupils reported by EAI and the figures reported by the BCPS that were used in subsequent analyses.

Most important in Table 9 are the figures indicating a large percentage of pupils in the EAI managed schools were economically disadvantaged. Current research in education finance suggests that "socio-economic status (SES) has persistently been the most consistent factor related to school outcomes" (Walberg 1986). Therefore, it was reasonable for us to conclude that significant gains in student achievement were unlikely in the first year of operation.

Determining the Cost of Education in Baltimore

The most important finding in this subsection is that an analysis of per pupil expenditures by school type for Baltimore's non-EAI schools yields results that are significantly lower than the EAI-contracted per pupil allowance. Furthermore, EAI's allowance per pupil was 26% above the district cost for elementary school students and 36% above the district cost for middle school students.

As reported earlier, EAI President John Golle claimed that the per pupil allotment for the nine EAI schools was simply the district average per pupil allotment. One way to determine whether the EAI schools had an expenditure advantage in per pupil terms is to calculate expenditures for the entire Baltimore school system based on EAI per pupil expenditures and gauge the impact on the total budget. The following "what-if" scenario simulates the impact on Baltimore's school budget if all schools spent the so-called "average per pupil allotment."

What-If Scenario: Comparing the expenditure levels of EAI and non-EAI schools in Baltimore. Appendix B displays a comparative analysis originally developed by an employee of the Board of Education from the Baltimore City Public Schools that we repeated for this study (Porter 1994). The budget totals for Baltimore's non-EAI schools were based on actual per pupil expenditures and compared with "what-if" budget totals based on the per pupil allowance received by EAI. The *Budget Totals* included reflect *site-based* allocations for the 1993-94 school year.[20] *Average FTE Expenditures* represent site-based costs per FTE pupil. Potential *EAI Budget* figures for each of the schools were derived relative to the EAI per pupil allowance and number of FTE pupils.[21] The *Difference Over/Under* represents the change in total budget for each institution. The author concluded that if such a funding program were to be implemented, schools then receiving in excess of EAI projected values would most likely be protected by a *Hold Harmless* provision. Potential losses to those institutions were represented under the *Hold Harmless* heading.

The analysis yielded a total of $432,676,607 in site-based budgets based on actual expenditure levels. The average site-based budget was $2,606,486. Using EAI's per pupil allowance, the analysis yielded a total of $545,998,656 in site-based budgets, creating a total difference of over $113 million, not including the hold harmless provision. If the hold harmless provision were included, then the total difference would increase to over $133 million. The average site-based budget would increase to $3,289,149, for a difference of 26%. The result tells us that the district average was skewed upward by a few schools where per pupil expenditure is exceptionally high. We found a few such schools, as we will discuss next.

What-If Scenario: Estimating per pupil cost by school type. The previous analysis suggests that allocations to EAI for the management of the nine schools did not accurately reflect educational expenditures throughout the Baltimore City Public Schools. Although Education Alternatives Inc. managed what were perceived to be among Baltimore's most difficult schools, each institution was still considered to be primarily a *regular education* institution that catered to a student population in grades K-8.

The assumption that per pupil expenditures for the BCPS could be accurately determined relative to the district total budget and the district total FTE pupils was misleading. Analysis of per pupil expenditures by school type for Baltimore's non-EAI schools yielded results that are significantly lower than the per pupil allowance contracted with EAI. In the following analysis, school types were defined as

- Elementary Schools K-5 (6)
- Middle Schools 6-8 (9)
- High Schools 9-12
- Special Facilities (primary and special education facilities)

Under that categorization, some schools within the district, such as elementary/middle schools, were omitted from the analysis. However, per pupil expenditures for those institutions closely followed spending patterns of the defined groups.

Table 10 displays a summary of per pupil expenditures for students in Baltimore's non-EAI elementary schools. For those 105 elementary schools, the average per pupil expenditure was $4,338 (Unit = School). The median per pupil expenditure was $4,282 (Unit = School). Per pupil expenditures for BCPS elementary schools ranged from $2,904 to $6,287, which suggests a great deal of intradistrict variation.

Table 11 displays a summary of per pupil expenditures for students in Baltimore's non-EAI middle schools. For those 24 middle schools, the average per pupil expenditure was $4,026 (Unit = School). The median per pupil expenditure was $3,952 (Unit = School). Per pupil expenditures for BCPS middle schools ranged from $3,442 to $5,342, again a surprisingly wide range of per pupil expenditure. The adjusted average, generated by excluding the highest spending school (Robert Poole Middle School, No. 56) dropped to $3,969. Expenditures for Robert Poole Middle School ($5,342) far exceeded the middle school average and exceeded their closest rival (Arnett Brown Jr. Middle School, No. 180) by over $560 per pupil.

Table 12 displays a summary of per pupil expenditures for students in Baltimore's high schools. For the 18 high schools, the average per pupil expenditure was $5,553 (Unit = School). The median per pupil expenditure was $4,204 (Unit = School). Per pupil expenditures for BCPS high schools ranged from $3,271 to $16,663. The adjusted average, gen-

TABLE 10

Summary of BCPS Elementary School Expenditures
(Non-EAI Schools)

	Total	Mean	Median	Standard Deviation
Site-Based Budget	$212,356,725	$2,022,445	$1,940,243	$701,756
FTE Pupils	50,256	479	441	183
Expenditures per Pupil	n.a.	$4,338	$4,282	$761

Source: Porter (1994) and 1993-94 site-based budgets.

TABLE 11

Summary of BCPS Middle School Expenditures
(Non-EAI Schools)

	Total	Mean	Median	Standard Deviation
Site-Based Budget	$84,514,126	$3,521,422	$3,348,372	$1,270,031
FTE Pupils	21,301	888	805	345
Expenditures per Pupil	n.a.	$4,026	$3,952	$461

Source: Porter (1994) and 1993-94 site-based budgets.

TABLE 12

Summary of BCPS High School Expenditures
(Non-EAI Schools)

	Total	Mean	Median	Standard Deviation
Site-Based Budget	$84,923,028	$4,717,946	$4,805,260	$1,622,250
FTE Pupils	19,418	1,079	1,242	536
Expenditures per Pupil	n.a.	$5,553	$4,204	$3,397

Source: Porter (1994) and 1993-94 site-based budgets.

erated by excluding the four highest per pupil schools (schools No. 115, 178, 415, and 451) dropped to $3,969. Each of the institutions excluded in this case provided specialized programming and as a result had either uncharacteristically high site-based budgets or low numbers of FTE pupils.

Per pupil expenditures for Baltimore's 11 *special facilities*[22] are displayed in **Table 13**. Though the number of those institutions would seem to be insignificant in affecting the district's average per pupil expenditure, their expenditure level (PPE = $14,448) did play a substantial role in elevating the district's total cost of education.

Per pupil expenditures in special facilities ranged from $4,229 to $29,743, with seven of 11 spending in excess of $10,000 per pupil. For that reason alone, a districtwide average per pupil expenditure rate was inappropriate for estimating the per pupil cost of regular elementary education program.

Conclusions and implications of the "what-if" analysis. As previously mentioned, all of the schools in EAI's Tesseract project are considered "regular" education institutions. Using the data previously presented in Tables 10 through 13 to represent the actual cost of education for BCPS elementary, middle, high school, and special education students, **Table 14** summarizes the difference between actual cost of education by grade level and EAI's allowance. The result of this comparison displays that EAI's allowance per pupil is 26% above the district cost for elementary

TABLE 13

Summary of BCPS Special Facilities Expenditures
(Non-EAI Schools)

	Total	Mean	Median	Standard Deviation
Site-Based Budget	$23,853,881	$2,168,535	$1,942,357	$1,032,909
FTE Pupils	2,608	237	107	228
Expenditures per Pupil	n.a.	$14,488	$14,714	$8,241

Source: Porter (1994) and 1993-94 site-based budgets.

TABLE 14

Comparison of Average BCPS Expenditures Per Pupil By Grade Level to EAI Expenditures Per Pupil

Grade Level	Average Expenditures	EAI Expenditures	Difference (Percent)
Elementary	$4,338	$5,474	$1,136 (26%)
Middle	4,026/3,969*	5,474	1,448 (36%)
High School	5,553/4,085*	No High Schools	n.a.
Special	14,488	No Special Ed. Schools	n.a.

* Second figure represents adjusted mean determined by removal of outlying schools in sample.

Source: Clarke, Mary Pat (1994).

school students and 36% above the district cost for middle school students.

As **Table 15** depicts, at the elementary level, 91% of non-EAI institutions fall below the EAI allowance and at the middle school level 100% fall below the EAI allowance. Of Baltimore's high schools, only four exceed EAI's allowance. Each of the four schools, the Francis Woods Alternative High School (FTE = 319), Baltimore School for the Arts (294), Venable Senior High School (FTE = 201), and Joseph Briscoe Senior High (FTE = 202), is classified primarily as either a special education or an alternative education institution.[23]

What-If Scenario: EAI were allocated funds according to calculated average expenditures (by school type). **Table 16** displays a comparison between EAI's contracted budget with the BCPS and a potential EAI budget determined by using Baltimore's average cost of education by school type.

Calculating EAI's allowance by that method would result in a total savings of $4.3 million (21%) to EAI elementary schools and $1.4 million (26%) to EAI middle schools for the BCPS per year. Conversely, EAI's total losses per year would exceed $5.7 million. From the fall of

TABLE 15

Summary of BCPS Non-EAI School Expenditures Compared With EAI Expenditure Levels

Grade Level	Number Above	Percent Above	Number Below	Percent Below
Elementary	9	9%	96	91%
Middle	0	0	24	100
High School	4*	22	14	78
Special	8	73	3	27

* Schools 115, 178, 415, and 451 cater primarily to special student populations.

Source: Clarke, Mary Pat (1994).

TABLE 16

WHAT-IF SCENARIO:
EAI Is Allocated Funds According to Average Expenditures, by School Type, for All Non-EAI Students

Grade Level	FTE (EAI Schools)*	EAI Average PPE	EAI Total Budget	Non-EAI Average PPE	Revised EAI Budget	Dollar Excess (Percent)
Elementary	3,790	$5,474	$20,746,460	$4,338	$16,441,020	$4,305,440 (21%)
Middle	969	5,474	5,304,306	4,026	3,901,194	1,403,112 (26%)
Total	4,759		26,050,766		20,342,214	5,708,552 (22%)

* Due to a lack of data on actual FTE for EAI schools, FTE values were derived relative to "Comparison Schools" indicated in the proposal of the Department of Research and Evaluation of the BCPS.

1994 through the end of the term of the contract the district's total savings would exceed $17 million.

What-If Scenario: EAI schools were compared with a control group of schools. Nine schools were identified by the BCPS Department of Research and Evaluation for comparative evaluation with the EAI schools. The Department of Research and Evaluation used the statistical technique of factor analysis to identify certain performance and demographic characteristics shared by both the control group and the schools then managed by EAI. As Table 16 depicts, only one of the nine comparison schools (Lakewood Elementary, No. 86) spent in excess of the EAI allowance of $5,739.

As **Table 17** demonstrates, the average per pupil expenditure level for the elementary comparison schools was $4,464, or on average about $1,010 less per pupil than EAI schools. One way to appreciate the potential impact of that difference on a classroom of 25 students is to note that a teacher in an EAI school had access to $25,250 more per year than the average classroom in comparison elementary schools. The differences were even greater for comparison middle schools.

What were the potential savings to the BCPS through the term of the EAI contract using each of the previous measures to determine "cost of education?" Using the previous analyses, a range of possible per pupil expenditures may be generated and applied to the eight EAI elementary schools and one middle school (See **Figure 2**). The middle school high-end expenditure is generated by the average expenditure of all BCPS middle schools (including outlying data), while the elementary school high-end expenditure is generated by the average of the comparison

TABLE 17

Summary of Comparison Schools
PPE Compared With EAI PPE

Grade Level	Comparison School PPE	EAI PPE	% of All Schools Above EAI PPE	% Below
Elementary	$4,464	$5,474	14%	86%
Middle	3,808	5,474	0	100

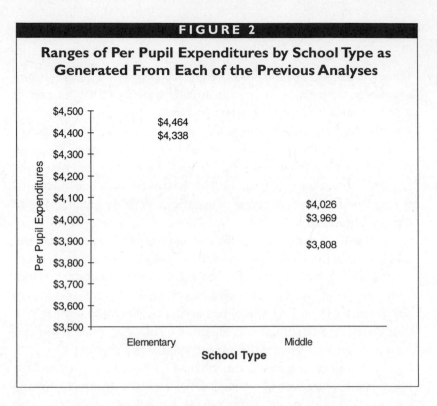

FIGURE 2

Ranges of Per Pupil Expenditures by School Type as Generated From Each of the Previous Analyses

school expenditures. The low-end expenditure for elementary schools ($4,338) is the average expenditure level of all elementary schools in the district, while the middle school low end ($3,808) is the average expenditure level of EAI's Comparison Middle School (Lombard Middle School, No. 57).

Applying those expenditure levels to EAI schools yields the results seen in **Table 18**. The total district savings under those conditions could be as high as $5.9 million per year.

With three years remaining on the EAI contract as of the fall of 1994, total savings to the Baltimore City Public Schools through the full term of the EAI contract could have been as high as $17.8 million (see **Table 19**). Even if the EAI allowance had been determined according to the low end of the calculated range, savings would have been approximately $15.7 million.

TABLE 18

Range of Potential Excess Allocations to EAI Annual Budget

Grade Level	Potential EAI High	Potential EAI Low	Range of Excess Compared to EAI Actual Budget
Elementary (FTE = 3,790)	$16,918,560	$16,441,020	$3,827,900 to 4,305,440
Middle (FTE = 969)	3,901,194	3,689,952	1,402,112 to 1,614,352
Total	20,819,754	20,130,972	5,231,012 to 5,919,792

TABLE 19

Possible Savings From Fall 1994 Through the Term of the Contract (Three Years)

Grade Level	Low	High
Elementary	$11,483,700	$12,916,320
Middle	4,209,336	4,843,056
Total	15,693,036	17,759,376

Conclusions and Recommendations

Each of the previous analyses indicate that serious discrepancies existed between the actual cost of educating Baltimore's youth and the allowance provided to Education Alternatives Inc. The implications are these:

- The cost of educating elementary and middle school students in Baltimore is significantly less than the average cost of education for all students in Baltimore.

- The method used for determining "fair contract value" for the EAI allowance was not necessarily appropriate.

- The Baltimore City Public Schools could have achieved substantial savings over the term of the EAI contract had they used alternative methods of calculating per pupil allowance.

- The validity of the performance comparisons between EAI schools and the selected comparison schools may be invalidated by spending inequities.

The conclusions imply that Education Alternatives Inc. was afforded a significant financial advantage in the management of its nine schools. Such an advantage decreased the district's ability to make a fair comparison between the EAI-managed schools and comparison schools. Moreover, because EAI was responsible for managing only nine of the district's schools, the financial advantage gained by EAI came at the expense of other schools in Baltimore.

In January 1995, John Golle of EAI responded to a report by Carl Stokes of the Baltimore City Council. Stokes had presented concerns that EAI had been provided excess expenditures compared with other schools in the district. Golle responded, however, that EAI was allocated funds *"using the district's existing formula*: gross operating dollars from all sources divided by the number of full-time equivalent students (FTEs)" (Golle 1995). Golle went on to suggest that in as much as EAI's contract was to include "a disproportionate number of schools with challenged students," EAI would *"not* be getting" its "fair share." That statement failed to recognize that many students within the district were "challenged" beyond the capacity of the city's "regular education" institutions, and the expenditure levels for those pupils (in special schools and out-of-district placements) often exceeded $20,000 per pupil/year. Golle suggested further that analyses of EAI's per pupil expenditures were performed using a "net to gross comparison." Golle indicated that a "gross to gross" comparison would have been more appropriate. In the absence of adequate data regarding centralized costs for BCPS institutions, each of the previous analyses presented a "net to net" comparison. Although, as Golle stated, "the sum cannot be greater/less than the parts," we have shown that averages with skewed per pupil expenditure data did result in a substantial financial advantage for EAI relative to other elementary and middle schools in Baltimore.

ANALYSIS OF INTERNAL EXPENDITURES

In this section, which compares EAI and non-EAI schools, our major findings are that EAI allocated a greater percentage of its resources to facilities, teacher training (Tesseract), and technology consulting than the BCPS administration and allocated a smaller percentage of resources to general instructional spending than the BCPS administration.

The manner in which an individual school or entire district spends its money reveals the priorities of its management. Our analyses were conducted to determine:

- spending trends of EAI schools before and after the EAI takeover

- spending trends of EAI schools compared with selected comparison schools

In the last section, the analysis of the contract between BCPS and EAI, we established that EAI received per pupil allocations significantly in excess of other BCPS institutions. In addition, EAI's total contracted budget changed according to full-time equivalent student enrollment number fluctuations and contract renegotiation. The growth in the total district budget from FY 1990 to FY 1994 averaged approximately 7% per year over the five-year period. That percent change in total budget was nearly three times the average rate of increase for per pupil educational expenditures on a national level, indicating that the district made substantial efforts to improve support for education (Hussar 1995). For the two years in which EAI was involved with the district, its percent of the district's total budget rose from 4.08% to 4.22% due to renegotiation of the central administration "payback."

Spending Trends in EAI Schools and BCPS Comparison Elementary Schools From FY 1991 to FY 1994

The following analyses were performed to compare EAI's spending priorities with those of the BCPS in general. Comparisons are based on BCPS and EAI data from FY 1991 through FY 1994. Detailed budgets for the nine EAI schools and nine comparison schools may be found in **Appendices C** and **D**, respectively. The objectives of the comparisons are:

- To determine EAI's spending priorities for the first year of the Tesseract program

- To compare EAI's spending practices with those of the previous managers of the EAI schools

- To compare EAI's spending practices with those of the managers of similar BCPS institutions.

Data acquired and cross-referenced from numerous sources were used to create reasonable comparisons. The research was complicated by the following data problems:

- Parallel budgets between comparison schools and EAI schools were not available for any of the years involved in this study.

- While comparison data are derived from proposed budgets, EAI data could be found fully reported only in the form of unaudited actual expenditure reports.

- Enrollment data were inconsistent among all sources, complicating the process of determining accurate per pupil expenditures.

Despite the awkward nature of the data, comparisons were made according to the sources displayed in **Table 20**.

Because of the necessity of using an alternative form of reported figures for EAI schools in FY 1993, specific line item comparisons required manipulation and in some cases aggregation of line items to achieve equivalents (i.e., aggregating *Salaries* and *Other Personnel* costs as they appear in the site-based budgets to create *Salaries and Other Personnel* as it appears in the EAI Expenditure Report).

Comparing Major Budget Areas and Shifts in Spending

Perhaps the most valid budgetary comparison that could be made is between the eight elementary schools managed by EAI and their eight BCPS counterparts. As suggested earlier, expenditure per pupil comparisons should be made between schools of similar type (elementary, middle, etc.). To account for spending variations that result from institutional differences, the elementary schools must be used. Peculiarities in

TABLE 20

Data Sources and the Structure of the Comparison Between EAI Schools and Their BCPS Counterparts

Fiscal Year	Comparison Schools	EAI Schools
FY 1991	Budgets and Enrollment: BCPS Site-Based Budget Book Proposed Budgets	Budgets and Enrollment: BCPS Site-Based Budget Book Proposed Budgets
FY 1992	Budgets and Enrollment: BCPS Site-Based Budget Book Proposed Budgets	Budgets and Enrollment: BCPS Site-Based Budget Book Proposed Budgets
FY 1993 First Year of EAI Contract	Data Not Available Report for FY 1993	Budgets: BCPS Expenditure Report No. 200 Unaudited Enrollments: BCPS Instructional Expenditure
FY 1994	Budgets and Enrollment: BCPS Site-Based Budget Book Proposed Budgets	Data Not Available

per pupil spending in EAI's Harlem Park Middle School and its counterpart Lombard Middle School will be discussed later. **Figures 3** and **4** are based on pupil-weighted means to account for the effect of school size (FTE) on overall budgeting practices.

A Closer Look at How EAI Chose to Spend

Figure 5 shows that while the EAI schools were already experiencing greater growth than their counterparts before FY 1993, upon the signing of EAI's contract with the BCPS, the eight EAI elementary schools experienced even greater growth in total budget. BCPS allocations to EAI schools appear to have widened the gap between EAI and non-EAI schools not only in year-to-year dollars, but in the rate of increase as well.

Figure 6 provides a closer look at the changes that occurred in instructional spending in EAI and comparison elementary schools. Instructional spending in comparison schools shows not only an increase in year-to-year dollars, as previously indicated, but an increase in rate of

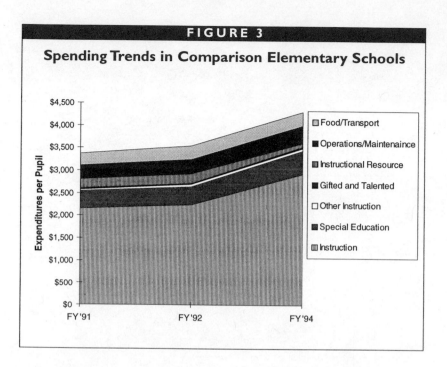

FIGURE 3

Spending Trends in Comparison Elementary Schools

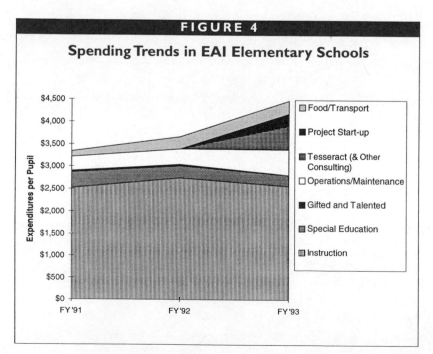

FIGURE 4

Spending Trends in EAI Elementary Schools

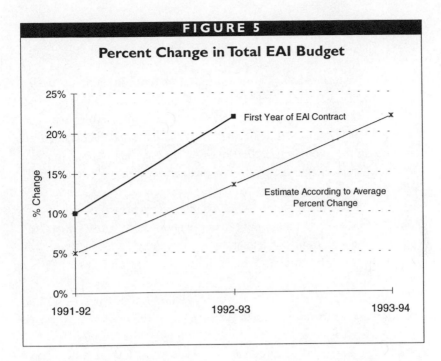

FIGURE 5

Percent Change in Total EAI Budget

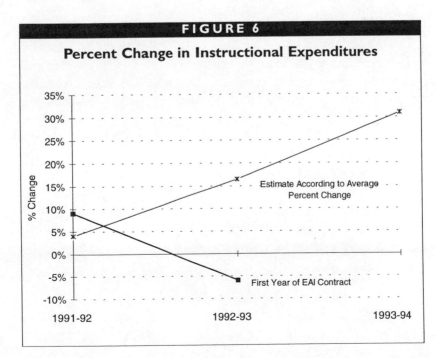

FIGURE 6

Percent Change in Instructional Expenditures

change over time. This rate of change may be interpreted as an "effort" factor, indicating that the management of BCPS significantly increased its instructional effort in recent years.

EAI, on the other hand, chose a different approach in spending. Again, the EAI schools experienced greater growth than their counterparts before FY 1993. The relatively high BCPS level of effort in the years preceding the EAI contract may be an indication of the special needs of the students in the schools inherited by EAI. In the first year of the EAI contract, however, instructional expenditures actually declined (-7%). Whether this is due in part to discrepancies in the reported forms of the data cannot be clearly determined, yet the differences in spending are sufficiently significant that minor discrepancies should not dramatically alter the apparent trends. Trends projected from EAI's limited tenure in Baltimore would be unreliable, so our data cannot be taken as more than descriptive.

EAI received much criticism from both the American Federation of Teachers and the Maryland State Department of Education regarding its special education spending practices. The bulk of the criticism (investigations and lawsuit) was directed toward spending at the middle school level, particularly Harlem Park Middle School. An analysis of special education spending at the elementary level shows a somewhat different picture. Although it is apparent in **Figure 7** that EAI special education expenditures experienced negative growth in FY 1993 compared with the strong positive growth in the comparison schools, EAI schools had experienced even greater negative growth in special education spending before FY 1993. Such spending fluctuations may be due to shifts in district policies regarding placement of special needs children or simply general demographic shifts.

Figure 8 depicts EAI's emphasis on operations spending (particularly facilities maintenance and repair) during the first year of its contract with BCPS. One possible explanation for the dramatic jump in operations spending is that EAI entered the project intending to ensure a clean and positive learning environment. There is little question that the facilities inherited by EAI were in dire need of attention. Another possible explanation for the rise in operations costs arises from discrepancies in the forms of the reported data. Because all budget items may not be matched on a line-for-line basis, it is questionable whether EAI, through its contract with the BCPS, chose to play a more significant role

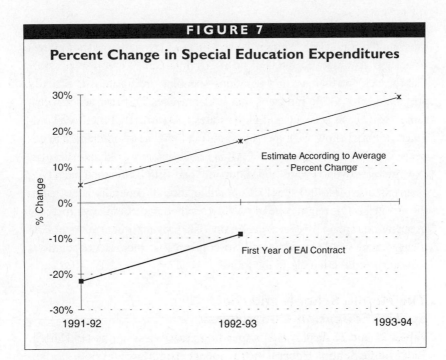

FIGURE 7

Percent Change in Special Education Expenditures

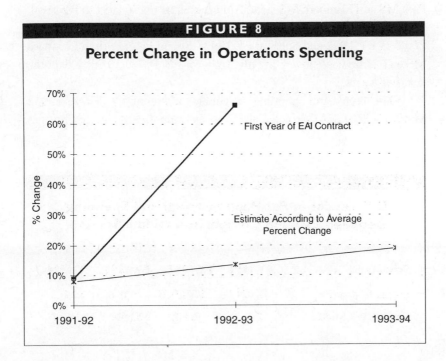

FIGURE 8

Percent Change in Operations Spending

in the operation and maintenance of its facilities. Given the information presented in John Golle's report, "The Myths and Realities of Baltimore's Education Alternatives Inc. Financial Arrangement," it is also possible that the percent increase in operations spending in Figure 8 is actually artificially low. Golle indicates that EAI practices "accrual accounting" rather than "cash accounting." Golle states, "Assume BCPS buys a computer. It would show the expenditure during the year of purchase and expense it in its entirety that year. EAI, in comparison, would amortize that expense over five (5) years and show only one-fifth of the total each year as an expense" (Golle 1995). This practice, though generally accepted in the private sector, might have ultimately resulted in a cumulative increase in operations spending over time. Again, data for subsequent years of EAI management would be necessary to confirm that increased operations spending would continue in the future.

The Middle Schools and the Special Education Controversy

Tables 21 and 22 display EAI's spending practices as applied to Harlem Park Middle School. General instructional expenditures for both Harlem Park MS and Lombard MS steadily increased from FY 1991 to FY 1994. The average rate of change for Harlem Park was approximately 7.1% (7.3% in FY 1992 and 6.9% in FY 1993). Spending growth in Lombard MS was somewhat slower, at only 3.9% for FY 1992 and 7.7% over the next two years.

While increasing spending on general instruction in Harlem Park Middle School, EAI attracted attention by dramatically decreasing spe-

TABLE 21

Differences in Per Pupil Instructional Spending Between EAI and Comparison Middle Schools

School	FY 1991	FY 1992	FY 1993	FY 1994
Lombard Middle	$2,021	$2,100	n.a.	$2,262
Harlem Park Middle	2,182	2,342	$2,503	n.a.

TABLE 22

Differences in Per Pupil Special Instructional Spending Between EAI and Comparison Middle Schools

School	FY 1991	FY 1992	FY 1993	FY 1994
Lombard Middle	$615	$630	n.a.	$590
Harlem Park Middle	703	809	$234	n.a.

cial education funding. The prior year increase had been at a rate of 15%. EAI's change in special education funding was -71% for FY 1993. Over the two-year period from FY 1992 to FY 1994 special education spending in Lombard Middle School (comparison school) decreased a total of 6.3%. What remains to be seen in this case is whether a court would have decided that special needs students were, in fact, deprived of appropriate opportunities. It is also possible that the dramatic shift in special education spending, coupled with a general increase in education funding, represented a new EAI approach to the education of special needs children.

Conclusions of the Budget Analysis

The internal budget analysis of EAI elementary schools demonstrates that EAI's spending practices in the first year of its contract with BCPS were significantly different from those of the nine BCPS schools selected for comparison with the EAI schools. Although interesting questions arise from the analysis of EAI's spending in Harlem Park Middle School, adequate conclusions may not be drawn on a single school basis. Assuming that elementary school spending practices reflected the priorities of school managers, the following conclusions may be drawn:

• EAI allocated a greater percentage of its resources to facilities than did the BCPS administration.
• EAI allocated a greater percentage of its resources to teacher training (Tesseract) and technology consulting—both provided by EAI itself—than did the BCPS administration.

- EAI allocated a smaller percentage of resources to general instructional spending than did the BCPS administration.

Because of the inconsistencies in EAI's special education spending practices between the eight elementary schools and one middle school, no reliable conclusions may be drawn. Excluding Harlem Park Middle School, it appears that EAI's special education spending policies did not differ significantly from BCPS policies. Overall it is difficult, if not impossible, to conclude whether any of the trends presented in this section are actually indicative of the future of Baltimore's EAI schools without data from subsequent years of EAI management. What is clear is that EAI entered into the Baltimore Tesseract project with a defined set of spending priorities that differed significantly from those previously established by the Baltimore City Public Schools.

SUMMARY AND RECOMMENDATIONS

This chapter explains the economic motivations of companies like Education Alternatives Inc. to seek markets in the public school sector and the economic motivations of school districts like the Baltimore City Public Schools to consider hiring them. We have attempted to describe the very complex relationship between Education Alternatives Inc. and the Baltimore City Public Schools, yet a good deal remains unexamined. Despite the limitations of our data, we have learned several noteworthy things.

In Section 2, we showed that EAI has a sophisticated corporate structure with support from powerful corporate allies including Simon and Schuster, Peat Marwick, and Johnson Controls. Further, EAI's leadership also established important linkages with corporate and financial leaders like Sam Walton Jr. and Piper Jaffray. We have shown that EAI has yet to demonstrate that it can make a profit running schools. To the extent that EAI did make a profit, it came from interest earnings and stock speculation. We concluded that EAI's optimistic self-promotion generated millions in profit through speculative stock sales.

Section 3 examined the contract between EAI and the Baltimore Public Schools. In particular, it discussed the contract's budget allocations and it compared actual per pupil expenditures by elementary, middle, and secondary school type in EAI schools and a comparison group of schools with similar student profiles. Section 3 concludes with an analysis showing that Baltimore public schools could have saved $17 million over the life of the contract by using more appropriate methods for calculating EAI's per pupil allocation.

Section 4 focused on a comparison of internal spending patterns in the nine EAI schools with nine other Baltimore public schools. The section examined expenditure trends in the total budget, instruction, personnel, maintenance, and operations. Our major findings were that EAI allocated a greater percentage of its resources to facilities, teacher training (Tesseract), and technology consulting than did the BCPS administration and allocated a smaller percentage of resources to general instructional spending than did the BCPS administration.

The following recommendations drawn from the research are addressed to policy makers, school district leadership, and government officials:

- Do everything possible to encourage competitive bidding.

- Carefully check the backgrounds, track records, and corporate structure of private providers, especially their financial stability.

- Do not turn large sums of cash over to private providers who are likely to invest it in ways that are riskier than your district's policies. Rather, schools should invest funds themselves and release it as needed to meet obligations.

- Collect good baseline data on student performance and school expenditures using both the privately managed schools, a group of control schools, and district averages for comparison.

- Require private providers to disclose in a timely fashion both detailed expenditure reports that use line items that parallel those used in the school district, and relevant personnel and student data.

- Write contracts that include accountability and performance standards.

- Establish per pupil cost comparisons by school type (e.g., K-6 elementary, 6-8 middle schools, 9-12 high schools, special education schools, alternative schools, and vocational technical schools).

Though these recommendations will not guarantee a positive outcome, they should dramatically reduce the risks associated with private contracting. These and other proposals are elaborated further in Chapter 4.

CHAPTER 3

Contracting and
Economic Efficiency

BY MAX B. SAWICKY

INTRODUCTION

Education reformers have been encouraged by privatization advocates to consider contracting the management of public schools to business firms. It is claimed that, according to widely accepted economic doctrine, business firms are better suited to manage schools than are public employees. Generally accepted economic theory, however, is altogether ambivalent on the validity of such an assertion. This should not be news to economists, but it is less well understood by policy makers and parents. This chapter hopes to motivate such readers to consider the ways of privatization as much as the initial decision to accept the approach. It also underlines the point that privatization is not necessarily the most promising approach to reform.

The basic economic premise under review here is that a business organization will supply better management of public schools because it is guided by the profit motive. The premise is criticized here by an appeal to elementary economic theory and a discussion of the real-world circumstances under which contracting actually has been conducted. The goal of this chapter is not to foreclose the contracting option, but to level the playing field on which it is compared with alternative reforms. Moreover, this and the following chapter suggest ways to employ contractors more effectively.

The basic conclusions are these:

- There is no case in economic theory that contracting the management of a school system or a group of schools necessarily improves educational outcomes or reduces costs.

- There is no empirical evidence that contracting the management of a school or group of schools has improved educational outcomes or reduced costs, because actual experience of this type has been limited.

- To date, competitive market conditions that might foster efficient production and distribution of goods and services have been largely absent from the actual practice of contracting in local public education. It is the obligation of the customer—local government—to create those conditions, and accomplishment in that area has been lacking.

The question is not whether a business can run a school acceptably. That clearly has been done, although there are remarkably few examples. Of course, many successful schools are run by nonprofit organizations. This chapter does not discuss whether the availability to parents of more choices of schools improves the effectiveness of education. The role of parental choice is beyond the scope of this study. There is a lively literature on school choice and a public debate that remains unresolved (Rasell and Rothstein 1993). The focus here is on contracting the management of public schools to for-profit business firms, without regard to whatever parental choice options may be available. Once again, our question is this: Can a contractor be expected to serve the public interest in education effectively by virtue of the fact that it is a business firm run for profit?

A basic obstacle to answering those questions is the nation's limited experience with contracting and the even more limited documentation of that experience. There is not enough information to predict with confidence that managing education under contract will or will not work. At this stage, we are reduced to collecting anecdotes. We have many of them, and we try to make as much sense of them as possible, but such stories are not a substitute for data obtained in well-organized experimental settings and subjected to statistical analysis. The chief value of our "data"—experiences with contracting to date—is to illustrate many of the things that can go wrong, as very little has gone right. That something can go wrong, of course, does not mean it must.

At a minimum, the almost uniformly negative experience with contracting should motivate education reformers to be more careful than they might otherwise be. Our lack of comprehensive data obliges us to focus on the economic logic of contracting out in education, rather than on the necessarily limited lessons of our insubstantial experience.

Our recurring question is whether markets can be expected to *improve* upon the public sector's performance. It might not seem fair to hold markets to a higher standard than the status quo, but we are choosing among alternatives from the starting point of the existing, public system. Transition to radically new arrangements would be costly, so any new system has to promise enough good to compensate for the upheaval associated with the switch. If we were beginning with a clean slate and choosing, for instance, the best way to bring the Internet to public schools, we would contrast public and private alternatives on a more level playing field.

WHAT ARE WE BUYING?

We begin by asking, what is special about public education in an economic sense? Then we consider how those characteristics are served by contracting. Parents could, of course, be organized (or compelled, if necessary) to select schools for their children, just as drivers are required to purchase auto insurance. At bottom, we would like to get some sense of the collective, public goals for education—in short, the national interest. From such a standpoint, the motives or capacity of parents to make decisions pertaining to their own children would not be taken for granted.

Contracting is a *means* of providing education. The question of how education is to be provided is distinct from the widely supported principle that education is in some way "public" and should be financed with tax dollars. The wisdom of contracting depends on how the goals underlying the public commitment to education can be efficiently met by business firms, nonprofit organizations, public employees, or some combination of these.

Four important public aspects of education are:

1. A concern underlies the well-being of every student;

2. Education ought to impart shared social values, particularly citizenship and patriotism;

3. The benefits of education or the extent of education provided by public or private suppliers are intrinsically complex—multidimensional—and difficult for the individual consumer (parents and children) to define, measure, and interpret;

4. The difficulty of evaluating the educational product elevates our interest in *how* education is provided. In other words, insofar as the benefits of education for students and the community are hard to measure, we are encouraged to infer what has been accomplished by examining the educational process itself.

We now consider these in turn.

Education for All

Universal education is commonly acknowledged to be in the national interest. Education is thought to provide benefits to society as a whole, not just to students and their families. In economic terms, a well-educated child is better equipped to make a productive contribution to the nation than is one who is not well educated. From a moral standpoint, universal education helps children to realize their potential. For both reasons, each child matters to all. None of this means that education must be provided by government employees, but it does underline a public interest. Two basic dimensions of the public interest are these:

- From an economic or ethical standpoint, a public commitment to universal education implies an interest in the way the benefits of education are distributed among students (Murnane 1981). Some level of achievement must be realized by all.

- Stipulating a requirement for a universal minimum level of educational accomplishment implies a common measuring rod—a standard by which to evaluate results (Ravitch 1994).

If we agree that each child must progress according to some common, minimum standard, it follows that the entire education system, including private schools, must be held to account. The national interest is no less pressing for a child who attends a religious school than for one who goes to a public school. There will always be students, parents, teachers, schools, local governments, business firms, and taxpayers who are indifferent to the general, public interest. Even for those with a direct stake in the education system, the public interest is always broader.

Education contractors and even private schools are paid in part with federal and state tax dollars. In light of interests that transcend the family and its community, the relationship between contractor and local government cannot be closed to oversight or regulation by higher levels of government. The same principle follows for any recipient of public support, including religious institutions.

Education for Citizenship

The purposes of education go beyond equipping children to be productive individuals. Our country also prospers because we agree to cooperate in certain essential ways—to practice the civic and social virtues. For instance, we agree to formulate and enforce in law common standards of moral behavior. As a democracy, we have a particular means by which we exercise self-government.

There is much disagreement over the proper interpretation of all such issues, but it remains widely recognized that in some way or another education should impart values, not just knowledge and skills. We may disagree on what the values ought to be, but we pursue such interests in any case. The question is whether it is possible to secure from a contract the same or better adherence to policy than is forthcoming in public education.

Outcomes Are Difficult to Measure, Interpret, and Attribute

Dissatisfaction with government has focused greater attention on the efficiency with which public services are provided. Business firms can measure some workers' productivity by comparing the quantity of goods or services sold to hours of work. Government's job in that respect is more difficult because its services are often as hard to measure as "the pursuit of happiness." If we do not know the amount of education produced, we are less able to reward or penalize workers, managers, government bureaus, or contractors for doing well or badly. In other words, it is not as easy to pay the provider according to measurable results.

Unlike other services, such as trash pickup, the educational "product" is difficult to define, measure, and interpret. Moreover, even if we knew exactly how much education had been produced, it would be difficult to determine which persons in the educational system deserved credit or blame.

Defining the product is plagued by the fact that there is more than one objective for education. With multiple dimensions, we are left to ponder how, for example, to weigh 1% more reading comprehension against 1% less mathematical proficiency. We could gather a wealth of productivity indicators, but there would remain the problem of how to weigh one against another. Devising ways to measure performance or productivity is costly and complicated. Disagreement persists over the best approaches, even in areas that might appear to be cut-and-dried, such as mathematics (Cohen 1995).

Definitions aside, measuring academic achievement is not easy. Course grades clearly have limited value. An "A" could mean different things coming from different teachers, earned in different subjects, or granted in different years. One alternative is evaluating students according to uniform procedures, such as standardized tests. Proper construction and evaluation of such tests is fairly complicated. Standardized tests can be helpful but are not definitive indicators of performance or productivity in education. Means for evaluating students other than standardized tests have been developed, and research proceeds in this area.

Insofar as we already have effective measurement methods, we still lack a system for conducting comprehensive assessments on a national basis. The same problem applies in many states. It will be necessary to organize new institutions to lay the basis for evaluating productivity in education.

The validity of assessment methods aside, the availability of such data sets the stage for a host of new problems. Students' scores can be compared, but a dizzying variety of such comparisons could be made, and a myriad of factors bear on the outcomes. A child could do well compared with his or her classmates but poorly compared with students in other classes, schools, or school districts, or worse than students in the same class and school in prior years. By contrast, a student who failed to impress the casual observer might have made extraordinary efforts to overcome adverse individual, family, or community circumstances. Untangling the various factors underlying test scores is a difficult analytical and statistical exercise. The same holds for teachers' performance. If student achievement is the gauge, teachers will perform more or less well if their students are more or less prepared, or if they labor under fewer or greater constraints.

Finding disappointing results in the educational system begs the question of how the quality of education might change under alternative arrangements. For instance, if a government chose the Edison Project over Education Alternatives Inc. to manage a school, or if parents move from Madison to Milwaukee for their child's journey through the third grade, how can we know whether the child would have been better off with Edison or by staying in Milwaukee? EAI could have a contract in another school, or in another town, but it does not have an identical child in a community with identical economic and social circumstances. What we would really like to know is the "value added" by the teacher, the school, and the school system (Hanushek 1994). That means the students' progress in meeting his or her maximum potential in light of all relevant obstacles.

Research on educational productivity has yielded diverse conclusions on some central considerations. Some scholars maintain, for instance, that education spending is not a major factor in determining the quality of educational outcomes (Hanushek 1986, 1989; Chubb and Moe 1990). These conclusions have been criticized or contradicted in other research (Ferguson 1991; Ferguson and Ladd 1996; Hedges, Laine, and Greenwald 1994, 1995; Hanushek 1994). Disagreement on the determinants of educational productivity extends to an entire range of factors (Porter 1995). Insofar as experts can disagree on such questions, it is safe to assume that local authorities could experience some difficulty in evaluating the effectiveness of their policies or their reform initiatives.

Some goals in education are not susceptible to measurement. Examples include the sorts of citizenship objectives noted, but they also encompass intellectual faculties not easily captured in tests. There is empirical evidence that test scores are poor predictors of lifetime earnings (Jencks et al. 1972). Educational outcomes are valued as investments, but their true future benefits are hard to predict. That such investments are the best available for most children underscores the urgency of reform but provides no guidance as to how best to pursue it.

It is presumed that if the provider has an incentive to do well, that individual in turn can pay his or her employees for their individual contributions. We noted the difficulty of measuring education's "product"; the difficulty applies in greater measure to individuals than to organizations. If teamwork is the root of productivity, then it is less feasible to measure fairly and accurately the contribution of any individual on the team (Simon 1991).

The difficulty of gauging educational productivity naturally recedes when schools are extremely good or very bad. In the former case there is less premium on measurement because norms of achievement are well satisfied. In the latter circumstance, the task of reform is grimly simple: construct schools that function or create effective escape routes for ill-served students. For this study, the use of private sector managers aims at the former remedy—to put schools that are clearly failing under more effective management. Precision measurement on the margin does not matter if one can distinguish between obvious failure and minimum functionality.

As we all note throughout this study, there has been, to say the least, no clear "breakaway" success story so far in education contracting, so we remain condemned to search for incremental gains. But insofar as the nature of education makes it difficult to pay for small portions of results, how do we determine what we are purchasing? We pay a provider who agrees to adhere to certain procedures. In other words, as discussed next, we regulate.

Obscurity of Outcomes Prompts a Consideration of How Education Is Provided

Problems in observing, measuring, and interpreting outcomes in education and other public services lead us to gauge outcomes by making inferences from the process by which the service is provided. For example, if we do not pay teachers for the number of A's their students receive (or for their scores on standardized tests), we might promulgate rules and regulations governing who is selected for the teaching profession, how they are trained, and what the curriculum must be. They could be called "input and process regulations." Such an approach currently dominates the way most public services, including education, are managed.

The preoccupation with inputs and process has been the focal point of attack by advocates of privatization and "reinventing government" (Osborne and Gaebler 1992), including critics of public education (Hanushek 1986; Hanushek et al. 1994). These writers point to difficulties in determining outcomes by monitoring "inputs." They say that if outcomes are not measured, they cannot be rewarded, and if they are not rewarded, public employees will have insufficient incentives to do a good job.

It is true that the connection between inputs and outcomes can be murky. But such criticism is only as good as the feasibility of alternatives that entail defining, measuring, and rewarding improvements in outcomes (productivity). As noted previously, there are important, perhaps insuperable, obstacles to those approaches in education.

Summary

We have suggested that the public interest in education has at least two crucial features that distinguish it from the public interest in, say, car ownership. One is that some minimum level of accomplishment is desirable for each child, so there is a proper concern with the distribution of the benefits of education. Furthermore, common standards of accomplishment must be set to determine the extent of such benefits. The second basic feature is that the content of education includes shared social values.

Concerning the nature of education as a "product," we have said that the quality of such a product is not easy to determine or to agree on. That dilemma leads us to consider how education is provided in order to gain insight into what we are getting.

The argument that public education is not quite like other products does not necessarily preclude a role for contractors. The goal of achieving universal satisfaction of minimum standards of educational achievement might well be pursued by employing contractors, just as universal health care could entail the participation of independent physicians and private hospitals. Nonpublic providers of education could be mandated to engage nonacademic areas of instruction. The difficulties in measuring education and the resort to "input and process" regulations apply in the public sector as well as the private.

It could be argued that concerns about values and measurement are luxuries compared with the public schools' core mission of providing adequate instruction in the most narrow sense, which is encompassed by the first feature of education discussed earlier. The primacy of results over values is well taken because problems with nonpublic providers in that vein may well be limited, and because other institutions in civil society, starting with the family, arguably have equal or greater responsibilities in that area. The determination of narrowly defined educational results, however, hinges directly on problems of definition, measurement, and evaluation, especially when clear and dramatic improvements are not customarily forthcoming.

In the next section, we consider the ways in which markets are believed to foster the efficient use of resources, and the respects in which that applies to managing public schools, keeping in mind the special features of education described.

MARKETS IN EDUCATION

U.S. Senator Phil Gramm (R-Texas), formerly a university professor of economics, uses the catch phrase that "markets are smart and governments are dumb," implying a broad distinction between the two ways of providing goods and services. Putting aside the question of who is smart or dumb, the line between "market" and "government" is blurred when we speak of contracting and education.

As things stand, governments always have made extensive use of markets to provide education. Governments buy books, computers, and educational materials from business firms. They arrange for construction firms to build their facilities. They often contract for custodians, food service, and security, among other things. They employ business firms and nonprofit organizations for explicitly instructional tasks, such as teaching disadvantaged students to read. They provide vouchers to parents of handicapped children with whom some public schools are not well equipped to deal.

So what is the big, new deal about markets and contracting? What's novel is the idea of using business firms to manage an entire public school, a group of schools, or a school system. At a minimum, the firm provides a team of managers. The new "market" therefore consists of the choice of teams for hire by public school authorities. Under the status quo in education, there is only one "team"—the public managers. The "team owners"—elected officials—can release and obtain individual players and they can shuffle personnel among positions in the line-up, but as a rule they do not engage or replace their entire corps of managers in one fell swoop. Contracting for management services makes the latter option more accessible, although in practice there must remain a layer of public bureaucracy between the public decision makers and the "provisional" contractor's managers. We discuss this potential redundancy of personnel below.

The idea of turning over educational management to for-profit firms seems new because it has not been tried for a while. As Rima Shore points out, there were a number of efforts in that vein some 20 years ago. Research on the fruits of the ventures turned up no improvements in educational outcomes (Gramlich and Koshel 1977; Peterson 1981[24]).

While markets and private management are pervasive in education, we noted above that very few private schools in the United States are run by for-profit business firms. The notion that profits will motivate business to provide effective management for education thus far lacks historical precedent.[25]

There is some public sentiment that profits do not belong in public education. This sentiment is not necessarily well founded. All who contribute to the nation's output of goods and services are self-seeking in a material sense. Workers want wages; managers want salaries; landlords want rent; investors want interest and dividends. Profit is simply the name for a type of financial reward reaped by a particular class of individuals—the owners of business firms.

Like markets, profits can already be found in public education. Schools buy plenty of things from business. Governments borrow money by selling bonds to profit-seeking investors. If a private business firm offered the services of a highly paid genius, a government would have to match such compensation to hire such a person directly. By and large, there is no escape from the cost of profits, with the exception of "supernormal" profits available to business monopolies. What's new is not the introduction of profit but the role being proposed for contracting: transferring managerial control to a profit-making concern.

Some suspicion of profit is understandable because contractors might increase profits at the expense of students, thereby violating the spirit, if not the letter, of their covenant with school authorities. But the same could be said of nonprofit organizations or public agencies that might overpay their executives or overstaff their ranks.

Another reason to deemphasize the influence of profits is that there are other ways a privately employed manager or business owner can make money for the firm or owner. Some of the alternative avenues to financial aggrandizement do not serve the interests of the customer, as discussed in Chapter 2.

The expectation that business firms will offer better services at a lower cost is founded on a vision of brisk competition for the public's purchase. In the public mind, quality and cost savings are complementary features of markets, but in economics they can be contradictory. For efficiently run firms, better quality could cost more and lower costs could entail inferior quality. In a lively market setting, there could well be a tradeoff between quality and cost. One often observes a range of products with variations in price and quality.

The drive to sell could encourage firms to temper or defer their lust for profits to match or beat their rival's price. In this scenario, prices are minimized because the nature of the product is taken for granted. Customers do not compare products—just prices. But cutthroat price competition might not afford much of a role for an "entrepreneur"—someone who finds innovative ways to provide more for less. Any such technique for reducing costs or improving quality might be readily emulated by competitors. Pressure to keep prices low might prevail indefinitely, all but eliminating the incentive to innovate.

For the profit motive to play a stronger role—for higher-than-average rates of return on investment to be possible—markets must be less competitive, not more. What draws investors is the chance to enjoy exceptional rates of return—not average ones. An entrepreneur may choose to manipulate a market for the purpose of suppressing competition. The individual may look for niches where competition is weak or lacking altogether. The competitor may seek to provide a service in ways that cannot be imitated.

Educational reformers shopping for private-sector management teams are dealing with business organizations that are no more eager to confront competition than the public agency is to be replaced. They prefer the appearance to the reality of competition. This is unavoidable and does not mean that contracting cannot work. As we will see, it does mean that the way contracting is organized by government makes all the difference.

An important feature of privatization debates has been the contrasting view of business firms and public agencies as organizations. Governments are thought to be hampered by a lack of flexibility, particularly in dealing with civil servants, but also more generally in "red tape" rules that limit the discretion of public managers to make sensible decisions. It is common to hear that "you can't fire anyone in government," or that managers are prevented from doing a better job because of the obligation to obey cumbersome rules.

In the first place, some negative attributes of public agencies can have positive ramifications. The difficulty of dismissing a worker, from the employee's standpoint, is job security, which enhances the appeal of the job and ought to attract a better class of worker. A business firm with a reputation for making snap judgments in employee discipline would be less attractive in this respect. Alternatively, a contractor could be subject to the same personnel rules as the local government, particularly if the contractor is required for one reason or another to manage the same front-line public employees formerly under public management. The latter has been the rule as far as teachers in public schools are concerned. In only one case (Wilkinsburg, Pa.) has the contractor tried to dismiss the entire teaching corps. Replacement of other types of workers, such as custodians, food service workers, and so forth, has been more common.

Rules governing the way workers do their jobs are intended to prevent undesirable behavior, while discretion (the lack of rules) can allow employees to do wrong as well as right. Large business firms are likely to have rules of their own governing how their employees function.

In general, it may be conceded that business firms have more flexibility in their personnel policies as far as their own employees are concerned. Whether they are able to devise superior methods of internal management that maximize the benefits of employee discretion and minimize the imposition of inefficient rules is open to question.

In the following sections, we discuss whether such market forces as competition and the profit motive could induce contractors to improve educational outcomes. First we evaluate contracting against criteria for competitive markets. Many private markets in the U.S. economy, however, are less than fully competitive, and nobody is contemplating their takeover by government. To be fair, we should consider whether noncompetitive markets could improve upon public sector performance, even while they fall short of the competitive ideal.

The following section discusses how a competitive market might serve public education. As noted above, the hallmark of such a market is cutthroat price competition with similar products. The subsequent section considers markets in which the services being offered differ and price competition is less consequential.

A technical literature on the subject of efficient contracting should be acknowledged (Sappington and Stiglitz 1987). Some work has focused specifically on contracting in education (Hill 1995). Delving into this literature is beyond the scope of our study. Contracting as currently practiced lacks the most elementary features of "efficient contracting," such as competitive bidding for a specified product. Any assessment of existing practice in such a rigorous framework would quickly doom the subject of investigation. A more modest goal for this chapter is the development of a basic understanding of how contracting and market competition might be hoped to advance education reform.

Will Contractors Really Compete?

What are the distinguishing features of an effective market? For the purposes of this discussion, they can be boiled down to the following: a lack of external consequences for the provision of the service, informed participants, a uniform product, many buyers and sellers, and low costs of "entry" and "exit" for buyers and sellers.[26]

Are there consequences for others? It should be clear that for consumer choice to be effective, the consumer must know what he or she is getting. But who is the consumer? In the context of this study, the customer in the narrow sense is the local government, acting on behalf of its constituents. In keeping with our remarks about the national interest in education for all children, however, the "customer" is really more than the parents or their local government—it is the nation as a whole. The success of each student in meeting or surpassing a minimum standard of accomplishment is of interest to all. From a social standpoint, the market "works" if the national standard is met. If local standards are inferior to national ones, local decisions will not serve the national interest.

It might be objected that every jurisdiction wants to provide education to all, or that state and local officials "care" as much as national ones. What is in question here, however, is not intent or motivation; it is results. There can be more and less education, as we have come to know all too well. National and state standards can induce states and localities to enhance their performance. Reporting how each school district compares with a common, external standard sends a strong signal that improvement by some means should be a priority.

Another objection stems from legal considerations. On some literal level, the U.S. Constitution vests responsibility for education in the states, not the national government. Of course, since the 1930s the national government has delved into a myriad of previously excepted roles in domestic policy. By some conservative views, federal policies were an encroachment on state prerogatives. One must ask, however, whether policies that were validated by constitutional procedure—Supreme Court decisions—can be unconstitutional in a substantive sense.

More compelling reservations about a wider federal role follow from practical considerations. The capacity of the national government to specify, impose, and regulate educational standards is limited by the enormous breadth and diversity of the nation. More realistic is the notion that the national government should provide leadership, specialized technical assistance, and general policy guidelines to be implemented with some latitude for the exercise of discretion by state and local governments. Indeed, this is the spirit of the Goals 2000 legislation (Cohen 1995). Even if Congress terminates such policies, their appeal will not disappear.

The rationale for contracting leans heavily on the idea of a "smart shopper." If the shopper is the best judge of what he or she needs, there is a case for facilitating transactions between the shopper and vender. In education, however, the independent, "local" shopper does not encompass and cannot serve the national interest. As noted, the national interest entails the universal attainment of minimum standards of accomplishment and the promotion of citizenship. This does not rule out contracting by any means; it only means that the shopper-vender relationship between local governments and contractors cannot escape the scrutiny of national and state governments.

A different sort of external consequence in the education market, as in all areas of public service provision, pertains to the regulatory interests of the public. In that sense, voters are "customers" for all interesting consequences of the provision of a service, not merely the benefits of the service itself. In areas such as labor standards, occupational health and safety, and environmental quality, among many others, the choice of provider of a public service raises the question of whether regulations routinely adhered to in the public sector will or should apply to a private contractor. In education itself, labor standards are one of the salient issues.

Labor standards in the public sector can have ramifications for local wages and economies. Higher public wages can leverage wages in the private sector, and vice versa. Taxpaying voters might be concerned that business firms paying low wages could shift such costs as health care to government. There has been a public interest in labor standards for the economy in general, not just for the public sector. An example is the debate over the minimum wage. Some commentators imply that private sector labor compensation is intrinsically natural, efficient, and therefore just, but others find it wanting.

As for other fields, contractors often promise to save money in education by economizing on labor costs. If their policies entail reduced pay for workers, and if a community is interested in elevating labor standards, then the local government is properly concerned with regulating the terms under which the contractor relates to public employees or hires its own workers. Failure to regulate would, from an economic standpoint, compromise the social efficiency of the market. A public interest in labor standards does not preclude the possibility of contracting. Contractors could be regulated or required by contract to adhere to specific, publicly set labor standards.

One local angle that comes up in debates is that the contractor is more likely to drain resources from the local economy than is a public bureaucracy. The contractor's profits are not likely to be invested locally. Economically distressed communities may want to compensate for the negligence of national and state governments, but that is not a major consideration. There is already plenty of profit in education, and such profit is not locally reinvested any more than the extra increment that would be reaped by a management contractor. A public employee's pension fund could be just as distant from the local economy as a contractor's personal financial portfolio.

In summary, external considerations in local public education do not disable the case for contracting. They do, however, imply that the relationship between local government and its contractor should not be shielded from the imperatives of national, state, or local education and social policy.

Do the customers know what they're buying? A basic rationale for contracting rests on the customer's ability to understand what is for sale. The purpose of contracting is to employ an organization which can function more effectively—with less supervision—than a public bureaucracy. The customer can afford to pay less attention to how the organization functions if he or she can see the results or their lack and act accordingly. Rather than closely supervise how a service is provided, as for an intrinsically governmental function, the customer can be satisfied with making the deal and receiving the product.

Even if there is no external interest in how a community educates its young, knowledge of the educational "product" remains elusive. As noted, obtaining information on the quality of the product is time-consuming, costly, and open to widely varying interpretations. Timeliness is further hampered in a reform situation because the advocates of reform can reasonably claim that their new approach will require an indeterminate length of time to bear fruit. All those factors undermine the power of the consumer—the local government—to deal with a contractor.

E.S. Savas, a prominent advocate of contracting, says: "Not every public service lends itself to contracting. It must be one for which it is possible to write specifications that are complete and understandable; moreover, it must be relatively easy to monitor the service and to enforce adherence to the specifications. Finally, it must be a service which allows sustained competition, either because there are already multiple providers or because a competitive market can be created" (1992; Allen 1995). All of these conditions are lacking in the case of public education. Savas believes that education (aside from food service, security, maintenance, etc.) happens to be a poor candidate for contracting out (Allen 1995).[27]

Problems in definition and measurement have direct, practical implications for contracting. The purpose of contracting is to hire, fire, and pay according to results. Contracts must be drawn to compensate the contractor for improvement and penalize him for regress. Insofar as results are hard to determine, rewards and penalties will be hard to institute. If contracts are bereft of educational performance criteria (as was the case for EAI in Baltimore and Hartford), there is less incentive for the contractor to do a good job.

Actual contractors in the education field customarily sell their *approach* to education—their "inputs and processes"—rather than request compensation geared to measured levels of accomplishment. The president of EAI claims the problem with education is that resources have been taken out of the classroom: too little is spent on technology or teachers are insufficiently trained (Golle 1994). When EAI was criticized in Baltimore for failing to improve local students' test scores, a company spokesperson said, "[T]he company should be judged on more than test scores, including the number of computers in classrooms, the availability of books and other materials, a 'clean and safe' school environment, and parental involvement." (*Baltimore Sun*, May 3, 1995) These are examples of gauging results by reference to inputs rather than outputs.[28]

Contractors in education management have preferred to be judged on an all-or-nothing basis: if you like what we do, you pay us as per our contract. If you do not like our performance, you can terminate our contract and pay us nothing. When Chester Finn was associated with the Edison Project, he said publicly that rather than be subject to performance measurement, the best proof of success for his organization would be whether local governments availed themselves of Edison's services. The implication was that Edison's services would be available on a take-it-or-leave-it basis.

Agreements that fail to reward or penalize the contractor for incremental changes in performance shift risk to the customer. If the contract turns sour, the customer must either retain the contractor and suffer substandard performance, or incur the costs of transition to a new or old arrangement. The transition costs afford the contractor space within which to provide mediocre service that falls safely short of the customer's threshold of tolerance. Although it is true that the contractor cannot earn exceptionally high rewards within the contract, he or she cannot lose badly either. The incentive is to do well enough to recover costs without being dismissed.

One helpful source of information in markets that is lacking in the education field is the reputation of its participants. Because contracting for school management is new, as recounted in Chapter 1, all the players are necessarily start-ups. The one with the most experience to date, Education Alternatives Inc., has never received the benefit of a positive verdict from any independent, rigorous evaluation.[29] Its self-touted educational methodology, "the Tesseract Way," has yet to be presented, much less vetted, in the professional literature (Shanker 1994).

Before being analyzed or evaluated, information on performance must first be reported. Reporting has been a problem in education contracting, both in the 1970s period, as Shore reports, as well as in recent years. The most prominent contractor in the field—EAI—has been criticized on a number of occasions for providing false or misleading information on enrollment, test scores, grade-level advances, attendance, and corporate revenues (*Wall Street Journal*, June 8, 1994; Richards 1991). Poor availability of information on the Baltimore arrangement moved City Council member Carl Stokes to subpoena EAI's financial records, and the mayor—who was instrumental in instigating the contract—supported Stokes' request (*Baltimore Sun*, May 28, 1995).

Contractors imply that the customer is free to evaluate results and act to retain or dismiss the contractor, but being free to do something and being able to do it are two different things. The question is whether the customer can easily evaluate results, and whether he or she can easily fire the contractor if performance is found wanting. In economists' jargon, the contractors are touting the customer's option of "exit," but the value of the option to the customer depends on its cost. The lower the cost, the more valuable it is. One cost of exit is the difficulty of obtaining information—without information, one would not know when to exit.

In principle, controlled experiments that facilitate the production of information about new approaches are possible. Indeed, efforts were made to structure the Baltimore arrangement as an experiment, and the launch did of course take place. Practical implementation of "social experiments" is difficult (Gramlich and Koshel 1977). In a public reform environment, nobody wants to be the "control group," no more than a terminally ill patient in a drug experiment wants the placebo. If one school or group of students gets the benefit of some new approach—especially if it entails additional resources (as it had in Baltimore, see Chapter 2)—others will demand some kind of parallel advantage.

If everyone is brought under the umbrella of some reform, the results will be more difficult to evaluate because there will be less of a vantage point for comparison. For instance, if a contractor is given control of an entire school system (as was the original intention, later abandoned, in Hartford), nobody can be sure what might have happened under some alternative arrangement, including the status quo. Barring exceptional changes in the measures of performance, supporters of the new order can claim it is better than what would have happened otherwise, and opponents can claim the contrary.

For smaller school districts the difficulty of comparison is greater. There are fewer schools to use as "controls," and the districts have fewer resources to commit to evaluation. Specific districts also have insufficient incentive to support such ventures, as the generation of good information from an experiment would be beneficial to school districts across the nation. As for a variety of basic research, there is an important role for state and national governments in organizing and financing rigorous trials of new approaches in local public education.

The purpose of experiments is to yield information that will inform future decisions, but innovations in education seldom have been organized to provide reliable information on results (Hanushek et al. 1994). Politicians fear being blamed for failure, so reforms are organized so that failure is "impossible." What this means is that experiments are not set up so that a clear judgment about success or failure is possible.

How should an experiment be done? Suppose a school district contemplated hiring the Edison Project to manage a school. To determine whether Edison succeeded or failed, the district ought to choose a number of similar schools where nothing new will be done. It can set out to collect data on outcomes in all of the schools and compare the "control group" with the Edison school. If significant improvements could be found, there would be a case for continuing and expanding the Edison contract.

A problem is that the politician who is responsible for choosing Edison in the first place could be torn between the desires of succeeding in reform and avoiding an association with failure, so both the politician and Edison will have an interest in preventing comparisons that would facilitate potentially negative judgments. As documented in Chapter 1, for such reasons very little evidence has been developed to support or reject the case for contracting in education. In Baltimore, there was a plan to organize the EAI contract as an experiment. Nine schools were chosen as a "control group." Once the contract was well underway, for unexplained reasons the control group was changed. The new schools in the control group tended to achieve lower test scores than those schools in the original group (Nelson 1994), so the change would appear to benefit EAI schools in comparison. As the official evaluators pointed out, changing the control group in the middle of an experiment is bad procedure (Williams and Leak 1995).

In summary, severe information problems in education hamper the effectiveness of markets for the management of education. The task of evaluating a contractor is complex and expensive; all but the largest local governments will require state assistance to pursue the option effectively. Questions of capacity aside, local governments are disinclined to organize and conduct rigorous, impartial evaluations. Where less is known about the product—the performance of managers in "real time"—there is less inherent rationale for instituting a system based on the rotation of management teams, in the form of hiring and firing competing contractors. Problems here for the competitive model are the nature of the product and the presently immature state of the market.

What about private schools? Are parents not able to choose such schools without difficulty, and do their students not compare well with those in public schools? The subject of this study is privatization options aimed at improving existing public schools. The "choice" option in this context is the choice of management team, either for a single school, a group, or an entire school district. The problem here is not how parents may distinguish among individual schools, but how local governments hire managers.

Does the existing private school market not make all these technocratic ruminations about measuring performance irrelevant? Would it not be simpler just to do away with public bureaucracy altogether and provide vouchers to individual parents? A short answer is that choices among Cadillacs, Lincolns, and BMWs are less difficult than other conceivable ranges of choice. Less expensive private schools, such as those run by religious institutions, are advantaged by selection; their family clientele is more motivated and better equipped financially to advance their children's education. I would argue that the central problem in public education is how best to serve families not falling into this category, those for whom problems of information, resources, and motivation are the most acute.

Even in the private school case, the right of parents to opt out of the public system reflects a gap in the public mission, not an extension of it. Such parents may succeed in securing adequate intellectual training for their children, but the fate of democratic and civic values is left to individual choice. I would hazard the guess that so far, in most schools run by religious organizations (e.g., Catholics, Jews, Mormons, Christian Fundamentalists), such values have been very well served. A concern is that expansion of such a system to encompass diverse social groups would bring problems.

Can the customer "comparison shop"? The information burden on the customer increases when the products under consideration differ. When products are identical, the consumer merely needs to find the one with the lowest price. In education contracting, the product is typically not a firm commitment to a specific, measurable performance result. The nature of education, especially in an experimental setting, is that any such commitment would be uncertain.

If a local government were to receive two bids by different contractors proposing very different approaches to education and chose not to employ performance criteria, it would be operating not in one market with two sellers, but in two markets, each dominated by a monopolist. As noted above, monopolistic markets exist but they would not be expected to work well—to provide services efficiently. Monopolistic markets might evolve in competitive directions, or they might not. At this point, it is difficult to foresee how the education market will develop.

As reported in Chapter 1 and noted above, the primary selling point of contractors is the way they propose to educate. Their claims rest on the uniqueness of their services, not on guaranteed results. A variety of choices does benefit the consumer, but the associated disadvantage is a diminished capacity to compare products for purposes of cost minimization.

Even with diverse choices or few choices, of course, it is possible to improve upon the status quo. In that event a market might not be competitive, but a desire to win and keep a contract could induce the contractor to perform well. That possibility is discussed next.

Lest nonuniformity seem a trivial matter, note that it automatically fosters two significant departures from the competitive market model. One is the information problem, with which we have dealt at length. Evaluating diverse products requires more information. The second is that diverse products split the market, reducing the number of sellers for any given product. We turn to this problem next.

Is there a choice of sellers? Nowadays, besides being described as dumb, governments are said to take after monopolies. Poor quality and inflated cost is said to afflict the taxpayer because she or he lacks alternative choices. The implication is that business firms would deliver a product with improved quality and lower cost—that they would not act as monopolies do. Of course, the term "monopoly" originated as a description of business firms in private markets. It should be obvious that a business firm can be a monopoly.

The notion that a contractor managing schools eliminates the public "monopoly" is wrong in one sense and right in another. It is wrong because at any given moment, a different management team allows no enlarged freedom of choice to parents. It is right in the sense that management can be replaced. The contractor could feel the competitive heat of his potential replacement. A question is whether the replacement option is sufficiently powerful to make the market effective.

What makes the replacement option viable? The same qualities characterizing a competitive market that we discuss in this section. A choice of alternative venders for the same product is available. The customer is able to remain informed about the quality of the service received, as well as the value of alternatives. And finally, it is easy to switch venders.

Presently the market for educational management is what economists call "thin," which means there are few sellers in comparison to the number of potential buyers. Moreover, as noted above, of those sellers currently soliciting business, their products differ in basic respects. Such a situation is understandable in a new industry of this type, but it undermines competition nevertheless. Where competition is lacking, some advocates of privatization have cautioned governments to contract no more than a portion of any given service so that there are at least two competitors—the contractor and the government agency (Savas 1992).

As Shore points out in Chapter 1, the number of sellers could increase in a short time if a few success stories succeeded in cracking open what is potentially a huge market. In Chapter 2, however, Richards demonstrated that the former industry leader—EAI—has yet to make money in the provision of education per se, although the principals of EAI have become rich at the expense of hopeful shareholders. EAI or other firms might do better in the future, but for the time being that remains a matter of speculation. If little or no money can be made, then contracting with business firms will have little future.

Even in markets with few sellers, economists allow for the possibility that markets characterized as "contestable" can generate sufficient competitive pressure to force sellers to minimize costs (Baumol 1982). The incentive to minimize costs or otherwise do better by the customer stems from a real, ever-present threat of new entrants—potential replacements for the firm currently garnering most of the business. For such a threat to be realistic, the costs of market entry to the potential seller must be low. It must also be easy for the customer to switch contractors. In economists' words, "entry" and "exit" for buyers and sellers must be easy and inexpensive.

Entry for new firms would not seem to be overly difficult. No gigantic capital investment is required to become a manager or management team for hire. One firm, Public Strategies Inc. in Minneapolis, offers the services of a single person to run a school system. A problem is that the contractor may be expected to bring more to the table than management expertise.

First, school authorities might expect contractors to have some new, proprietary approach to teaching. Implicitly, such intellectual property must be founded on some capital investment by the contractor. The two major players both make large claims to pedagogical innovation. The Edison Project has spent $40 million in assembling what it calls the "best practices" employed in education throughout the world. EAI has its own proprietary approach, the "Tesseract Way." Whatever the merits of the offerings, they have set a hurdle which competitors must either match or demonstrate to be without value.

Second, the contractor has to bring money to the table. Both EAI and Edison have appealed to customers by promising to upgrade schools' physical plant and computer facilities. That hurdle makes competition more difficult for nonprofit organizations, small business firms, labor unions, or groups of teachers who might organize to bid for a management contract.

Even if entry were easier, the opportunities for many sellers to compete may be deliberately reduced by the customer. The public agency can limit competition by withholding information about the work it wants to contract. The contractor's ability to bid for the job of managing schools depends heavily on information about historic costs available only from the local government. For some public officials with decision-making power, the option of contracting has evidently taken shape not as a general principle but in the form of a specific provider. The selection process is subsequently "wired" to guarantee that provider the job.

Why would the local government limit its options? Before accepting any bid, the public agency must acquire information about potential applicants. That is costly, so the agency has an interest in limiting the number of competitors. The agency might content itself with the first viable contractor it finds, the better to avoid the costs of evaluating additional ones. Education officials involved in contract negotiations have been known subsequently to obtain employment with contractors. Contractors play an obvious role in local politics and raise the possibility of graft.

Competition appears to have been stifled in both Baltimore and Hartford, where the city governments initiated consultations and provided information to a single prospective contractor—Education Alternatives Inc.—for an extended time before making a token effort to solicit competing bids. In Hartford, a request for proposals was released with a three-week deadline after the Board of Education had been working with EAI for four months (*Hartford Courant*, June 2, 1994). In 1995 a similar scenario became visible in Washington, D.C., where the superintendent announced a desire to hire EAI in advance of any competitive bidding process. As Shore reports, advocates of privatization have described those experiences as "sole-source contracting."

A noncompetitive pattern can be found in broad areas of public service contracting, even where the service involved satisfies Savas's requirement that it can be defined for contractual purposes in a straightforward manner (Van Horn 1991; Goodman and Loveman 1991; Sclar 1995). "No-bid" contracting is pervasive. Rules intended to foster competition and ethical behavior are difficult to formulate and enforce. Costs are not studied to determine whether contracting provides real savings.[30] In an extensive study of public services in New Jersey, Van Horn (1991) found that cost and quality were often (e.g., more than half the time) not the motivation for contracting. Other explanations included political mandates or a lack of resources, which are both founded on an a priori political decision to contract.

A less base political motive for restraining competition is that the notion of organizing a competitive market suffers from abstractness, whereas the idea of investing special expectations in a unique "man with a plan" is more comprehensible to voters. In this setting, the public official's political well-being can become wound up with the perceived worth of the contractor.

It is obvious why sellers should favor such practices. There are very few of them at present, and 15,000 potential customers (school districts). There is more than enough potential business for all. It would be foolish for a firm to poach in a territory where somebody else had developed a head start.

In the fullness of time, there are factors that mitigate both for and against an increase in the number of sellers. To be sure, the positive example of companies making money will attract additional investment and new entrants. On the other hand, the relationship between specific providers and their clients could ossify over time (Williamson 1975). Established providers will have an information advantage over outside competitors. They will have solidified relationships with influential public officials and developed community support.

Large and successful providers in a thin market will have the capacity to employ predatory pricing against potential rivals. That practice will be difficult to police because the customer will be a short-term beneficiary of such practices. A profit-seeking provider will seek to exploit such advantages up to, but short of, the point of overt abuse.

With fewer prospective contractors, there are fewer benefits to contracting. If the replacement option is weak for lack of suitable replacements, if the market is not really "contestable," there are fewer viable contractors from whom to choose and less to encourage the contractor to perform well at low cost.

Is it easy to switch sellers? The consumer has a low cost of exit when he or she can switch sellers or do without the product in question at acceptably low cost. There are problems for public education in this context. Organizing schools is a protracted process requiring time, information, and resources. Local governments cannot monitor, evaluate, and switch the management of school systems at will.

Baltimore's contract with EAI provides anecdotal evidence on the "exit" problem. The city's contract with EAI gave it legal authority to end the arrangement at any time without cause. The implied disruption to the school year was undoubtedly some deterrent from doing so. The mayor asked that the contract be rewritten to reflect performance requirements (*Baltimore Sun*, March 18, 1995). If the "dismissal" option had been effective, the threat to "fire" EAI should have gotten the desired results. It did not, and the city was forced to terminate the arrangement. In the end, EAI evidently preferred dismissal in Baltimore and Hartford to agreement on their customers' terms. The right to terminate the contract, therefore, was not useful in governing EAI's behavior— only in getting rid of the contractor.

A more tangible example of an obstacle to exit has proven to be the expenditures undertaken by EAI under the rubric of "investment." In Hartford, termination of the contract was feared to entail a contractually obligated "exit fee" of $4 million. The figure was based on the value of capital improvements made by EAI (chiefly computers) for which the city would be liable. The *Courant* reported: "That reminder went a long way in convincing the mayor and city council to back EAI's continued presence in the city" (*Hartford Courant*, May 28, 1995). After Hartford terminated EAI's contract, the issue descended to the level of farce when the city felt it necessary to lock out EAI personnel to prevent them from removing computer equipment (*Hartford Courant*, January 26, 1996).

The political harm to public officials with a stake in the success of the contract is another potential obstacle to easy exit. The job tenure of big-city superintendents, for instance, is nearly as brief as the terms of elected officials.[31] Insofar as the fates of political leaders and specific venders become linked, the public sector loses its capacity to make purchasing and contracting decisions objectively. In contrast, with a service that is routinely contracted for, the public official who dismisses a nonperforming contractor will suffer less political harm.

In education contracting, a product of paramount importance with special, not entirely transparent qualities is being purchased. The political decision maker is accorded credit for having the vision to divine those qualities. If the product turns sour, the public official is in trouble to a greater extent than if the city finds it has been paying too much for, say, its trash removal.

In two of the three most prominent cases to date—Baltimore and Hartford—great political controversy surrounded the contracting initiatives. Politicians backing the experiment were returned to office in heated elections, but they enjoyed relatively strong margins of victory. So our picture of local political pressures may be overdrawn. On the other hand, the same politicians terminated the contracts. They might simply have a sense of timing superior to that of their political adversaries.

The costs of exit bias decisions toward the status quo, meaning retention of the contractor, but they also tend to preclude the initiation of contracts by forward-looking public officials. In either case, the contractors' boast that "you can fire us any time" is bluff to some extent. The customer is not prevented from dismissing, of course, but has incentives to make concessions before doing so.

Extended tenure for any contractor could lead to rising costs, as Sappington and Stiglitz (1987), among others, point out. As time passes, the contractor develops a better understanding of the costs of the job than potential competitors on the outside. The contractor gains a competitive advantage that repels potential rivals and narrows alternatives for the contracting government. Empirical evidence of savings from contracting dwindling over time can be found in Pack (1989).

In time, the school bureaucracy will have a short-term incentive to shed personnel that are made redundant by the contractor's operations, including those who perform oversight and evaluation functions. By so doing, the bureaucracy will become more dependent on the continued service of the contractor and face greater difficulty—higher exit costs— if it should decide to switch providers. If the contractor's knowledge of the costs of the job outstrips that of the government, the latter will come to be increasingly less well equipped to bargain and renew contracts to the advantage of the taxpayer. Indeed, a prime explanation of much contracting is that the public sector has been barred from providing a service directly. In contrast, expectations of lower cost and higher quality often fail to explain why contracting is pursued (Van Horn 1991).

None of this means that public providers are better than private ones— only that the costs of entry and exit make contracting less effective than it would otherwise be—less like a competitive market and more like the status quo of public management.

Summary. The market for educational management bears little resemblance to real-world competitive markets, let alone ideal models of efficient markets. It lacks the supreme advantage of competition—the customer's ability to play one seller against another to obtain a product at the lowest possible price. The local government is hampered by fundamental information problems: the evaluation of the quality of the product is difficult and requires extended periods of time. The customer cannot readily switch providers. There are not many providers from which to choose, and switching requires information and consumes resources.

National interests in local education are not fatal to the contracting enterprise, although they do undermine its rationale to some degree. Contractors can be required to collect the same data the school would be mandated to report under public management, for state and national governments to ascertain the strength of the school system's commitment to universality and minimum standards. Education under contract could also be monitored to promote satisfaction of citizenship goals.

National concerns are more salient in the context of school choice, where the educational process is located one further remove from public scrutiny because it is more decentralized and fragmented. The principal problems and opportunities for contracting lie in the areas of quality and cost.

Competition is not the sole advantage of employing private contractors, although it is the principal rationale for contracting. Even where competition is lacking, private solutions for educational management could prove superior to public ones. To be viable, contracting does not absolutely have to be competitive; it only has to be superior to alternatives. Insofar as local governments despair of creating competitive conditions, there is more of a premium on monitoring and evaluating results according to solid experimental criteria. We next consider the potential benefits of markets that fall short of the competitive ideal.

Waiting for Entrepreneurs

Although an emerging industry like contracting out for education management bears little resemblance to competitive models, an education contractor might still have advantages over public management. If we acknowledge that competitive pressures are weak, we can still look to the potential strengths of business firms in noncompetitive markets, such as the ability to innovate, to cultivate managerial expertise, and to finance capital improvements. In theory, the core incentive to do a good job stems from the opportunity to earn profits. Even if entrepreneurs fail to minimize costs, they might improve upon the status quo. In this section we temper our emphasis on competitive forces to consider how the qualities of firms in imperfectly competitive markets might play out in the educational arena.

Do profits serve the public good? One hopes that the desire to earn profits will encourage the business firm to win the loyalty of its customers by providing a good product at an acceptable cost. Sources of motivation for the contractor are (1) a contract that stipulates performance incentives, or (2) an effective threat of dismissal in the event of poor performance.

On the first count, as noted earlier information about productivity in education is neither easy nor inexpensive to develop and interpret. In fact, a prominent critic of public education has said regarding Baltimore and Hartford's arrangements with EAI, "Little evidence exists on the best way to structure such contracts so that performance is improved while the possibility of unintended adverse consequences is minimized" (Hanushek 1994). One provision whose necessity has been validated in Baltimore and Hartford is the dismissal option. Another might be the financial protections the Hartford school system won in its own contract with EAI, although the ultimate result was still a termination of the relationship.

On the second point, the threat of dismissal is no more real than the availability of alternatives. With little or no competition, the business firm does not have to be the best of its breed. It only has to be perceived as superior to the public sector's alternatives. We are back to the question whether the public sector's alternatives exert sufficient pressure on the contractor. Ironically, the more bereft the local government, the more desperate it is, the less the contractor must do to provide an alternative that compares favorably with the status quo.

Although few firms seek to manage public schools for profit, local governments do have other sorts of alternatives. For instance, rather than hire contractors to run schools, the local government could hire contractors to take over assorted niche functions within a school system, such as teaching reading to disadvantaged students, educating students with disabilities, and so forth. School authorities might seek to hire nonprofit organizations to manage schools, as noted in Chapter 1. Choice might be enhanced within the public system in different ways (e.g., magnet schools and the like). Entirely different reform strategies could be entertained, such as vouchers or school-based management. Those options do imply some pressure on for-profit contractors to perform well.

A basic political drawback of the incremental options is that they are not persuasive sources of wholesale, comprehensive reform. If the school system as a whole is viewed with extreme disfavor, the public may be hostile to anything short of a sweeping change. Incremental remedies might be disdained as bureaucratic flourishes by the discredited education establishment. The same could be said for plans involving decentralization within the public system, in the form of parental choice or school-based management.

A full-blown choice system by means of vouchers for private schools is a radical reform of the status quo, but opposition to vouchers may help make the case for contracting out. Fear of vouchers could elevate contractors rather than pressure them to do a better job.

The general principle is that the fewer the viable alternatives available to it, the less a contractor must to do please the customer and earn a profit. Insofar as doing a better job raises costs and reduces profits, the contractor's best business strategy is to do only as well as necessary, not as well as possible. Thus the opportunity to make money in and of itself is only a limited source of market-like discipline on the contractor. On the whole, the diverse options available to school districts would seem to imply some pressure on contractors, especially as they have yet to prove themselves.

The preceding discussion begs a question to which economists have devoted much attention: in public firms that are owned by shareholders, managers without an ownership interest do not benefit from higher profits. Therefore, the "profit motive" is lacking in those upon whom the success of the contract depends (Sappington and Stiglitz 1987). For instance, if a contractor forges an agreement to split savings with a local government, the manager may benefit less by an incremental rise in profits than by an increase in, say, executive compensation at the expense of profits. Conflict between shareholders and managers in many business firms has a long and colorful history.

Economists have shown that profits or financial incentives of some kind or another are not a necessary wellspring of productivity. Simon (1991) points to accumulated evidence against the notion that profits and individual rewards are all-consuming factors in explaining productivity, including productivity comparisons in for-profit, nonprofit, and public organizations (Weisbrod 1988, 1989), and comparisons of business profits in which the firms were owner-controlled or share ownership was widely diffused. An example of a for-profit organization that could neglect productivity would be a firm under absentee ownership (e.g., stockholders) in which substantial control is afforded to managers without major ownership interests (Demsetz and Lehn 1985). Another would be a contractor enjoying a "cost-plus" arrangement of the type that has been notorious in defense spending.

It happens that some principals in EAI and Edison are also shareholders. On the other hand, some EAI shareholders, including chief executive John Golle, have already "cashed in"—they have reaped windfalls from their exercise of stock options. Similar problems attend to public managers, where there is not even a profit indicator that would shed light on their performance. The general point is that setting financial incentives in private sector organizations, as opposed to public ones, is not as simple, effective, or essential as it is made out to be.

Can education contractors profit from innovation? As we have been saying, in education the "product" encompasses the desired result—the educated student—but also the means by which such a result is fostered. Accordingly, interest attaches not only to doing a set job at reduced cost, but to finding innovative ways to do better.

Strong disagreement prevails as to what, if anything, is wrong with pedagogical methods in the first place. Different, appealing departures from the status quo could be very much at odds with each other. One contractor, for instance, might emphasize discipline and order for the sake of a "basic skills" approach, while another might celebrate flexible problem solving and multidisciplinary approaches. The question is whether school authorities can figure out what sort of problem they really need to solve.

As pointed out above, the normal concept of a competitive setting mitigates against innovation. Cutthroat price competition dissuades firms from devoting resources to investments with delayed, uncertain payoffs. It is more in monopolistic or oligopolistic industries that firms have the ability to finance innovation internally, precisely because they are earning above-average, super-competitive rates of return. Without question, there are investors willing to support the development of innovative methods for a chance at such returns. The two leading companies—EAI and the Edison Project—have been well-capitalized in advance of reaping any profits from contracting. Indeed, if we believe that what schools need is not merely better management of orthodox education practice, but creative departures, then competition could be more of a hindrance than a help. In this case, the priority for the prospective customer would be to evaluate the contractor's claims to innovation.

The most prominent focus of innovation has been pedagogy, including computer-assisted methods. If a school system is considering a contractor who promises such improvements, it needs to convince itself that such inputs would be more valuable than whatever costs they might displace—such as the compensation of instructional personnel.[32] As the empirical analysis in Chapter 1 demonstrates, the tradeoff was evident in the Baltimore experience; it also loomed on the horizon in Hartford.[33]

The next question, in the context of this study, is why such devices could not be purchased separately. In other words, if schools ought to have more computers and fewer teachers, why must they hire new managers for the school system? The same goes for a better accounting system, maintenance service, or almost any other facet of a school system.

The former industry leader—Education Alternatives Inc.—has its own proprietary, pedagogical approach, the "Tesseract Way." But EAI does not suggest that Tesseract is the only legitimate method. (How could it?) In its contract proposal to the city of Hartford, EAI promised to implement any of eight different pedagogical models, or one to be named later by the Hartford Board of Education, and still do an exemplary job. If the author of a proprietary pedagogical approach acknowledges that it is but one of many potential solutions, the indispensability of the contractor logically narrows to its management expertise, as opposed to its creativity in formulating and instituting curriculum and educational methods.

EAI participated in a five-year consulting arrangement with Dade County, Fla., that involved a single school—South Pointe Elementary. EAI had long showcased its role in Dade County. The actual contract, however, entailed not management of the school but rather the provision of support for curriculum in the form of the Tesseract model. Although described as successful by EAI and its client, the arrangement was terminated in 1995, reportedly because the county could not afford to continue.

At least three conclusions are possible from the Florida episode. One is that EAI's program requires higher spending to be effective; otherwise there would be no budget problem in retaining them. A standard rhetorical commitment of contractors, EAI included, is that they will do better with existing resources.[34] Public officials, for their part, could promise to improve if their funding were increased. In South Pointe, EAI did in fact receive a disproportionate infusion of funds relative to schools not receiving its services ("School ends experiment," *Miami Herald,* June 20, 1995).

The second possible conclusion is that South Pointe does not need EAI any longer—that EAI brought some useful innovations which the school district can now carry on without EAI. The *Baltimore Sun* (May 2, 1995) reported: "EAI itself said the school staff can 'carry the Tesseract principles forward' to continue the 'sound educational experience.'" The Associated Press reported: "'I think you could find in any good school many of the good practices,' said Pat Parham, Dade County schools' director of early childhood programs. She said that EAI pulled those practices together but did not invent any techniques." (*Minneapolis Star-Tribune,* June 16, 1995). In other words, the core of EAI's educational innovations is not protected by copyright or patent, nor does it require a continuing role for the company. If that is so, how can EAI commercialize its pedagogical discoveries? On that account, if educational contractors are to make money, it would be as the equivalent of evangelists for new methods rather than permanent local pastors.

A third possibility is that officials responsible for shepherding the EAI arrangement do not want to admit the venture failed. In fact, the Tesseract program was found by evaluators to have made no difference in student achievement, and EAI itself ended up losing money on the deal (Abella 1994; *Hartford Courant*, May 5, 1995). Although anecdotal, that evidence looms somewhat larger in light of EAI's heavy use of its Dade County arrangement for promotional purposes.

The Edison Project, for its part, does not claim to have invented new approaches so much as synthesized information on "best practices." Whether such information can be exploited for profit remains to be seen. Once Edison imparts its discoveries to a public school, we could ask what prevents the school district from replicating the methodology and helping others to do likewise, as EAI claims its Florida client has done. From that standpoint, the commercial failure of contractors could still benefit public education, but the life of the industry would be short.

In the case of pedagogy per se, as EAI acknowledges, a school need not pay for access to new methods. Much research on pedagogy is in the public domain. Much has been financed by government. A school system may need nothing more than consulting services to institute new methods, as opposed to contracting out for new management. There may be plenty of scope for entrepreneurs in the consulting field, as contrasted with management services.

A different type of innovation claimed by contractors is superior knowledge of what the school system ought to be purchasing. Once the broad brush strokes of such a secret are established, however, one could also question its commercial viability. If entrepreneurs cannot profit from educational innovation—by doing more for less—we have to worry that their profits will be based on doing less for more.

An added problem is that those eager to manage and recommend what school districts should buy have interests that go beyond giving good advice so that their management services will be valued highly. They may also profit because some of their purchases are their own goods—particularly software and teacher training. They may also receive commissions for certain types of purchases. They may also contract for guaranteed returns on funds they advance to the school district, which is nothing but another kind of markup. Just as one is wise to make sure one's financial planner is not receiving commissions by selling a particular investment product, it is preferable for the consultant one engages on educational reform not to be also in the business of profiting from the volume or composition of purchases brokered for the school system—on his or her advice—from the consultant's or other firms.[35]

If the public sector's problem is held to be a deficiency of managerial expertise, a school system could hire managers with suitable credentials. Any such persons will cost them no less under private contract than public. It is true that the organizational separation of the contractor from the customer expands the manager's scope of discretion, but discretion is always a double-edged sword: it permits doing bad as well as doing good. A less defensible function of contracting out would be to mask the true compensation paid by the public, which contravenes the whole idea of a smart buying public choosing better providers for its services.

It is plausible that business firms have developed expertise in such fields as accounting, procurement, or the management of physical plant. That could be tested by the interested school district without hiring managers to oversee instruction (or vice versa). The practice of bundling school reform, maintenance of physical plant, food service, accounting, and so forth. makes it more difficult for the school district to identify savings and efficiencies by function. There is always the possibility that losses in one area could be subsidized by economies in another. The school district should retain contractors who bring savings and dismiss those who do not. Contracting separately for diverse functions makes more feasible an analysis of where money is saved or lost.

In summary, the claims of educational innovation by private contractors are weak, and the need for school districts to pay for such information is questionable. School authorities should seek independent, expert validation of claims to pedagogical innovation. Contractors' advice on procurement is liable to conflicts of interest. Possible savings by contracting in any area should be tested in a framework in which the relevant results can be identified and evaluated.

Are the contractor's deep pockets a boon to the customer? A common inducement for business firms selling education reform is the promise of "investments," especially in physical plant. The school system must ultimately pay the full cost of any such investments, including the implied, accumulated interest and the expected cost of the investment risk, or else the provider cannot make money. If the provider did not expect to get its money back, it would not offer any such "investments."

Besides limiting competition, this entry cost to sellers—the inducement of a contractor's "investment" in schools, in the form of such things
as computer hardware or other capital improvements—is no real economic advantage to the customer. School districts and local governments
can borrow money to make the same investments themselves. After all,
over the course of their contract they would pay no less in the costs
associated with such debt, as the contractor is obliged to recover all
such costs from the government in question. Insofar as taxpayers are
more indulgent of such arrangements, it reflects their failure to pierce
the veil of the public sector's indirect capital budgeting.

The advance of resources by a contractor is more valuable if the
contractor is compelled to risk its capital on its performance, as was the
case in one sense in Hartford. The public sector's "payback" obligations
would ideally be contingent on the contractor fulfilling preset performance criteria in education, among its other roles. The city of Hartford
protected itself to some extent in their arrangement with EAI because
the Hartford contract provided for some financial performance incentives. EAI failed to document their avowed achievements in saving money
and pulled less money out of Hartford than it put in.

Sappington and Stiglitz (1987) point out that private sector borrow-
ers have a greater risk of default than the federal government. That means
that a higher risk premium increases their costs of finance, and they
must pass along such costs in contracts they establish with governments.
Any government enjoying a more favorable credit rating than the contractor with which it is dealing is throwing money out the window on
that account. By employing privately owned capital in some kind of
leasing arrangement, or by accepting advances of funds in the guise of
the firm's "investments," the government is paying a premium over its
own costs of borrowing.

As noted elsewhere in this study, the city of Hartford did commit
that error in its relationship with EAI—paying more interest on the advance of resources than it is charged when it borrows directly—although
there were offsetting financial benefits to the city in the contract. For all
but local governments in the rockiest financial condition, it could be
expected that governments will usually face lower finance costs borrowing directly rather than through a contractor.

An exception might appear to lie in the case of a relatively credit-
worthy contractor and a fiscally stressed local government. In that case

a lender would indeed deal with greater confidence and demand less of a risk premium from the deep-pocket borrower—the contractor—but the obligation would remain for the contractor to recover its capital costs from the school district, including that same risk premium.

For example, suppose lenders demand 10% from a school district but only 8% from a well-capitalized education contractor. If 10% is the correct, competitive, risk-adjusted return for the school district, it is that 10% that the contractor must recover. Insofar as the contractor systematically discounted risk premiums in its investments in school districts, it would average a subcompetitive rate of return. It would be allocating its capital inefficiently. The error is tantamount to choosing an investment yielding 6% return when one has access to another providing 8%.

A fundamental distinction between public and private capital financing for local governments is the fact that private capital is subject to federal and state taxation, while public capital (or capital owned by non-profit organizations) is not. An exception is the exemption of interest on some state and local bonds, but this benefit is typically not available to contractors marketing services to governments. The bond interest exemption only benefits contractors who participate in projects financed directly by bonds. Indeed, for that reason some economists have proposed that the federal government tax state and local governments to erase their advantage in capital costs over the private sector (Hulten and Schwab 1991). An arcane exception to that advantage would be a case in which the federal tax system confers an effectively negative rate of taxation on capital required to provide services to or at the behest of state and local governments.

Education contractors claim that their advance of capital to school districts is an incentive for them to reduce other costs if their fees are capped in advance. That is supposed to result in the school district getting more for less. Pitfalls of the logic follow:

- It is based on the premise that the contractor is getting the same or less to begin with. Otherwise, increased spending by the school is simply recouped by the contractor for capital advanced (including interest). As Richards showed in Chapter 2, the contractor can obtain more resources while claiming the contrary.

- To some extent the new facilities are removable. Computers and network hardware, for instance, can by prior agreement be carted away if a contract is terminated.

- The pressure to recover capital costs is an incentive to reduce other costs, not necessarily an incentive to do more for less. It is easier to change the composition of a school budget (e.g., more capital, less labor) than to use resources more efficiently.

In general, the school district or local government cannot hope to reduce its capital costs through the mediation of a private business financing. Any such savings in cases in which loans come in the guise of up-front investment in the schools are illusory; the business firm must extract its competitive pound of flesh sooner or later. The school jurisdiction would have better luck through some kind of state or federal program like a loan guarantee that would effectively shift (but not eliminate) the costs of its risk premium to a higher level of government.

The converse point is that the local government does not forgo capital costs by employing public management. One type of capital cost is interest on debt. It is obvious that the public sector pays interest if it borrows money or forgoes interest if it uses cash for current expenditure rather than maintaining a reserve. It should be clear that if some business firm does so in its stead the cost will still be absorbed by the taxpayer. Suppose a local government buys computers from a manufacturer who charges a 10% markup over production costs. That 10% is the source from which the manufacturer recovers the costs of purchasing and maintaining its own plant and equipment. If the local government manufactured its own computers, it would face the same costs.

The preceding arguments follow if the contract between a school district and a business firm specifies no more than a total fee. In the case of EAI, however, capital charges have been specified explicitly. EAI's original proposed contract language to Hartford was this:

"Education Alternatives Inc. would be reimbursed for its expenses as they relate to the project, including but not limited to...amortization of capital investments....These amounts will represent out-of-pocket costs to EAI without markup. In addition, Education Alternatives Inc. would expect a return of 9% on the capital it invests. (That is to say, if Education Alternatives Inc. invests $4 million of its own capital to purchase [not lease] something for the district, then the company would expect to receive $360,000 as a return on its investment.—M.S.). This return would not create any ongoing, economic obligation to the district should there be a cancellation, nor would it represent an incremental expense of doing business. In essence, this return would be in lieu of floating a bond or issuing a COP (certificate of participation). In this case, however, Education Alternatives Inc. would be acting as a creditor on an unsecured basis." (EAI 1994)

A few comments are in order. EAI forgoes what it calls a markup for its investment, but the classification of the 9% as return on capital or interest and zero as markup is utterly arbitrary. Obviously, EAI hoped to make money on the spread between its own costs and the 9% it wanted to charge the school district. This is made obvious in the final sentence quoted: EAI wants to be the school system's banker. It would be wiser for local governments to steer their banking business to a real, insured bank—not to a venture capital start-up! The final agreement with Hartford specified a lower interest rate, but it turned out that the agreed-upon rate exceeded the city's own cost of funds in the bond market (*Hartford Courant*, May 16, 1995). It should not prove difficult for local governments to avoid such problems in the future.

The advance of funds is clearly a means by which the contractor can change the composition of the education budget in favor of services also sold or brokered by the contractor and against such things as labor compensation, on which the contractor makes no money. The fact that the school district can get resources sooner rather than later may provide some inducement, but we have seen that the taxpayer does not escape the implicit borrowing costs underlying such an arrangement.

A more dramatic downside of a financial relationship with a privately capitalized entrepreneur is the risk of bankruptcy. To some extent, the public sector becomes a stakeholder in the contractor's firm. Lately we have witnessed some spectacular failures in the financial world, encompassing legendary banks (Barings), giant corporations (Daiwa), and local governments (Orange County, Calif.).

To some extent, contractors will be handling the public's money. Their outlays will never coincide with disbursements from the public treasury, creating the opportunity for creative cash management by the contractor. This threatened to sink to the level of absurdity when EAI proposed that the city of Hartford, by allegedly overfunding an insurance reserve fund (e.g., building a financial nest egg for emergencies), could "save money" by turning over excess savings to EAI (*Hartford*

Courant, July 29, 1995). Presumably the inclination of venture capitalists and entrepreneurs toward risk entails some risk for the customers of entrepreneurial for-profit firms in the education field. The same problem would not ordinarily pertain to nonprofits in the same business. A taste of this concern was reflected in news that EAI had lost $12 million by speculating in derivatives in the last quarter of 1994, as Richards discusses in Chapter 2.

Presently the national government is removing itself from state and local public policy. Local governments have complained of neglect from their state governments. A contractor might be the only friend a local school district had, but this says less about the merits of contracting than it does about the evolution of our federal system.

Advocates of privatization have in fact promoted a policy of stranding local governments by reducing federal or state aid so that they must rely more on private capital (Young 1989). Another factor spurring privatization has been the contraction of federal aid to state and local governments and the reduced value of exemptions of interest on public debt in the federal personal income tax (Young 1989; Kenyon 1995).[36]

Deterioration of the cash flow of state and local governments induced by conservative national and state policy has no relevance to the social value or cost of public services or privatization. When abandoned by federal or state governments, school districts will have an increased dependence on private financial capital. This is an unfortunate and unnecessary turn of events, not a natural advantage of contracting.

In summary, there are scant advantages in contracting owing to the superior financial flexibility of firms in noncompetitive markets. In seeking such advantages, local governments would be well advised to bank with a real banker, to follow prudent financial practices, and to discount the financial advantages of contractors' investments.

Summary. The more limited a school district's options, the less incentive there is for a contractor in a thin market to perform well. The potential for profiting from investments in pedagogical innovation seems dubious. The general financial power of a contractor is not necessarily beneficial to his customer. There seems to be no systematic theoretical reason why noncompetitive markets should provide good management services. Success will not be impossible, but it is more likely to be a creature of chance than of design.

A CASE FOR PUBLIC MANAGEMENT

The case for public management of education can be made in light of the basic qualities of education recounted at the beginning of the chapter—the things that make education different from economic goods and services routinely provided in markets.

Public Education Is Universal and Democratic

Three basic aspects of universal, democratic education are universal access, universal satisfaction of national standards of accomplishment, and the passing on of social values. Given those national concerns, the relationship between a government and its contractor cannot be a purely local affair. Education of each child in each school district in the United States is everybody's business, although the scope for "outside" intrusion is clearly limited by practicality, the law, and the proper prerogatives of local self-government.

There are ample precedents for concern that local governments can fail to serve national interests of various types. Local governments, for example, have discriminated against minorities in the provision of education. A local government's incompetence and corruption could move higher levels of government to act in defense of victimized citizens. The 104th Congress, for instance, feels compelled to intervene in the local education policy of the District of Columbia. Without passing judgment here on the wisdom of specific decisions, it cannot be denied that the Federal government and the states have suspended local political control of school systems, among other public functions. Here we are speaking of a far less radical proposition: oversight and regulation of local contracting governments.

National interests do not rule out contracting. They do breach the autonomy of the contracting relationship. Private management is intrinsically more insulated from public view and control, so it is less consistent—if not altogether inconsistent—with the national interest in education.

Accountability

Contractors have been used as vehicles for unpopular decisions that public officials would prefer not to make. Insofar as politicians escape responsibility for their policies, the democratic process is weakened. It might be argued that such power could be used to good end—to do things that need to be done but are politically difficult. This begs the question of who ought to make such decisions in a democratic society. If real-world politics is thought to be a consistent obstacle to the democratic will, then there is a much deeper problem in our system of government than bad education policies.

Contracting is one way for an education official to "look busy." The impulse to "try anything" has actually been celebrated by newspaper columnists on the grounds that "things can not get any worse." Of course, *things can always get worse.*

Contractors provide public officials with scapegoats for shortcomings in the provision of public services, as Shore points out in Chapter 1. Where the contractor turns around and subcontracts, the chain of responsibility is weakened further. Elected officials and their appointees should be accountable for their policies—there should be nobody left to blame. One intriguing idea in this vein for strengthening accountability is for school boards themselves to be chartered (Shanker 1994). That would highlight the proper focus of responsibility and reduce the ability of school officials to shield themselves from accountability by, in effect, hiring somebody else to do their jobs. Another idea is to require that boards be elected as teams, although a drawback is that the resulting board would allow for little diversity of views or dissent.

Educational Output Is Hard to Measure

The core rationale for contracting is the improvements that incentives would bring, particularly the profit motive. For profits to bring about improvement, however, they must in some way depend on the extent of improvement. In other words, it is necessary to measure productivity if one is to reward it. Insofar as educational "output" is hard to measure, the feasibility of contracting is diminished and the logic of public management strengthened.

If public education is viewed as a national interest, there should be some standard of accomplishment, and the implementation and enforcement of such a standard requires some intrusiveness by national or state government. The implied educational system would be more centralized. The use of private firms sacrifices information and accountability in hopes of cost minimization and innovation, among other objectives.

Those considerations notwithstanding, the public sector ought to pursue systematic assessments of the quality of their services, including surveys on the satisfaction of their constituents, as Osborne and Gaebler (1992) usefully emphasize. There is a difference in degree of difficulty between fostering such research, on the one hand, and using such information to implement a contract compensation system.

Outcomes Are Inferred From Process

The identity of the manager matters for productivity. A manager motivated by profits will not behave the same as one guided by publicly set rules. Rules for public managers are one alternative to paying private managers for productivity. Productivity is measured in educational "output," but insofar as output is hard to measure, rules and regulations must be resorted to.

In some respects, the means of education are themselves part of the product of education. For example, an educational process that attempts to instill certain values has no readily identifiable product. The contractor can be counted on to deliver such a product only if he or she is monitored and regulated, but such measures go against the grain of contracting.

If it is possible to define a desired standard for accomplishment in ways that could be verified without reference to the contractor's mode of operation, then there is more scope for contracting. An obvious mode of verification is external testing or other types of assessments, but suppose the contractor emphasizes preparation for such procedures to the neglect of other national objectives for education? We are back to the necessity of evaluating performance by monitoring provision of the service. In other words, whoever cares about the results of education must investigate the means by which such results are obtained. In general, contracting economizes on the information required by the customer, but that is not helpful insofar as such information (e.g., the way services are provided) is of interest to the customer.

Education as a Calling

The assertion that "you can not fire anyone" in public service has a logical, equally exaggerated corollary—that you can always fire anyone in a private firm. As noted above, the public sector's rigidity has a positive side and the private sector's flexibility a negative. The logic of contracting is that labor costs can be reduced by a greater capacity for exerting labor discipline on the part of the employer—the contractor. That is due to the contractor's ultimate weapon—dismissal. In other words, the prospect of labor turnover is the key to reducing labor costs. A problem is that labor turnover levies its own cost on productivity.

In an organization in which any employee can be fired at will, employment security will be low and labor turnover high. Workers value job security, so a heightened risk of separation cannot be a positive factor in morale, and morale has a bearing on productivity. Pride in one's job and organization, whether it is a business firm, a nonprofit group, or a government agency, is also a component of productivity (Simon 1991). Such pride depends on job tenure, among other things.

If we agree that for its workers the educational enterprise is something more than a way to gain income, we ought to acknowledge the role of job security and long-term job tenure in productivity. Of course, many business firms maintain such policies by choice, and an education contractor could do likewise. But in so doing a contractor would become more like the public agency to whose mission it lays claim.

That labor costs can be reduced without compromising quality has been contradicted by empirical research. Lower pay levels are not likely to maintain the same quality of workforce. Pack (1991) found that under contracting, wage reductions increased labor turnover which, in turn, reduced the quality of services.[37] Turnover is doubly harmful in public services where the relationship between the front-line service provider and the public benefits from stability. Examples are daycare, nursing-home care, counseling, and the focus of this study—education. As Shore writes in Chapter 1 regarding the difference between technology and teachers: "But at the heart of public schooling is an irreplaceable phenomenon—the words and looks and gestures exchanged between children and teachers, as they construct meaning together."

Problems also may arise in occupations in which productivity depends on senior workers training newer ones (Thurow 1976). High turnover exacerbates the fear of the older worker that by training his colleague, he renders himself more dispensable to his employer. Turnover is less of an issue in lower-skill occupations which do not entail the relationships noted above. There has clearly been scope for reducing labor costs in some areas by contracting out, but issues of external considerations discussed above (e.g., cost-shifting by private employers, the adequacy of wages from an ethical standpoint, the public sector's labor standards and labor relations) are properly raised.

Advocates of education reform usually warn that for changes to be successful, the good will and cooperation of participating employees must be secured. This will not be possible if collective bargaining and civil service standards are casualties of reform. The circuitous means by which such policies are pursued affronts the concept of democratic accountability. Public officials should take responsibility for their labor policies (Starr 1987).

Thus far the labor relations record of education contractors is very mixed. In Baltimore unionized maintenance workers were offered continued employment by the non-union contractor Johnson Controls at reduced wages. EAI replaced unionized paraprofessional teachers' aides with non-union interns. In Hartford, EAI called for the elimination of 300 positions (*Hartford Courant*, December 2, 1994, "Unions Upset by EAI's Hiring Plans"; "Custodians' Union Files Complaints About EAI"). In Wilkinsburg, Pa., the contractor proposed to summarily dismiss the entire teaching corps at the outset. This decision is being fought in court.

It is possible for contractors to have civil, if not always harmonious, relations with teachers unions. Examples include EAI and the AFT in Dade County, the Edison Project in its four new contracts, and the Minneapolis contract. The political significance of opposition to contracting by teachers unions can be overemphasized. As noted, political leaders in Baltimore and Hartford maintained their support for EAI and prevailed in elections campaigns. Their subsequent decision to dismiss EAI therefore cannot be easily ascribed to political pressure from unions.

One Should Not Pay for What Is Free

Private firms have limited incentives to conduct research on pedagogy because such research may not easily be exploited for profit. Successful methods could be emulated. The value of any pedagogical discovery is not obvious in the same way as, say, a miracle drug, so the commercial appeal of the former is more limited. For the same reasons, there is a public sector role in subsidizing such research, and this has been done. Research on educational reform and pedagogy is substantially in the public domain. School authorities have little need to purchase proprietary methods when there are free ones available. They may benefit from outside consulting services, a different kind of arrangement than the employment of outside managers.

New Vested Interests Are Not Desirable

The contracting arrangement places a new, self-seeking actor in the local political arena: the for-profit business firm marketing management services. All the old ones are still there: consumers, public employees, public sector bureaucrats, and politicians. Contractors can legally pursue their narrow economic interests just as bureaucrats can—by lobbying to maximize the share of public revenues allocated to their sector (Niskanen 1972). This can add to pressure for some combination of less noneducation public spending and higher taxes. In this vein, for-profit organizations seem to have more sway than nonprofits because the former have more scope for making legal financial contributions to candidates for public office (Van Horn 1991).

It is customary for vested interests to promote their interests in a form that seeks to embody the general interest. An example is the idea that schools should use more technology and less labor. That could prove to be true, but local governments ought to satisfy themselves on that score before seeking advice from contractors. We would not, after all, knowingly accept a proposed defense budget crafted by defense contractors!

An example of such influence can be found in San Diego, where EAI board member and stockholder John Walton (son of Sam Walton) funded school board candidates who supported privatization; also, EAI worked with a local African American parents' group called "We, the Collective" to take over some schools (*San Diego Union-Tribune*, November 9, 1994). The *Hartford Courant* (August 15, 1994 editorial) noted that EAI asked Hartford elected officials to recommend local subcontractors while a decision was pending before City Council and Board.

In Hartford, EAI became a player in labor-management conflict by joining the city in calling for give-backs from the teachers' union (*Hartford Courant*, November 23, 1994; "Hartford Board, EAI Talk Tough to Unions.") In Baltimore, EAI President John Golle said, "Just try to take that [the EAI innovations] away from the have-nots. Just try. I dare you, you just try," referring to an organization known as the "Tesseract Parent Coalition" (*Baltimore Sun*, June 6, 1995).

Another form of influence is the employment of former government officials by contractors. This kind of "revolving door" became infamous in the case of federal defense spending and can be observed in the states as well (Van Horn 1991). Contractors who employ persons with whom they had previously dealt in an official capacity ought to be automatically suspect; the conflict of interest is manifest. A stark example can be found in Baltimore, where Superintendent Walter Amprey publicly disclosed that EAI had promised him employment if he left his position with the Baltimore public school system ("Amprey a Fervent Convert to EAI," *Baltimore Sun*, June 6, 1995).

Then there is the prospect of outright illegal behavior from contracting. If public officials have approved the transfer of materials or services from Bureau X to Agency Y, no money changes hands, so there is less scope for kickbacks and similar crimes.

Another potential abuse accentuated by contracting is the exploitation of workers for political purposes. That is less feasible under civil service regulation or union protection, although in the latter case union leaders might make political decisions that are unpopular with their membership. Employment standards make it less easy for public or private employers to hire on a basis other than merit.

It is possible, out of fear of corruption, to bind public employees up with so many rules that effective performance becomes impossible (Kelman 1990). But reform of such rules within the public sector remains an option; contracting is not the only possible solution. At the same time, contracting has always been and will remain pervasive in the U.S. public sector. The problems are worth trying to solve whether or not business firms ever run public schools.

Local Labor Markets Matter

Are there legitimate public concerns in the manner of provision, over and above the actual educational complex itself? One is the effect of the contract on the local labor market. A decision to use cheaper labor or nonlocal labor diminishes local employment opportunities. Such concerns ought to be stronger for communities with dimmer job prospects and weaker labor markets. For the residents of communities who have ready access to jobs and high employment levels, such concerns would be less pressing.

The most fiscally stressed localities would do well to interest themselves in the extent to which their public sector exports jobs and income. For instance, by employing a suburbanite rather than a community resident, a locality is exporting a job and most of the tax revenue that would be recaptured from the person holding that job. Our federal system as currently organized is not effective in addressing the fiscal drain on cities. As noted above, the repatriation of profits is much the more minor consideration. The bulk of school expenditures will always be devoted to labor compensation and bread-and-butter purchases of supplies and the maintenance of physical plant. Buying locally aggrandizes the local economy, admittedly at some possible extra cost to taxpayers.

Conclusion

Like privatization in general, contracting is first and foremost a matter of cases. Some public services or components of services ought to be contracted and others not. Theory alone is usually an inadequate guide to what should or should not be privatized in some way or another. Extensive experimentation, evaluation, and risk are unavoidable costs of considering such options. Education management remains unproven as a candidate for contracting, although neither can it be rejected.

The expectation that competition routinely bolsters contracting is likely to be disappointed. To benefit from competitive forces, local governments and their constituents need to take fairly elaborate steps to organize the setting in which such forces can blossom. How they might do so is discussed in the next, concluding chapter.

Although contracting cannot be rejected as a potential source of educational progress, it is not the only potential source and not necessarily the most promising one. Given the urgency of the goal, local governments cannot be faulted for a willingness to consider a wide range of alternatives. For the same reason, however, this chapter has tried to show that experimenting with contracting should not rank as the most prominent possibility. The elaboration of alternatives to contracting is largely beyond the scope of this study, although limited discussion of them is offered in Chapter 1 and the next chapter.

CHAPTER 4

Implications for Policy

BY MAX B. SAWICKY,

CRAIG E. RICHARDS,

& RIMA SHORE

In this final chapter we summarize the findings of our study, explore their implications, and offer recommendations to state and local governments considering the use of private contractors to advance education reform.

MAJOR FINDINGS

There is no empirical evidence supporting the case for contracting the management of public schools. The most basic limitation is the dearth of experience with contracting for management services; another is the lack of support for research on the costs and benefits of contracting. Of course, that will be true for any really new sort of education reform. The point is that school authorities and parents should be aware that contracting for management remains an experimental option the effectiveness of which has yet to be demonstrated. Some may be eager to experiment, while others may prefer initiatives for which some evidence of effectiveness is available.

The current state of private contracting for educational management bears little resemblance to the standard economic model of a well-functioning market. Competitive contracting systems in education have yet to be organized by local governments. Contracts have been nominally competitive at best. Without competitive forces or effective government regulation, contractors are unlikely to contribute much to education reform.

The legal authority to dismiss a contractor at will is not necessarily an effective source of discipline on the contractor's operations. One reason is that dismissal has negative and disruptive consequences for the school district and its students. For example, the computers supplied to Baltimore schools by Education Alternatives Inc. were leased and might be withdrawn after the arrangement was terminated. The district must either replace them or risk demoralizing students and teachers. Another reason is that public officials may believe that a negative verdict on a contractor's performance may reflect badly on their own judgment and impede their own political careers.

Many local governments and school districts will not have the technical capacity to structure contracts so that they generate useful data on contract performance. Local governments have been lax in documenting the results of their policy innovations in education. Politics mitigates against the organization of valid experiments, as here again the experiment's results can be taken as a criticism of public officials held responsible for the policy.

The lack of labor productivity incentives in public education stems to an important extent from the difficulties inherent in a service with the special characteristics of public education, difficulties faced by public and private managers alike. Private contractors have yet to establish any such incentives in the education field.

The power of contracting to facilitate the reduction of labor standards in such areas as compensation, working conditions, and job security has proven so far to be illusory. Education Alternatives Inc. attempted to eliminate union jobs in Baltimore and Hartford and fared badly in the resulting political warfare. Public employees may not forfeit political sway under contracting. To facilitate experimentation, local governments and contractors need cooperative relations with their workers, which means supporting civil service standards and collective bargaining with public employee organizations.

About Education Alternatives Inc.

- EAI is a sophisticated corporate structure with financial, reputational, and managerial support from highly respected corporations. Despite those qualities, EAI has yet to demonstrate that it can make a profit running schools. Its actual profits derive primarily from interest earnings and speculative financial transactions. In spite of its impressive corporate connections, EAI's survival has been brought into question in light of the fall in the price of its stock from $48 in 1993 to less than $4 per share, following news of its dismissal from Baltimore in December 1995.

- EAI did not break the law or violate what are known as generally accepted accounting practices, but it did represent its cash flow and income projections in a highly optimistic manner that promoted speculative interest in EAI's stock and millions in profit for EAI and its principals.

- An analysis of Baltimore's payments to EAI in light of the cost history of the Baltimore public school system shows that EAI's fee per pupil in Baltimore was 26% above the average district cost for elementary school students and 36% above the average district cost for middle school students. That was because the cost of educating elementary and middle school students in Baltimore is significantly less than the average cost of education; the latter includes high schools and special education, both of which carry above-average per pupil costs. Thus, the method used for determining fair contract value for the EAI—a fee based on spending per pupil—was not based on appropriate cost comparisons. Baltimore City Public Schools could have achieved substantial savings over the term of the EAI contract had they calculated average per pupil costs by the appropriate type of school.

- EAI emphasized the role of adequate facilities in providing quality education in Baltimore. While every child deserves a clean, safe school facility, such circumstances are not sufficient to promote ongoing progress in student achievement. Additional dollars are best used to increase student time on learning tasks. EAI spending on facilities came at the cost of lower average spending on general instruction than in the Baltimore City Public Schools comparison schools.

Organizing Competition in the Public Interest

- For contracting to work, the business firm must be induced to act in the public interest. The merits of contracting do not rest in ownership or control of the vender organization; what matters is the setting in which the contractor is obliged to operate (Goodman and Loveman 1991). The primary responsibility for creating appropriate conditions falls to the local government. Those conditions depend on the relationship between buyer and seller, particularly the contract itself, and the ways governments and voters are organized to monitor the contract. Crucial elements include the contractual stipulation of performance requirements and the comprehensive and timely public disclosure of information on all aspects of the contractor's operations.

- A basic virtue of markets—when they work—is flexibility. Arrangements that cease to satisfy can be recast. Today's seller can be replaced tomorrow. The customer—in our study the school authorities—*must be prepared to develop good contracts by a process of costly, experimental trial and error.* For errors to be visible, information must be available. Plans must be made in advance for collecting, analyzing, and disseminating such information. That applies to any reform of public services, not just contracting in education. In fact, it should apply to school systems whether there is reform in progress or not, simply from the standpoint of the taxpayer/consumer's right to know.

- The national and state interest in quality education, as discussed in Chapter 3 and articulated in reports like *A Nation at Risk*, requires guidelines for the definition of education that measure up to the challenges posed by today's global economy. Standards should guide each school district's formulation of appropriate benchmarks for the success of all students. School authorities must be held accountable for adherence to such standards, whether or not they employ contractors.

- Decentralization of education, even if it results in greater parental control, cannot satisfy the need for standards. From the standpoint of either standards or decentralization, contracting is neutral at best. Contractors' sensitivity to either national standards or parental control will be mediated through the institutional and political priorities of its customer—the school authority.

- Because of the novelty of privatized management in education, as noted, cost comparisons between private management corporations are not yet available. As a result, school authorities must rely on their own cost history to determine fair contract value. Paying higher-than-average costs to a private contractor can be justified, depending on the goals of the district. Indeed, as we have shown in the case of Baltimore, there can be a wide variance in per pupil spending from one school to another. However, higher-than-average per pupil fees should be included in any comparison of student outcomes with schools that do not have extra resources. The standard procedure for such a comparison is a cost-effectiveness analysis (Levin 1983). If cost-effectiveness analysis is not used, the validity of performance comparisons between schools managed by different parties will be invalidated by spending inequities.

POLICY RECOMMENDATIONS

In this section we extrapolate from our major findings to make policy recommendations to local governments, state legislators, and school boards struggling with education reform. We begin with some general considerations about the whys and wherefors of competitive strategies. We then recommend ways to improve accountability when private contractors are employed.

Begin at the Beginning

• The desire for rapid, sweeping reform can distract policy makers from thinking about how the reform might work in practice.

• A school district considering private contracting ought to step back and first decide exactly what problems it sees in its schools. Dissatisfaction with results is not a sufficient guide to appropriate action. For instance, committing the school system to graduating more students is not a reform but a goal. Concentrating the best teachers in the upper grades is a reform but not necessarily an effective means to the stated goal.

• For the sake of public understanding of education reform, public officials must stress that the essence of contracting is the process of public decision making, not the adoption of a specific vender. The latter should be understood as readily disposable, not exalted as long-term partners. That has not been an easy task in previous endeavors. Hanushek (1994) illuminates the problem as follows: "[I]nstead of selling voters a solution to the problems of schools, legislators must instead convince voters to embark on the search for a solution, a search that will require considerable effort, and some risk, on the part of voters themselves."

Smart Contracting

• Contracting benefits from market-like discipline, but well-functioning markets do not necessarily take shape automatically—especially for such a unique "product" as public education. Markets in the provision of public services must be *organized by government*. Citizens must demand efficiency in that dimension just as they would for a publicly provided service. The responsibility of the contractor is to make money and to uphold its contracts and related agreements— not to recruit competition for its own business or to establish self-regulation that is contrary to its own interests.

- Local governments must give careful thought to how they expect to harness competitive forces in the public interest. Contracts should stipulate performance outcomes, rewarding success and penalizing failure. Developing proper measures, data collection practices, and evaluation methods will require some prior work and expense by the school district (see below).

- The best way for a school district to obtain a good contract is to consider a range of venders simultaneously. Opportunities must be made available for all prospective contractors to obtain and analyze information about the school system. In the same vein, such information should be made available to the interested public so that the political process surrounding contracting will be better informed. Sufficient lead time must be afforded to potential bidders for the preparation of proposals. Finally, the services offered for bidding must be comparable so that the district can focus on cost minimization.

- Because education is a national concern, local governments will need to link the contractors' performance and modus operandi to national objectives through regulation, among other means. There also will be local public objectives that cannot be quantified or precisely stipulated in a contract requiring similar treatment.

- Competition requires information. Districts that report out school-based performance indicators—both qualitative indicators like the perceptions of teachers and students about school climate and quantitative indicators, such as test scores—provide school leaders, teachers, and parents with important basic information about school performance. Pride is often a sufficient motivation if one is given the necessary information to make valid and informed comparisons about school performance. The key to perceptions of validity is that similar schools be compared.[38]

- Full and timely public disclosure on all aspects of contract implementation should be required, in cooperation with independent auditors, analysts, and evaluators designated by the school district or sponsoring parties in higher levels of government. Data should also be made available gratis to any outside researchers who want to study the arrangement. Disclosure of inaccurate information should be subject to financial penalties.

- Left to their own devices, district superintendents may not be anxious to cooperate in releasing data to outside evaluators, or even to elected government officials. For-profit firms have wide leeway in the way that they must report income and expenditures for tax or regulatory purposes. Unless the financial reporting parallels the line items of the school district, appropriate comparative analysis will be difficult or impossible.

- Rules for timely, comprehensive disclosure should be set in the contract itself. Contracting parties should agree on school-based budgeting formats for the reporting of financial data that permits school-by-school comparisons. If the district does not currently have site-based budgeting in place, it should be introduced at least a year before the first year of a private management contract. That will also facilitate the development of the appropriate average per pupil expenditure data required to negotiate a good contract. Competition might successfully serve the laudatory function of forcing the school system to specify in detail the extent and nature of the management contract, its primary goals and performance expectations, and the way performance will be measured.

- When functions are merged under one contractor, inefficiency in one area can be masked by gains in another. Custodial services, security, curriculum development, pedagogy, and management are distinct tasks that are best assigned to proven specialists in each area, whether public or private, so that costs and productivity can be accurately assessed. Bundling of functions by contractor should be avoided. The school district should strive to hire contractors only for what they do well.

- Contractors have appealed to school districts by offering advances of funds in the form of expenditures on facilities, computer equipment, and educational software. Impoverished school systems may be tempted to supplement their funds in this way, but they should weigh the risks. So-called "investments" by contractors may allow the customer to "buy now, pay later." Because the contractor must recover the interest costs of any funds advanced, such an arrangement is analogous to deficit spending. Contractors are not the best intermediaries for such transactions. Moreover, such offers from contractors may be mere contrivances aimed at shifting education expenditures among line items for the sake of the contractor's bottom line, to the potential detriment of the curriculum.

• How private companies invest their cash should be important to a public school district since risky investments can undermine the ability of a contractor to fulfill its obligations. Certainly if an Orange County government can suffer a sharp financial reversal, so can a business firm beholden to venture capital. It is important to come to agreement in advance about the contractor's allowable short-term cash investments. Public funds should be segregated in accounts managed by the local government until needed for disbursement to the contractor, subcontractors, and public employees for purchases and services rendered. Inquiries should be made about the company's cash management strategies; they should not expose the local government to inordinate financial risk. That is especially important if the contractor is handling the school system's large, routine financial transactions, such as payroll. The contractor might be required to post a bond. As reported in Chapter 1, a $1 million bond, for one school no less, was demanded in Wichita, Kan., of the Edison Project for use as "transition money" if it became necessary to dismiss the contractor. The downside of such requirements is that they might reduce competition from nonprofit organizations or associations of public employees.

• Per pupil fees specified in contracts between private providers and school districts should be comparable to per pupil fees at similar schools if the school district has the goal of comparing the private contractor's performance to the previous performance of the schools or to the concurrent performance of a control group of schools. A school district should (1) sign no contracts permitting a vender to manage all the schools of a particular type in the district; that would make it difficult to develop appropriate comparison data; (2) collect good baseline data on student outcomes before the private contractor entered the district; (3) make certain that the agreed-upon outcome measures, including kinds of tests taken and other indicators, can be compared against benchmarks of desired performance; and (4) establish a comparison group of schools with a profile similar to those managed by the private provider to provide another point of reference for measuring progress. It may be the case, for example, that test scores are rising in all elementary schools in the district because of other school reforms being implemented concurrently with the reforms initiated by the private manager. In that case, the relevant comparison is whether the private manager is providing a greater added value than other reform initiatives in the district.

- Testing is a complex business. Comparison of education outcomes by reference to students' scores on different types of tests is tantamount to comparing quarts to liters. It adds unnecessary complications to the evaluation process. Tests used by the district before the contract to evaluate performance, as well as other measures like dropout rates, attendance, and disciplinary actions, should be adopted for use under the contract and reported by procedures and standards that conform to precontract practices. Competition and the concomitant expectation of improved student achievement are goals that do not require the private provision of education itself. Districts can explore other ways of using competition. For example, they can investigate charter schools and school choice plans that seek to exploit competitive forces, keeping in mind that those approaches are not without risks of their own (Rasell and Rothstein 1993). Although the literature on individual teacher merit pay plans is almost uniformly negative, school-based incentive plans have shown some positive outcomes (Richards and Sheu 1992). The use of school-based incentives to promote student achievement should be explored.

- Contracting cannot escape the real world of politics. Business firms with limited political support, especially if they lend themselves to the "outsider" label, will be no more able to implement controversial personnel policies than politicians. Furthermore, the discord resulting from abrogation of such standards will imperil the contracting enterprise. Labor standards for contractors should mirror those in the public sector, in general. As such standards have been the product of the democratic process, they should not be preempted by alternative management arrangements.

- Contracting is an experiment, and experiments that are not mined for information are a waste. School systems in some large cities have research and evaluation capacity, but resources for these functions tend to be limited—especially as pressure mounts for districts to cut overhead and staff. It is therefore unrealistic to expect systematic data collection and analysis by local school systems. This is more appropriately a task for state and local governments, which have greater technical and financial resources. Cohen (1995) points out the abandonment by the 104th Congress of federal educational reforms set in the 1980s and the likely ripple effects in state governments. State governments appear to be threatened by severe cuts in grants-in-aid that will poison the environment for policy innovations. School districts abandoned in this way may feel they have no choice but to try new things. The tragedy lies in the dim likelihood that such experiences will be sufficiently endowed to be informative. Innovations should be tested in rigorous, professionally designed experimental settings. Evaluations should be conducted by objective third parties.

The public and the press do not have the time or resources to become technical experts in education, economics, and accounting, but there are some red flags that they can watch out for. These simple indicators provide for informal assessment of a contracting arrangement:

- How many bidders attempted to win the contract? If there were few, competitive pressure will be lacking or absent altogether.

- Were public employees given a fair opportunity to participate in the bidding? If not, competition is inhibited and the public, in general, may not be fully informed of important, potentially controversial details of the contracting process.

- Does the contractor promise dramatic improvements within five years or less? Because such a commitment is patently unrealistic, any such promise signals the possibility of bad faith on the part of the seller.

- Does the contract contain specific performance requirements, or is the issue of performance left entirely to the discretion of public officials whose political well-being will be affected by popular perceptions of whether or not the contract is successful? If the latter is the case, getting out of a bad contract will be more difficult.

- Are any types of termination costs stipulated in the contract? Obviously such costs should favor the customer rather than the seller.

- Does the contractor claim no special advantage over comparison schools within the jurisdiction by virtue of being paid the "average per pupil expenditure"? As noted in Chapter 2, the systemwide average has no bearing on the costs of running any subset of schools.

- Is the arrangement being organized so that it can be rigorously tested from a comparative standpoint? Who is to decide by whom the evaluation of the contractor will be conducted? Clearly, those being evaluated (the contractor and his or her sponsors, patrons, and boosters in local government) should not control the choice of who will conduct the evaluation.

- How, by whom, and when will information about the progress of the contract be designed, collected, analyzed, and disseminated? Comprehensive, timely, and convenient disclosure to all is the best guarantee that the true value of the contract will be transparent to the public.

- Does the contractor employ former public officials, including education administrators, who were previously involved in evaluating and negotiating contracts in their official capacities? "Revolving-door," conflict-of-interest issues arise.

- Has the contractor or those with an ownership interest in the contractor made political contributions to local candidates for public office?

CONCLUSION

Private contracting has been tried but it has yet to be truly tested. It should be tested because it is relevant to concerns about cost and quality in local public education. We need more research about contracting in education, as for other types of privatization. In particular, we need careful studies of costs and educational outcomes under well-formulated experiments. Education contracting promises innovations in pedagogy, curriculum, and cost control, among other areas. Such claims should be evaluated.

Private contracting will not solve the problems of poor leadership, conflicts of interest, and especially corruption. To the extent that poor or corrupt political leadership dominates a system, its contracts are likely to reflect the same deficiencies. At the same time, reform-oriented leadership may feel it needs to resort to private contracting to stimulate the competitive juices of a moribund school system.

Private contracting is not a risk-free strategy. When poorly implemented—as in Baltimore—matters can become worse. Much of this report has referred to experiences with a single firm—Education Alternatives Inc. Indeed, most contemporary experience with contracting the management of public schools has been with that company. The future of contracting should not be generalized from such a narrow beginning, and, indeed, other private companies, like the Edison Project, may prove to serve the public interest more successfully. Our purpose is to point out how the theory of market efficiency can be compromised in practice when government's method of contracting is flawed. That is not to say that contracting cannot work. What remains to be seen is whether governments can effectively organize competition among their own suppliers in the educational arena. The record to date is not good.

Although we have documented numerous lapses in the case of EAI's role in Baltimore and Hartford, the moral of our story is that government itself is responsible for such irregularities. If governments are able to organize competition, firms—including EAI—could yet prove to be important contributors to education reform. The slogan "caveat emptor"—let the buyer beware—is appropriate to contracting. What's different about contracting for public services of any type is the added burden on the customer—the government—when well-functioning markets are lacking. Because the customer must learn by trial and error, the more salient motto is: "Fool me once, shame on you. Fool me twice, shame on me."

Appendix A
The Informal Structure of Education Alternatives Inc.

The Informal Structure of Education Alternatives Inc.

In addition to its formal business relationships, EAI executives have a number of interesting informal connections and relationships that add some insight into the emergence of EAI's recent successes. In particular, it was necessary to examine stock ownership among affiliated companies; individuals who are or were on the board of one or more companies; individuals formerly employed by affiliated companies; and personal business relationships among individuals connected with affiliated companies and contractees.

Some of those complex corporate relationships are depicted in **Figure A**. One example of the complexity and unpredictability of such networks is EAI's efforts to secure a contract with the Piscataway, N.J. school district. Philip Geiger, EAI's East Coast vice president, was the former superintendent in Piscataway, where he was a proponent of full privatization of noninstructional services. He succeeded in privatizing transportation and cafeteria services and unsuccessfully attempted to privatize custodial and maintenance services. Johnson Controls employs the former business manager of Piscataway, N.J. public schools, Guy Vander Vliet. EAI has been unable to parlay those linkages into a contract with the Piscataway public schools.

Another example is John Walton, an EAI director, major stockholder, and the son of Sam Walton, founder of Wal-Mart. John Walton is a Wal-Mart heir and vice president of Walton Enterprises II LP. Walton is an Arkansas resident and was seen as an asset to negotiations with the Little Rock public schools, which, so far, have been unsuccessful.

The Walton family has long been involved with educational projects. The proceeds from Sam Walton's book *Made in America* are dedicated to the New American Schools Development Corp., a private effort to improve education. In 1994, Walton bankrolled the campaigns of two San Diego, Calif., school board candidates. While Walton's candidates were able to spend twice as much as their opponents, they still lost. According to newspaper reports, EAI pursued a management contract in San Diego.

A third interesting business relationship is the one between Piper Jaffray and John Golle. Jaffray is extremely well-connected in corporate circles. Norwest Bank, EAI's transfer agent, is the seventh largest of 26 institutional stockholders of Piper Jaffray, EAI's investment banker. Both companies are based in Minneapolis, Minn. John Golle, a prominent Minneapolis businessman, is a director of 26 Piper Capital Man-

agement trusts, funds, and portfolios. As a director of those 26 regis-
tered investment companies, Golle's income during the calendar year
ended December 31, 1994 was $59,500. Furthermore, EAI had approxi-
mately $36 million invested in risky derivatives through Piper Jaffray. In
a court suit settled with investors, the fund was to pay back 50 cents on
a dollar invested. This means that EAI stood to lose approximately $18
million. Golle's response at the time the losses were disclosed was, "In
retrospect, looking into a crystal ball, maybe we shouldn't have made
the investments because of the decline of the market value. We do not
own the exotic derivatives like Orange County." Obviously, EAI was
only one among many companies and institutions that lost money investing in derivatives. However, for school districts contemplating long-
term contracts than involve the private management of public funds, it is
extremely important to ensure that such funds are in secure investments.

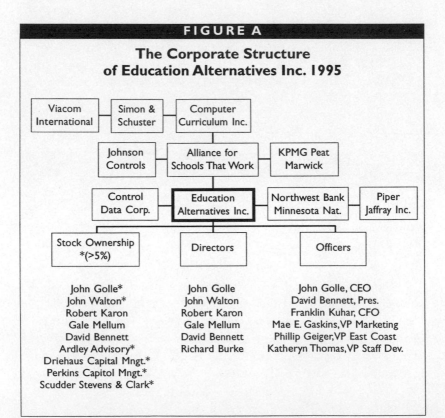

FIGURE A

The Corporate Structure
of Education Alternatives Inc. 1995

Viacom International	Simon & Schuster	Computer Curriculum Inc.		
	Johnson Controls	Alliance for Schools That Work	KPMG Peat Marwick	
	Control Data Corp.	**Education Alternatives Inc.**	Northwest Bank Minnesota Nat.	Piper Jaffray Inc.

Stock Ownership *(>5%)	Directors	Officers
John Golle*	John Golle	John Golle, CEO
John Walton*	John Walton	David Bennett, Pres.
Robert Karon	Robert Karon	Franklin Kuhar, CFO
Gale Mellum	Gale Mellum	Mae E. Gaskins, VP Marketing
David Bennett	David Bennett	Phillip Geiger, VP East Coast
Ardley Advisory*	Richard Burke	Katheryn Thomas, VP Staff Dev.
Driehaus Capital Mngt.*		
Perkins Capitol Mngt.*		
Scudder Stevens & Clark*		

Appendix B
What-If Analysis

Adaptation of Judson Porter's (BCPS) Data 1993-94 Site-Based Budgets

School #	School Name	Grade Level	Status EAI/Partner	Actual Budget	FTE Pupils	Average FTE Expenditures	EAI Budget	Difference Over/Under	Hold Harmless
4	Steuart Hill Elem.	1		$2,529,315	510	$4,959	$2,791,740	$262,425	$0
5	Langston Hughes Elem.	1		1,462,248	342	4,282	1,869,371	407,123	0
7	Cecil Elem.	1	1	2,459,967	632	3,892	3,459,568	999,601	0
8	City Spring Elem.	1		2,552,403	446	5,729	2,438,667	(113,736)	113,736
10	James McHenry Elem.	1		2,224,975	531	4,190	2,906,694	681,719	0
11	Eutaw-Marshburn Elem.	1		2,424,139	607	3,984	3,330,929	906,790	0
12	Lakeland Elem./Middle	2		2,313,675	534	4,333	2,923,116	609,441	0
13	Tench Tilghman Elem.	1		2,562,346	569	4,503	3,114,706	552,360	0
14	Park Heights Elem.	1		1,530,635	361	4,240	1,976,114	445,479	0
16	Johnson Square Elem.	1	1	2,621,432	556	4,719	3,040,807	419,375	0
19	Lexington Terrace Elem.	1		1,861,231	376	4,957	2,055,487	194,256	0
21	Hilton Elem.	1		1,902,008	586	3,246	3,207,764	1,305,756	0
22	Geo. Washington Elem.	1	1	1,917,220	386	4,967	2,112,964	195,744	0
23	General Wolfe Elem.	1		1,137,420	221	5,147	1,209,754	72,334	0
24	Westside Elem.	1		2,442,813	626	3,744	3,571,785	1,128,972	0
26	Madison Square Elem.	1	1	2,007,184	477	4,208	2,611,098	603,914	0
27	Comm. John Rodgers Elem.	1		3,638,995	798	4,563	4,365,515	726,520	0
28	Wm. Pinderhughes Elem.	1		1,735,486	370	4,691	2,025,380	289,894	0
29	Matthew A. Henson Elem.	1		1,943,382	502	3,871	2,747,948	804,566	0
30	George Street Elem.	1		1,838,106	352	5,222	1,926,848	88,742	0
31	Coldstream Park Elem.	1		2,210,131	569	3,888	3,111,969	901,838	0
34	Charles Carroll, Barrister Elem.	1		1,631,800	321	5,083	1,757,154	125,354	0
36	Harford Heights Elem.	1		6,628,463	1,562	4,244	8,550,388	1,921,925	0
39	Dallas F. Nicholas, Sr. Elem.	1		1,996,875	402	4,967	2,200,548	203,673	0
40	Lake Clifton/Eastern Sr. High	4		8,334,816	2,044	4,078	11,188,856	2,854,040	0
41	Hamilton Middle	3		4,344,156	1,233	3,523	6,749,442	2,405,286	0
42	Garrison Middle	3		3,225,752	790	4,083	4,324,460	1,098,708	0

Adaptation of Judson Porter's (BCPS) Data 1993-94 Site-Based Budgets (cont.)

School #	School Name	Grade Level	Status EAI/Partner	Actual Budget	FTE Pupils	Average FTE Expenditures	EAI Budget	Difference Over/Under	Hold Harmless
43	Hampstead Hill Middle	3		$4,061,417	1,010	$4,021	$5,528,740	$1,467,323	$0
44	Montebello Elem.	1		2,271,908	646	3,520	3,533,467	1,261,559	0
45	Federal Hill Elem.	1		1,380,873	52	5,480	1,379,448	(1,425)	1,425
46	Chinquapin Middle	3		5,340,675	1,238	4,314	6,776,812	1,436,137	0
47	Hampstead Hill Elem.	1		2,344,957	639	3,670	3,497,886	1,152,929	0
49	Northeast Middle	3		3,815,780	1,098	3,475	6,010,452	2,194,672	0
50	Abbottston Middle	3		1,848,811	461	4,015	2,520,777	671,966	0
51	Waverly Elem.	1		1,597,418	461	3,473	2,518,040	920,622	0
53	Margaret Brent Elem.	1	1	1,908,424	492	3,883	2,690,471	782,047	0
54	Barday Elem.	1		1,752,394	405	4,327	2,216,970	464,576	0
55	Hampden Elem.	1		1,856,558	542	3,429	2,964,171	1,107,613	0
56	Robert Poole Middle	3		3,488,303	653	5,342	3,574,522	86,219	0
57	Lombard Middle	3	1	3,621,428	951	3,808	5,205,774	1,584,346	0
58	Ashburton Elem.	1		938,542	257	3,652	1,406,818	468,276	0
60	Gwynns Falls Elem.	1		1,964,221	386	5,095	2,110,227	146,006	0
61	John Eager Howard Elem.	1		2,190,867	504	4,347	2,758,896	568,029	0
62	Edgecombe Circle Elem.	1		2,040,761	530	3,854	2,898,483	857,722	0
63	Rosemont Elem.	1		1,844,092	412	4,476	2,255,288	411,198	0
64	Liberty Elem.	1		2,513,061	601	4,181	3,289,874	776,813	0
66	Mt. Royal Elem./Middle	2	1	2,436,588	620	3,930	3,393,880	957,292	0
70	Southern Sr. High	4		5,371,417	1,362	3,944	7,455,588	2,084,171	0
75	Calverton Middle	3		4,917,444	1,339	3,672	7,329,686	2,412,242	0
76	Fr. Scott Key Elem./Middle	2		3,089,104	804	3,842	4,401,096	1,311,992	0
77	Herring Run Middle	3		6,246,385	1,390	4,494	7,608,860	1,362,475	0
79	William H. Lemmel Middle	3		4,888,335	1,356	3,605	7,422,744	2,534,409	0
80	W. Baltimore Middle	3		5,802,380	1,686	3,442	9,229,164	3,426,784	0
82	Greenspring Middle	3		4,407,325	963	4,577	5,271,462	864,137	0

83	William Paca Elem.	1		2,797,971	807	3,469	4,414,781	1,616,810	0
84	Thomas Jefferson Elem.	1		1,870,433	486	3,849	2,660,364	789,931	0
85	Fort Worthington Elem.	1		2,465,757	477	5,169	2,611,098	145,341	0
86	Lakewood Elem.	1	1	1,122,006	195	5,739	1,070,167	(51,839)	51,839
87	Windsor Hills Elem.	1		1,281,914	233	5,502	1,275,442	(6,475)	6,475
88	Lyndhurst Elem.	1		1,981,779	431	4,593	2,362,031	380,252	0
89	Rognel Heights Elem.	1		1,723,208	392	4,396	2,145,808	442,600	0
95	Franklin Square Elem.	1		1,960,282	448	4,376	2,452,352	492,070	0
97	Collington Square Elem.	1		2,377,302	439	5,415	2,403,086	25,784	0
98	Samuel F.B. Morse Elem.	1		2,576,833	593	4,345	3,246,082	669,249	0
101	Elmer A. Henderson Elem.	1		2,580,652	530	4,869	2,901,220	320,568	0
102	Thomas G. Hayes Elem.	1		2,316,283	417	5,555	2,282,658	(33,625)	33,625
105	Moravia Park Elem.	5		2,865,243	678	4,229	3,708,635	843,392	0
107	Gilmor Elem.	1		2,124,019	490	4,335	2,682,260	558,241	0
115	Venable Senior High	4		2,129,362	201	10,594	1,100,274	(1,029,088)	1,029,088
122	Sam Coleridge-Taylor Elem.	1		2,708,561	453	5,986	2,476,985	(231,576)	231,576
124	Bay-Brook Elem.	1		998,332	191	5,227	1,045,534	47,202	0
125	Furman L. Templeton Elem.	1		2,407,093	394	6,109	2,156,756	(250,337)	250,337
130	Booker T. Washington Middle	3		3,176,601	819	3,879	4,483,206	1,306,605	0
133	Paul Laurence Dunbar Middle	3		2,828,877	763	3,708	4,176,662	1,347,785	0
134	Walter P. Carter Elem.	1		1,932,804	416	4,646	2,227,184	344,380	0
135	Luther C. Mitchell Primary Ctr.	5		713,051	88	8,103	481,718	(213,339)	213,339
138	Harriett Tubman Elem.	1		1,967,680	409	4,811	2,238,866	271,186	0
139	Charles C. Carrollton Elem.	1		3,200,817	704	4,550	3,850,959	650,142	0
142	Robert W. Coleman Elem.	1		2,146,768	417	5,148	2,282,658	135,890	0
144	James Mosher Elem.	1		1,947,906	375	5,194	2,025,750	104,844	0
145	Alexander Hamilton Elem.	1		1,868,015	441	4,236	2,414,034	546,019	0
150	Bentalou Elem.	1		2,610,246	552	4,733	3,018,911	408,665	0
157	George G. Kelson Elem.	1		2,266,041	554	4,090	3,032,596	766,555	0
159	Cherry Hill Elem.	1		1,417,555	297	4,773	1,625,778	208,223	0
159	Cherry Hill Elem.	1		1,417,555	297	4,773	1,625,778	208,223	0
160	Carter G. Woodson Elem.	1		1,392,796	262	5,326	1,431,451	38,655	0

Adaptation of Judson Porter's (BCPS) Data 1993-94 Site-Based Budgets (cont.)

School #	School Name	Grade Level	Status EAI/Partner	Actual Budget	FTE Pupils	Average FTE Expenditures	EAI Budget	Difference Over/Under	Hold Harmless
162	Diggs-Johnson Middle	3		$2,212,024	569	$3,888	$3,114,706	$902,682	$0
163	Patapsco Elem.	1		1,930,277	409	4,725	2,236,129	305,852	0
164	Arundel Elem.	1		1,511,396	258	5,869	1,409,555	(101,841)	101,841
177	Geo. McMechen Middle-Senior	3.5		4,146,110	224	18,509	1,226,176	(2,919,934)	2,919,934
178	Francis M. Woods Alt. High	4		1,948,168	319	6,107	1,746,206	(201,962)	201,962
180	Amett J. Brown Jr. Middle	3		2,543,038	532	4,780	2,912,168	369,130	0
201	Dicky Hill Elem.	1		1,423,163	357	3,992	1,951,481	528,318	0
202	Lafayette Elem.	1		1,771,393	369	4,807	2,017,169	245,776	0
203	Maree Garnett Farring Elem.	1		1,600,425	457	3,506	2,498,881	898,456	0
205	Woodhorne Elem.	1		1,453,907	405	3,590	2,216,970	763,063	0
206	Furley Elem.	1		2,430,014	621	3,913	3,399,354	969,340	0
207	Curtis Bay Elem.	1		1,446,213	365	3,962	1,998,010	551,797	0
209	Winston Middle	3		2,708,534	651	4,161	3,563,574	855,040	0
210	Hazelwood Elem.	1		1,940,243	621	3,127	3,396,617	1,456,374	0
211	Gardenville Elem.	1		1,280,498	379	3,379	2,074,646	794,148	0
212	Garrett Heights Elem.	1		1,725,952	336	5,144	1,836,527	110,575	0
213	Govans Elem.	1		1,207,613	386	3,133	2,110,227	902,614	0
214	Guilford Elem.	1		1,779,427	439	4,053	2,403,086	623,659	0
215	Highlandtown Elem.	1		2,513,284	709	3,547	3,878,329	1,365,045	0
216	Frankford Intermediate	3		1,619,028	451	3,590	2,468,774	849,746	0
217	Belmont Elem.	1		1,618,833	355	4,560	1,943,270	324,437	0
219	Yorkwood Elem.	1		2,158,771	528	4,092	2,887,535	728,764	0
220	Morrell Park Elem.	1		1,839,315	486	3,785	2,660,364	821,049	0
221	Mt. Washington Elem.	1		1,192,449	392	3,042	2,145,808	953,359	0
222	Pimlico Middle	3		3,470,991	880	3,944	4,817,120	1,346,129	0
223	Pimlico Elem.	1	1	2,649,680	576	4,600	3,153,024	503,344	0
224	Grove Park Elem.	1		1,814,326	423	4,294	2,312,765	498,439	0
225	Westport Elem.	1		2,695,126	639	4,218	3,497,886	802,760	0

226	Violetville Elem.	1	1,109,073	295	3,766	1,612,093	503,020	0
228	John Ryhrah Elem.	1	1,735,211	381	4,560	2,082,857	347,646	0
229	Holabird Elem.	1	1,509,619	316	4,777	1,729,784	220,165	0
230	Canton Middle	3	2,887,081	729	3,960	3,990,546	1,103,465	0
231	Brehms Lane Elem.	1	1,737,389	435	3,999	2,378,453	641,064	0
232	Thomas Jefferson Elem.	1	1,255,588	404	3,108	2,211,496	955,908	0
233	Roland Park Elem./Middle	2	5,095,821	1,536	3,318	8,408,064	3,312,243	0
234	Arlington Elem.	1	1,905,449	527	3,619	2,882,061	976,612	0
235	Glenmont Elem.	1	1,682,426	470	3,583	2,570,043	887,617	0
236	Hamilton Elem.	1	1,865,967	504	3,706	2,756,159	890,192	0
237	Highlandtown Elem.	1	631,290	171	3,692	936,054	304,764	0
239	Benjamin Franklin Middle	3	1,751,334	418	4,190	2,288,132	536,798	0
241	Fallstaff Middle	3	2,740,211	749	3,658	4,100,026	1,359,815	0
242	Northwood Elem.	1	2,138,091	704	3,039	3,850,959	1,712,868	0
243	Armistead Gardens Elem.	1	2,524,382	402	6,287	2,197,811	(326,571)	326,571
245	Leith Walk Elem.	1	2,368,582	741	3,196	4,056,234	1,687,652	0
246	Beechfield Elem.	1	3,101,334	1,068	2,904	5,846,232	2,744,898	0
247	Cross Country Elem.	1	2,237,976	649	3,451	3,549,889	1,311,913	0
248	Sinclair Lane Elem.	1	2,867,437	703	4,082	3,845,485	978,048	0
249	Medfield Heights Elem.	1	1,383,561	374	3,704	2,044,539	660,978	0
250	Dr. Bernard Harris Sr. Elem.	1	2,511,830	493	5,095	2,698,682	186,852	0
251	Callaway Middle	1	2,018,693	623	3,240	3,410,302	1,391,609	0
254	Dr. Martin Luther King Jr. Elem.	3	3,114,491	774	4,024	4,236,876	1,122,385	0
255	Southeast Middle	1	2,568,216	572	4,490	3,131,128	562,912	0
256	Calvin M. Rodwell Elem.	1	1,084,310	288	3,765	1,576,512	492,202	0
260	Frederick Elem.	1	1,679,464	384	4,379	2,099,279	419,815	0
261	Lockerman-Bundy Elem.	1	2,006,556	400	5,023	2,186,863	180,307	0
301	William S. Baer School	5	3,955,862	133	29,743	728,042	(3,227,820)	3,227,820
303	Upton School	5	3,259,415	246	13,277	1,343,867	(1,915,548)	1,915,548
304	Harbor View School	5	1,175,724	52	22,610	284,648	(891,076)	891,076
307	Claremont School	5	1,942,357	107	18,153	585,718	(1,356,639)	1,356,639
313	Lois T. Murray School	5	1,535,499	71	21,627	388,654	(1,146,845)	1,146,845
314	Sharp-Leadenhall School	5	1,383,136	94	14,714	514,556	(868,580)	868,580

Adaptation of Judson Porter's (BCPS) Data 1993-94 Site-Based Budgets (cont.)

School #	School Name	Grade Level	Status EAI/Partner	Actual Budget	FTE Pupils	Average FTE Expenditures	EAI Budget	Difference Over/Under	Hold Harmless
315	Dr. Lillie M. Jackson School	5		$1,332,017	83	$16,146	$451,605	($880,412)	$880,412
400	Edmondson-Westside High	4		6,205,797	1,344	4,617	7,357,056	1,151,259	0
401	Northwestern Sr. High	4		3,968,154	964	4,116	5,276,936	1,308,782	0
402	Northern Sr. High	4		5,200,854	1,140	4,562	6,240,360	1,039,506	0
403	Balt. Polytechnic Institute	6		4,459,320	1,113	4,007	6,092,562	1,633,242	0
405	Patterson Sr. High	4		6,056,590	1,725	3,511	9,442,650	3,386,060	0
406	Forest Park Sr. High	4		3,931,455	874	4,498	4,784,276	852,821	0
407	Western Sr. High	4		4,409,665	1,348	3,271	7,378,952	2,969,287	0
410	Mergenthaler Sr. High	4		6,745,250	1,529	4,412	8,369,746	1,624,496	0
411	Wallbrook Sr. High	4		5,315,366	1,410	3,770	7,718,340	2,402,974	0
412	Southwestern Sr. High	4		5,921,621	1,380	4,291	7,554,120	1,632,499	0
413	Harbor City Learning Ctr.	5		2,913,214	535	5,445	2,928,590	15,376	0
414	Paul Laurence Dunbar High	4		3,773,443	922	4,093	5,047,028	1,273,585	0
415	Baltimore School for the Arts	4		2,766,695	294	9,411	1,609,356	(1,157,339)	1,157,339
450	Frederick Douglas Sr. High	4		3,986,664	1,000	3,987	5,474,000	1,487,336	0
451	Joseph Briscoe Sr. High	4		3,366,002	202	16,663	1,105,748	(2,260,254)	2,260,254
454	Carver Voc-Tech Sr. High	4		5,491,709	1,360	4,038	7,444,640	1,952,931	0
456	Fairmont-Harford Institute	5		2,778,363	522	5,323	2,857,428	79,065	0
457	Laurence G. Paquin Mid/Sr. High	3.5		1,616,285	178	9,080	974,372	(641,913)	641,913
480	Baltimore City College	6		3,871,944	1,153	3,358	6,311,522	2,439,578	0
	Totals			$432,676,607	99,744	$861,789	$545,998,656	$113,322,049	$19,846,171
	Mean			2,606,486	601	5,192	3,289,149	682,663	119,555
	Median			2,218,500	498	4,238	2,723,315	655,560	0
	Standard Deviation			1,346,489	370	3,658	2,022,882	982,219	453,835

Note: Grade Level and Status columns have been added for sorting purposes.

Appendix C
Sample EAI Budget Worksheet

Browne Elementary Spending History

Code	Line		1990-91 Total	1991-92 Total	1992-93 Total	1993-94 Total	1990-91 Per Pupil	1991-92 Per Pupil	1992-93 Per Pupil	1993-94 Per Pupil
743	Instruction		$967,491	$1,106,867	$753,078	n.a.	$2,749	$3,525	$2,339	n.a.
	Salaries and Personnel Costs		933,678	1,085,718	707,404	n.a.	2,652	3,458	2,197	n.a.
	Salaries and Wages									
	Other Personnel									
	Instructional Resource									
744	Salaries and Wages (Other)									
	Personnel Costs (Other)									
	Contractual Services		3,100	2,329	6,786	n.a.	9	7	21	n.a.
	Materials and Supplies		20,318	18,820	38,888	n.a.	58	60	121	n.a.
	Equipment Replacement		10,395	0	0	n.a.	30	0	0	n.a.
	Tesseract Training	025114/025214	0	0	45,250	n.a.	0	0	141	n.a.
	Mandated Transportation		0	0	0	n.a.	0	0	0	n.a.
	Noninstructional Equipment		0	0	6,219	n.a.	0	0	19	n.a.
	Project Administration (EAI)	025118	0	0	57,488	n.a.	0	0	179	n.a.
	Instructional/School (Profit?)		0	0	0	n.a.	0	0	0	n.a.
756	Special Instruction		163,008	145,119	98,643	n.a.	463	462	306	n.a.
	Salary/Other Personnel Costs		161,532	143,774	98,643	n.a.	459	458	306	n.a.
	Other		1,476	1,345	0	n.a.	4	4	0	n.a.
758	Gifted and Talented		0	0	0	n.a.	0	0	0	n.a.
754	Vocational		0	0	0	n.a.	0	0	0	n.a.
	Instructional/School	025113	0	0	1,004	n.a.	0	0	3	n.a.
	Computer Lease & Consultant	025154/025254	0	0	19,400	n.a.	0	0	60	n.a.
	Noninstructional Contract Services	02156	0	0	5,619	n.a.	0	0	17	n.a.

Browne Elementary Spending History (cont.)

Code	Line	1990-91 Total	1991-92 Total	1992-93 Total	1993-94 Total	1990-91 Per Pupil	1991-92 Per Pupil	1992-93 Per Pupil	1993-94 Per Pupil
Nonallocated Contract Services (b)	025158	0	0	61,841	n.a.	0	0	192	n.a.
Nonallocated Professional Services	025159/025259	0	0	12,737	n.a.	0	0	40	n.a.
Transportation (Non-Mandated)	025163	1,301	555	85	n.a.	4	2	0	n.a.
Operation and Maintenance	025175	$144,994	$154,796	$234,690	n.a.	$412	$493	$729	n.a.
Fuel		5,472	51,404	57,811	n.a.	16	164	180	n.a.
Staff		71,408	75,135	88,401	n.a.	203	239	275	n.a.
Repairs		27,180	28,257	0	n.a.	77	90	0	n.a.
(Johnson Controls) JCWS		0	0	61,779	n.a.	0	0	192	n.a.
Other		40,934	0	26,699	n.a.	116	0	83	n.a.
BCPS Overhead Payment	025177	0	0	1,200	n.a.	0	0	4	n.a.
Project/Office Materials	025178	0	0	600	n.a.	0	0	2	n.a.
Project Startup (Op. & Maint.)	025179	0	0	42,453	n.a.	0	0	132	n.a.
School Security		0	0	0	n.a.	0	0	0	n.a.
Project/Contract Administration	025179/025299	0	0	32,056	n.a.	0	0	100	n.a.
Food Service		83,161	95,104	100,220	n.a.	236	303	311	n.a.
Total		$1,502,441	$1,472,583	$1,359,955		$4,573	$4,785	$3,864	

Appendix D
Sample Comparison
School Budget Worksheet

Cecil Elementary Comparison School Spending History

	1990-91 Total	1990-91 Per Pupil	1991-92 Total	1991-92 Per Pupil	1992-93 Total	1992-93 Per Pupil	1993-94 Total	1993-94 Per Pupil
General Instruction								
Salaries and Wages	$1,363,307	$1,931	$1,446,399	$2,156	n.a.	n.a.	$1,434,281	$2,269
Other Personnel Costs	261,701	371	299,712	447	n.a.	n.a.	355,985	563
Contractual Services	13,762	19	4,116	6	n.a.	n.a.	500	1
Materials and Supplies	52,599	74	43,553	65	n.a.	n.a.	30,161	48
Equipment Replacement	989	1	950	1	n.a.	n.a.	0	0
Subtotal	1,692,358	2,397	1,794,730	2,675	n.a.	n.a.	1,820,927	2,881
Other Instructional Services								
Salaries and Wages	0	0	36,475	54	n.a.	n.a.	0	0
Other Personnel Costs	0	0	12,537	19	n.a.	n.a.	0	0
Subtotal	0	0	49,012	73	n.a.	n.a.	0	0
Special Education								
Salaries and Wages	128,049	181	122,182	182	n.a.	n.a.	125,521	199
Other Personnel Costs	14,554	21	15,255	23	n.a.	n.a.	24,742	39
Contractual Services	255	0	108	0	n.a.	n.a.	0	0
Materials and Supplies	1,661	2	1,100	2	n.a.	n.a.	0	0
Equipment Replacement	240	0	146	0	n.a.	n.a.	0	0
Subtotal	144,759	205	138,791	207	n.a.	n.a.	150,263	238
School Social Work Services								
Salaries and Wages	0	0	0	0	n.a.	n.a.	36,918	58
Other Personnel Costs	0	0	0	0	n.a.	n.a.	7,277	12
Subtotal	0	0	0	0	n.a.	n.a.	44,195	70

Cecil Elementary Comparison School Spending History (cont.)

	1990-91 Total	1990-91 Per Pupil	1991-92 Total	1991-92 Per Pupil	1992-93 Total	1992-93 Per Pupil	1993-94 Total	1993-94 Per Pupil
Transportation	0	0	0	0	n.a.	n.a.	0	0
Contractual Services	0	0	0	0	n.a.	n.a.	4,755	8
Subtotal	0	0	0	0	n.a.	n.a.	4,755	8
Transportation	$2,601	$4	$14,815	$22	n.a.	n.a.	$2,166	$3
Operations Staff	83,049	118	75,135	112	n.a.	n.a.	26,149	41
Food Services	178,964	253	204,796	305	n.a.	n.a.	213,269	337
Instructional Resource	112,164	159	111,854	167	n.a.	n.a.	44,195	70
Fuel/Utilities Costs	45,394	64	40,731	61	n.a.	n.a.	46,598	74
Repairs 90		49,840	71	51,549	77			56,963
Cleaning	0	0	0	0	n.a.	n.a.	48,930	77
School Security	0	0	0	0	n.a.	n.a.	0	0
Total	$2,309,089	$3,271	$2,481,413	$3,698	0	0	$2,458,410	$3,890

ENDNOTES

1. This concept is discussed more fully in Chapter 1, in the section, "Public and Private."

2. In this study we distinguish between contracting out the management of existing public schools from establishing entirely new schools by charter in cooperation with business firms and nonprofit organizations. The Edison Project is a partner in a charter school, in addition to the three public schools it manages under contract.

3. Comments attributed to individuals but appearing without citation are taken from interviews conducted in person or by telephone in February 1995.

4. Charles Blaschke, who takes credit for inventing the term, says he originally called it "performance turnkey contracting" to stress that the capacity for implementing contractors' projects would, over time, be transferred to the school.

5. Guttenberg, "Performance Contracting: Why the Gary School Board Bought It: And How." See also *American School Board Journal* (January 1971, 21). According to Jost (1994), more than 100 school districts in 23 states signed performance contracts with about 15 companies.

6. A fuller discussion of the Gary experiment is contained in "Performance Contracting: Why the Gary School Board Bought It: And How." *American School Board Journal* (January 1971, 19-21).

7. In the interim, there had been a smattering of interest in contracting. One company that stepped briefly into the market was the Education Corporation of America, a mid-1980s spinoff of the Massey-Burch Fund, a venture capital firm. I am indebted to John McLaughlin for this information.

8. NASDC is a single-purpose, private organization dedicated to transforming American public education, using private monies to meet public goals. NASDC has no public funding. Chaired by David Kearns, former Xerox chief executive officer and former deputy secretary of education, it has received $70 million to support the initiatives of the nine development teams. After three years of development, NASDC is now beginning the process of disseminating its projects. In the 1995-96 school year, the nine development teams were scheduled to "roll out" successful examples that other schools and school districts could begin to replicate. See Doyle, 1994b, p. 130.

9. In an overview of privatization, John McLaughlin associates new interest in education contracting with the end of the Cold War.

10. Those who want to retain government control over the day-to-day operation of schools reject this analogy. They argue that the effectiveness of privatiz-

ing government services hinges on the nature of the service and on whether or not the service is a public good. As Richard C. Hunter has written, "Public education is one of the most important of all public goods and services produced and consumed by society." Because education has such a huge and direct impact on the nation's economic growth and prosperity, the public has an overriding interest in controlling its delivery.

11.   Walsh (1995) based his article, in part, on a June 1994 interview with Judson Porter, the Baltimore school system's finance officer at the time the EAI contract was awarded. Calling the contract process with EAI "extremely odd," Porter commented: "It was clear it was an initiative the superintendent wanted to proceed with, and the negotiations really weren't what you would call hard bargaining."

12.   Minneapolis Public Schools. "Payment Proposal for the 1994-95 District Improvement Agenda," October 28, 1994. Provided by the Minneapolis Public Schools.

13.   The report notes that it is "based exclusively on testing, staffing, and financial information obtained by the AFT from the Baltimore City Public Schools."

14.   The Educational Testing Service in Princeton, N.J., is formally a nonprofit organization. However, that is more a distinction related to tax implications than it is a matter of making money on the testing of schoolchildren.

15.   Sources for this section included the following: Clark, Kim and Gary Gately (December 17, 1994), and Gately, Gary (February 20, 1995), *Baltimore Sun*; telephone conversation, Clark, Kim (February 21, 1995), reporter, *Baltimore Sun*; telephone conversation, McLaughlin, John M. (February 2, 1995), president, Education Investing Inc.; personal communication, Schedule I, Education Alternatives Inc., 10-K for fiscal year ended June 30, 1994.

16.   Schedule I, p. 15, of the 10-K for the fiscal year ended June 30, 1994.

17.   1993-94 Site-Based Budgets, Baltimore City Public Schools.

18.   Includes Francis Woods Alternative High School (No. 178), School for the Arts (No. 415), Venable Senior High School (No. 115), and Briscoe Senior High School (No. 451).

19.   Our written request for data, with repeated phone calls, was not responded to by the Baltimore public schools. However, as many of the documents are public, we were able to obtain them elsewhere.

20.   1993-94 Site-Based Budgets.

21.   Figure represents allowance after payback using March 23, 1994 contract.

22.   In this analysis, schools catering solely to primary populations, although providing regular education, have been included as special facilities.

23. School Instructional Expenditure Report (Program ID: AABD0007.1).

24. Quoted in John Hilke (1993). Peterson found small academic gains in some areas, losses in others, and no cost savings. Hilke's report was published by the Reason Foundation, a leading proponent of privatization in the United States. Peterson's is the only evidence reported on cost savings in the privatization of education as of 1993, which is some grounds for confidence that no positive empirical evidence is available.

25. Exceptions include the numerous schools specializing in particular vocational skills or particular types of students, but our focus here is on the "general education" for work and college provided by the typical U.S. public school.

26. There is also the technical issue of increasing marginal costs, which is beyond the scope of this paper.

27. Savas favors the use of vouchers for local public education.

28. The conventional wisdom on problems in education is that too much has been spent on the quantity and quality of teachers (Hanushek et al. 1994).

29. It was not until the summer of 1995 that an evaluation was done of the Baltimore experience with EAI (Williams and Leak 1995). The study was put up for competitive bidding (unlike the EAI contract itself), to which there was only one respondent. The respondent was awarded the contract by public officials whose prestige stood to rise if the EAI contract was successful. EAI had a veto over the choice of evaluator. There is no evidence that the evaluation was improperly conducted, but it is not good practice to allow those with a stake in a policy initiative to choose their own critics. As it turned out, the evaluation was replete with criticisms of EAI. On basic performance indicators used in the evaluation, EAI schools were marginally better in a few respects, and worse in others.

30. Even conservative advocates of contracting concede that contracting could increase public spending, as the case of defense procurement has illustrated so vividly over the past 40 years (Butler 1991).

31. The *Baltimore Sun* reports the average stay of a big-city superintendent in the United States to be two-and-one-half years, and for all superintendents six-and-one-half (April 29, 1995).

32. Kathleen Fulton, an expert with the U.S. Congress's Office of Technology Assessment, has said: "... the presence of new computers in a school isn't what improves test scores....What it depends mostly on is the teachers and how much they are supported....What else is going on in the classroom....If you really want to make an impact you should have one computer for the teacher and others for the kids in the classroom" ("The Big Plunge Into Technology for City Schools," *Hartford Courant*, April 9, 1995).

33. "EAI asks to cut 320 jobs" (*Hartford Courant*, April 20, 1995).

34.   EAI Chairman John Golle was quoted in *USA Today* (June 7, 1995) as follows: "Our position is you do not have to spend more money. You have to spend it differently—more on children, less on things like administration."

35.   "In spite of deficit, EAI is busy buying," (*Hartford Courant*, December 23, 1994): "[T]he company earns a fee or interest on the money that it advances to the system to lease computers."

36.   "Perhaps the most important pressure for privatization is the declining attractiveness of public ownership. . . free money [e.g., federal subsidies.—M.S.] [T]he policy objective in all fields should be the further reduction of these grants [for public works—M.S.], and, if possible, their outright abolition (Young)." Young is an advocate of privatization.

37.   High turnover among the interns hired by EAI in Baltimore has been a concern. The interns are college students and graduates who replaced unionized paraprofessional teachers aides. The latter tended to reside in their school's community environs. The new hires receive substantially lower pay than the aides and few fringe benefits.

38.   Attention also needs to be paid to different ways of presenting outcomes, including whether they are easily interpreted, performance-based, improvement-based, or equity-based (Richards 1991).

BIBLIOGRAPHY

Abella, Rudolpho. 1994. *Evaluation of the Saturn School Projects at South Pointe Elementary School*. Miami, Fla.: Dade County Public Schools.

Allen, Michael. 1995. "Pro and Con: An Ardent Advocate of Privatization Squares Off Against a Staunch Opponent." *Wall Street Journal*, October 2.

American Federation of Teachers. 1994. *The Private Management of Public Schools: An Analysis of the EAI Experience in Baltimore*. Washington, D.C.: AFT.

American Federation of Teachers. 1995. *How Private Managers Make Money Off Public Schools: Update on the EAI Experiment in Baltimore*. Washington, D.C.: AFT.

Amprey, Walter. 1990. *Superintendent's Budget Requests to the Board of School Commissioners for School Year 1990-91 (Site-Based Budgets)*. Baltimore: Baltimore City Public Schools.

Amprey, Walter. 1991. *Superintendent's Budget Requests to the Board of School Commissioners for School Year 1991-92 (Site-Based Budgets)*. Baltimore: BCPS.

Amprey, Walter. 1992. *Superintendent's Budget Requests to the Board of School Commissioners for School Year 1992-93 (Site-Based Budgets)*. Baltimore: BCPS.

Amprey, Walter. 1993. *Superintendent's Budget Requests to the Board of School Commissioners for School Year 1993-94 (Site-Based Budgets)*. Baltimore: BCPS.

Amundson, Robert, John Trent, and Robert Gilman. 1988. In Richard Green, "Answering to the Children: Shared Accountability for Public Education." *CSA Education Review*.

Apple, Michael. 1993. *Official Knowledge: Democratic Education in a Conservative Age*. New York: Routledge.

Applebome, Peter. 1995a. "Employers Wary of School System." *New York Times*, February 20.

Applebome, Peter. 1995b. "Private Company Given Power to Pick Teachers." *New York Times*, April 9.

Baltimore City Public Schools, Educational Data Processing Center. 1993. *School Instructional Expenditure Report (Program ID: AABD0007.1)*. Baltimore: BCPS.

Bary, Andrew. 1994. "Trading Points: Florida Setback." *Barron's*, May 23, 30.

Battelle Columbus Laboratories. 1972. "Final Report on the Office of Economic Opportunity Experiment in Educational Performance Contracting." Reprinted in Myron Lieberman, ed., *Privatization and Educational Choice* (1989), pp. 88-89.

Baumol, William J. 1982. "Contestable Markets: An Uprising in the Theory of Industry Structure." *American Economic Review*, Vol. 72, No. 1, pp. 1-16.

Beales, Janet R. and John O'Leary. 1993. "Making Schools Work: Contracting Options for Better Management." Reason Foundation.

Beales, Janet R. 1995. "By Request: How to Get What You Want for Your RFP." *The American School Board Journal* (February), pp. 25-28.

Behr, Peter. 1995. "Solving the Privatization Puzzle." *Washington Post*, Feb. 13.

Branch, Eleanor. 1991. "Can Business Save Our Schools." *Black Enterprise* (March), pp. 38-50.

Bretts, Ann. 1992. "Can Private Company Run Public Schools?" *Duluth News Tribune*, April 26.

Brown, Frank and A. Reynaldo Contreras. 1991. "Deregulation and Privatization of Education: A Flawed Concept." *Education and Urban Society* (February), pp. 144-58.

Brown, Frank. 1995. "Privatization of Public Education: Theories and Concepts." *Education and Urban Society* (February), p. 117.

Butler, Stuart. 1991. "Privatization for Public Purposes." In William T. Gormley Jr., ed., *Privatization and Its Alternatives*. Madison, Wis.: University of Wisconsin Press.

Callahan, Raymond. 1962. *Education and the Cult of Efficiency*. Chicago: University of Chicago Press.

Carson, Robert B. 1980. *Economic Issues Today: Alternative Approaches*. New York: St. Martin's Press, p. 246.

Chubb, John E. 1988. "Why the Current Wave of School Reforms Will Fail." *Public Interest*, Vol. 90. (Winter), pp. 28-49.

Chubb, John E. and Terry M. Moe. 1990. "Politics, Markets & America's Schools." Washington, D.C.: Brookings Institution.

Clark, Kim and Gary Gately. 1994. "EAI Falls Victim to Derivatives Market." *Baltimore Sun*, December 17.

Clarke, Mary Pat. 1994. *EAI/Tesseract Contract Adjustments and Modifications.* Baltimore: Board of Estimates, Office of the President of the Baltimore City Council, March 23.

Cohen, David K. and Carol Barnes. 1995. "High Standards, All Children, and Learning: Notes Toward the History of an Idea." Unpublished paper prepared for the Carnegie Corporation of New York.

Cohen, David K. 1996. "Standards-Based School Reform: Policy, Practice, and Performance." In Helen F. Ladd, ed., *Holding Schools Accountable: Performance-Based Reform in Education.* Washington, D.C.: Brookings Institution.

Coleman, James S. and Thomas Hoffer. 1987. "Public and Private High Schools: The Impact of Communities." New York: Basic Books.

Conlin, Elizabeth. 1991. "Educating the Market." *Inc.*, pp. 62-7.

Cremin, Lawrence A. 1989. "Education As Politics." *Popular Education and Its Discontents.* New York: Harper and Row, p. 92.

Crowson, Robert L. and William Lowe Boyd. 1993. "Coordinated Services for Children: Designing Arks for Storms and Seas Unknown." *American Journal of Education* (February), pp. 140-79.

Cullis, John G. and Philip R. Jones. 1987. "Microeconomics and the Public Economy: A Defense of Leviathan." Oxford: Basil Blackwell.

Demsetz, H. and K. Lehn. 1985. "The Structure of Corporate Ownership: Causes and Consequences." *Journal of Political Economy*, Vol. 93, pp. 1155-77.

Dewey, John and Evelyn Dewey. 1915. *Schools of Tomorrow.* New York: E. P. Dutton and Co., p. 312.

DiIulio, John Jr., Gerald Garvey, and Donald F. Kettl. 1993. *Improving Government Performance: An Owner's Manual.* Washington, D.C.: Brookings Institution.

Donlan, Thomas G. 1994. "Education Alternatives: Adding "Inc." to a Good Idea Doesn't Always Improve It." *Barron's*, March 28.

Doyle, Denis P. 1994a. "The Role of Private Management Companies in School Reform." Testimony before the Senate Appropriations Subcommittee on Labor, Health and Human Services, and Education and Related Agencies, January 25.

Doyle, Denis P. 1994b. "The Role of Private Sector Management in Public Education." *Phi Delta Kappan* (October), p. 132.

Drucker, Peter F. 1992. *Managing for the Future: The 1990s and Beyond.* New York: Truman Talley Books/Dutton, pp. 18-9.

Du Pont, Pete. 1989. "Education in America: The Opportunity to Choose." In Edward H. Crane and David Boaz, eds., *An American Vision: Policies for the '90s.* Washington, D.C.: Cato Institute.

Educational Researcher. 1994. "Money Might Matter Somewhere: A Response to Hedges, Laine, and Greenwald." Vol. 23 (May), pp. 5-8.

Education Alternatives Inc. (EAI). 1994. "A Vision for Hartford's Children: Proposal for a Partnership." RFP No. 4071. Submitted to the Hartford Board of Education and the City of Hartford, Management of School System.

Elmore, Richard F., Charles H. Abelmann, and Susan H. Fuhrman. 1995. "The New Accountability in State Education Reform: From Process to Performance." Paper presented at Brookings Conference on Performance-Based Approaches to School Reform, Washington, D.C., April.

Farkas, Steve and Jean Johnson. 1993. *Divided Within, Besieged Without: The Politics of Education in Four American School Districts.* New York: Public Agenda Foundation.

Farrell, Walter C., James H. Johnson Jr., Clyzelle K. Jones, and Marty Sapp. 1994. "Will Privatizing Schools Really Help Inner-City Students of Color?" *Educational Leadership* (September), pp. 72-5.

Ferguson, Ronald F. 1991. "Paying for Public Education: New Evidence on How and Why Money Matters." *Harvard Journal on Legislation*, Vol. 28 (Summer), pp. 465-97.

Ferguson, Ronald F. and Helen F. Ladd. 1996. "How and Why Money Matters: An Analysis of Alabama Schools." In Helen F. Ladd, ed., *Holding Schools Accountable: Performance-Based Reform in Education.* Washington, D.C.: Brookings Institution.

Garms, Walter I. and Richard Guttenberg. 1970. *The Sources and Nature of Resistance to Incentive Systems in Education: Final Report on an Investigation Under Contract HEW 05-69-94.* New York: Teachers College, Columbia University.

Garber, Michael. 1995. "Opening the Education Marketplace." *Education Week*, March 29, p. 34.

Geiger, Keith. 1995. "Privatization: An Interim Report Card." *Education Week*, March 29, p. 34.

Glazer, Judith S. 1994. "The New Politics of Education: School Districts For Sale." *Education Week*, November 9.

Golle, John. 1992. Letter of Intent to Walter G. Amprey, Superintendent, Baltimore City Public Schools, Baltimore, Md., June 3.

Golle, John. 1994. "The Role of Private Management Companies in the School Reform Movement." Hearing before a Subcommittee of the Committee on Appropriations, U.S. Senate, January 25.

Golle, John. 1995. *The Myths and Realities of Baltimore's Education Alternatives, Inc., Financial Arrangement.* Unpublished paper, January.

Good, T. L. and J. E. Brophy. 1986. "School Effects." In *Handbook of Research on Teaching.* 3rd ed. New York: Macmillan, pp. 570-602.

Goodman, John B. and Gary W. Loveman. 1991. "Does Privatization Serve the Public Interest?" *Harvard Business Review*, Vol. 69, No. 6, pp. 26-8.

Graham, Patricia Albjerg. 1993. "What America Has Expected of Its Schools Over the Past Century." *American Journal of Education* (February), p. 86.

Gramlich, Edward M. and Patricia P. Koshel. 1975. *Educational Performance Contracting.* Washington, D.C.: Brookings Institution.

Gramlich, Edward M. and Patricia P. Koshel. 1977. "Is Real-World Experimentation Possible? The Case of Educational Performance Contracting." In Robert H. Haveman and Julius Margolis, eds., *Public Expenditure Analysis, 2nd Edition.* Chicago: Rand McNally.

Green, Richard. 1988. "Answering to the Children: Shared Accountability for Public Education." *CSA Education Review.*

Green, Rick. 1995. "Board Chief to Push Plan for EAI to Run Five City Schools." *Hartford Courant*, June 16.

Grumet, Madeleine R. 1988. *Bitter Milk: Women and Teaching.* Amherst, Mass.: University of Massachusetts Press.

Guttenberg, Richard. 1971a. "Incentive Systems for Educational Personnel." Final Report on an Investigation Under Contract OEC-0-71-3319. New York: Teachers College, Columbia University.

Guttenberg, Richard. 1971b. *Performance Contracting: A Systems Approach to Management in Education.* New York: Teachers College, Columbia University.

Hamburg, Sandra Kessler. 1994. "Putting Learning First: Governing and Managing the Schools for High Achievement." New York: Committee for Economic Development Research and Policy Committee.

Hanushek, Eric A. 1986. "The Economics of Schooling: Production and Efficiency in Public Schools." *Journal of Economic Literature*, Vol. 24, No. 3, pp. 1141-77.

Hanushek, Eric A. 1989. "The Impact of Differential Expenditures on School Performance." *Educational Researcher*, Vol. 18 (May), pp. 45-65.

Hanushek, Eric A. 1994. "Education Investment and Education Reform." *Jobs and Capital*, Vol. 3 (Fall), pp. 36-8.

Hanushek, Eric A. et al. 1994. *Making Schools Work: Improving Performance and Controlling Costs.* Washington, D.C.: Brookings Institution.

Havighurst, Robert J. 1972. "Joint Accountability: A Constructive Response to Consumer Demands." *Nation's Schools* (May).

Hedges, L.V., Laine, R.D., and Greenwald, R. 1994. "Does Money Matter? A Meta-Analysis of Studies of the Effects of Differential School Inputs on Student Outcomes." *Educational Researcher*, Vol. 23, No. 3, pp. 5-14.

Hedges, Larry V., Richard Laine, and Rob Greenwald. 1995. "Dollars and Sense: A Reanalysis of Hanushek." Mimeo.

Hilke, John. 1993. *Cost Savings From Privatization: A Compilation of Study Findings.* Reason Foundation: Privatization Center.

Hill, Paul T. 1994. *Reinventing Public Education.* Santa Monica, Calif.: Rand Institute for Education and Training.

Hill, Paul T. and Josephine Bonan. 1991. *Decentralization and Accountability in Public Education.* Santa Monica, Calif.: Rand Institute for Education and Training.

Hinden, Stan. 1995. "This Educational Firm's Stock Is Running a Clinic." *Washington Post*, July 31.

Hulten, Charles R. and Robert M. Schwab. 1991. "A Haig-Simons-Tiebout Comprehensive Income Tax." *National Tax Journal*, Vol. 44, No. 1, pp. 67-78.

Hunter, Richard C. 1995. "Privatization of Instruction in Public Education." *Education and Urban Society* (February), pp. 176-91.

Hussar, William. 1995. *Projections of Education Statistics to 2005.* Washington, D.C.: U.S. Department of Education, National Center for Education Statistics.

Immerwahr, John, Jill Boese, and Will Friedman. 1994. "The Broken Contract: Connecticut Citizens Look at Public Education." New York: Public Agenda.

Innerst, Carol. 1994. "Hartford Schools Turned Over to a For-Profit Firm." *Washington Times,* October 5.

Jencks, Christopher et al. 1972. *Inequality: A Reassessment of the Effect of Family and Schooling in America.* New York: Basic Books.

Johnson, Ian. 1994. "Shareholder Suit Alleges Deceptive Practices at EAI." *Baltimore Sun*, February 25.

Johnson, Ian. 1994. "EAI's Promising Future Begins to Look Bleak." *Baltimore Sun*, March 6.

Johnson, Jean. 1995. *Assignment Incomplete: The Unfinished Business of Education Reform.* New York: Public Agenda.

Jost, Kenneth. 1994. "Private Management of Public Schools." *CQ Researcher*, March 25, p. 276.

Judson, George. 1995. "In Hartford's Schools, a Company Installs Symbols of Change." *New York Times*, January 1.

Judson, George. 1996. "Private Business, Public Schools: Why Hartford Experiment Failed." *New York Times*, March 11.

Kelman, Steven. 1990. *Procurement and Public Management.* Washington, D.C.: American Enterprise Institute Press.

Kenyon, Daphne. 1995. *The Decade of Declining Federal Aid.* Washington, D.C.: Economic Policy Institute.

Kershaw, J. A. and R. N. McKean. 1959. "Systems Analysis and Education." In Richard Guttenberg, ed., *Performance Contracting.* Santa Monica, Calif.: RAND Corporation, Memorandum RM-2473-FF, p. 7.

Kolderie, Ted, Robert Lerman, and Charles Moskos. 1993. "Educating America: A New Compact for Opportunity and Citizenship." In Will Marshall and Martin Schram, eds., *Mandate for Change.* Washington, D.C.: Berkeley Books.

Kotter, John P. and James L. Heskett. 1992. *Corporate Culture and Performance.* New York: Free Press, pp. 3-9.

Kozol, Jonathan. 1991. *Savage Inequalities: Children in America's Schools.* New York: Crown Publishers.

Kuhn, Susan. 1994. "He Lost How Much?" *Fortune*, September 19.

Ladd, Helen F., ed. 1996. *Holding Schools Accountable: Performance-Based Reform in Education.* Washington, D.C.: Brookings Institution.

Lankford, Hamilton and James Wyckoff. 1995. "The Allocation of Resources to Special Education, Administration, and Regular Instruction." Paper presented at Brookings Conference on Performance-Based Approaches to School Reform, Washington, D.C., April.

Legters, Nettie and Robert E. Slavin. 1994. *Elementary Students at Risk: A Status Report.* Baltimore: Center for Research on Effective Schooling for Disadvantaged Students, Johns Hopkins University.

Lessinger, Leon. 1970. "Engineering Accountability for Results in Public Education." *Phi Delta Kappan* (December), pp. 217-25.

Levin, Henry. 1978. *Cost Effectiveness Analysis.* Beverly Hills, Calif.: Sage.

Levin, Henry. 1983. *Cost Effectiveness: A Primer.* Beverly Hills, Calif.: Sage.

Levine, Marsha and Denis P. Doyle. 1982. "Private Meets Public: An Examination of Contemporary Education." In Jack A. Meyer, ed., *Meeting Human Needs: Towards a New Public Philosophy.* Washington, D.C.: American Enterprise Institute, pp. 272-329.

Levitan, Sol and Garth Mangum. 1969. *Federal Training and Work Programs in the Sixties.* Ann Arbor, Mich.: Institute of Labor and Industrial Relations.

Lewis, Anne C. 1992. "Public Education and Privatization." *Phi Delta Kappan* (April), pp. 580-1.

Lieberman, Myron. 1989. *Privatization and Educational Choice.* New York: St. Martins Press.

Lieberman, Myron. 1993. *Public Education: An Autopsy.* Cambridge, Mass.: Harvard University Press.

Lim, Grace. 1995. "School Ends Experiment." *Miami Herald*, June 20.

Linowes, David F. 1988. *Privatization: Toward More Effective Government.* Report of the President's Commission on Privatization. Washington, D.C.: U.S. Government Printing Office.

Marcial, Gene G. 1994. "A Very Bad School Report." *Business Week*, February 28.

McLaughlin, John M. 1994. "Commentary: Private Management Overview." *Education Investor*, Vol. 2, No. 6, pp. 1-7.

McLaughlin, John M. and Michael M. Norman. 1995. "Responsibility 101: Seven Ways to Hold Your Contractor Accountable." *American School Board Journal* (February), pp. 28-31.

Mickler, Mary Louise. 1984. "Accountability: Perceptual Changes Over a Decade." *Educational Horizons* (Spring).

Minneapolis Public Schools. 1994. *District Improvement Agenda: First Quarter Report on Performance.* Minneapolis: MPS.

Minneapolis Public Schools. 1995. *District Improvement Agenda: First Quarter Report on Performance.* Minneapolis: MPS.

Moe, Michael. 1994. *White Paper.* Educational Alternatives Company Report. Lehman Brothers Inc., October 24.

Molnar, Alex. 1994. "Education for Profit: A Yellow Brick Road to Nowhere." *Educational Leadership* (September), pp. 66-71.

Molnar, Alex. 1996. *Giving Kids the Business: The Commercialization of America's Schools.* Boulder, Colo.: Westview Press.

Moore, JoAnne. 1994. "Evaluation of Empowerment in the Detroit Public Schools." Detroit Public Schools, Office of Research, Evaluation and Testing.

Morley, Jefferson. 1994. "Taking Public Schools Private: How It Would Work— And Why D.C. Didn't Do It." *Washington Post*, March 13.

Murnane, Richard. 1981. "An Economist's Look at Federal and State Education Policies." In John M. Quigley and Daniel L. Rubinfeld, eds., *American Domestic Priorities: An Economic Appraisal.* Berkeley, Calif.: University of California Press.

National Commission on Excellence in Education. 1983. *A Nation At Risk.* Washington, D.C.: U.S. Government Printing Office.

Nelson, Howard. 1994. *The Private Management of Public Schools.* Washington, D.C.: American Federation of Teachers.

Niskanen, William A. Jr. 1972. *Bureaucracy and Representative Government.* Chicago, Ill.: Aldine-Atherton.

Odden, Allan. 1994. "Trends and Issues in American School Finance." Unpublished paper prepared for the Carnegie Corporation of New York.

Odden, Allan R. and Eleanor R. Odden. 1995. *Educational Leadership for America's Schools: An Introduction to Organization and Policy.* New York: McGraw Hill, Chapter 6.

Osborne, David and Ted Gaebler. 1992. *Reinventing Government: How the Entrepreneurial Spirit Is Transforming the Public Sector.* Reading, Pa.: Addison-Wesley.

Pack, Janet Rothenberg. 1989. "Privatization and Cost Reduction." *Policy Sciences*, Vol. 22, pp. 1-25.

Pack, Janet Rothenberg. 1991. "The Opportunities and Constraints of Privatization." In William T. Gormley Jr., ed., *Privatization and Its Alternatives.* Madison, Wis.: University of Wisconsin Press.

Payzant, Thomas W. 1994. "The Role of the Private Sector in Reforming Education." Testimony to the Senate Appropriations Subcommittee on Labor, Health and Human Services, and Education and Related Agencies, January 25.

Peterson, George. 1981. *Pricing and Privatization of Public Services.* Washington, D.C.: Urban Institute.

Porter, Andrew. 1995. "The Uses and Misuses of Opportunity-to-Learn Standards." *Educational Researcher*, Vol. 24, No. 1, pp. 21-7.

Porter, Judson. 1994. *Baltimore City Public Schools: Budget Worksheet.* Baltimore: BCPS.

Public Agenda. 1994. "The Broken Contract: Connecticut Citizens Look at Public Education." New York: Public Agenda, p. 28.

Putka, Gary and M. Stecklow. 1994. "Fast Learner: Do For-Profit Schools Work? They Seem to for One Entrepreneur." *Wall Street Journal*, June 8.

Rasell, Edith and Richard Rothstein, eds. 1993. *School Choice: Examining the Evidence.* Washington, D.C.: Economic Policy Institute.

Ravitch, Diane. 1994. *National Standards and Assessment in American Education.* Washington, D.C.: Brookings Institution.

Rebell, Michael. 1982. "Educational Voucher Reform: Empirical Experience from New York City's Schools for the Handicapped." *Urban Lawyer* (September).

Richards, Craig E. 1991. "The Meaning and Measure of School Effectiveness." In Bliss, Firestone, and Richards, eds., *Rethinking Effective Schools: Research and Practice.* Englewood Cliffs, N.J.: Prentice Hall.

Richards, Craig E. and Dennis Encarnation. 1986. "Teaching in Public and Private Schools: The Significance of Race." *Educational Evaluation and Policy Analysis,* Vol. 12, No. 4.

Richards, Craig E. and Dennis Encarnation. 1987. "Teaching in Public and Private Schools: The Significance of Race." In Henry Levin and Thomas James, eds., *Comparative Perspectives on Public and Private Education.* London: Falmer Press, Vol 1.

Richards, Craig E. and Sheu. 1992. "South Carolina School Incentive Reward Program: A Policy Analysis." *Economics of Education Review,* Vol. 11, No. 1, p. 71.

Richards, Craig. E. and Robert White. 1989. "Are Vouchers More Efficient: The Case of New Jersey Funding System for Private Providers of Special Education." *Journal of Education Finance*, Vol. 14 (Spring), pp. 484-99.

Richardson, Joanna. 1994. "Superintendent for Hire." *Education Week*, February 9, pp. 31-3.

Rigert, Joe. 1994. "EAI Gets Five-Year Deal With Hartford Schools." *Minnesota Star Tribune*, August 30.

Rothstein, Richard and Karen Hawley Miles. 1995. *Where's the Money Gone? Changes in the Level and Composition of Education Spending.* Washington, D.C.: Economic Policy Institute.

Ruffini, Stephen J., Lawrence F. Howe, and Denise G. Borders. 1994. *The Early Implementation of Tesseract: 1992-93 Evaluation Report* (January). Baltimore, Md.: City of Baltimore, Department of Education.

Russo, Charles J., Rosetta F. Sandidge, Robert Shapiro, and J. John Harris III. 1995. "Legal Issues in Contracting Out for Public Education Services." *Education and Urban Society* (February), p. 128.

Saks, Judith Brody. 1995. "Scrutinizing Edison." *American School Board Journal* (February), pp. 20-5.

Sappington, David E.M. and Joseph E. Stiglitz. 1987. "Privatization, Information, and Incentives." *Journal of Policy Analysis and Management*, Vol. 6, No. 5, pp. 567-82.

Savas, E.S. 1992. "Privatization and Productivity." In Marc Holzer, ed., *Public Productivity Handbook*. New York: Marcel Dekker Inc., pp. 79-97.

Schmidt, Peter. 1995. "E.A.I. Proposes to Scale Back Hartford Plan." *Education Week*, June 21, p. 10.

Sclar, Elliott D. 1995. "Why a Simple Idea Can't Solve a Complex Problem: The Case of Public Service Privatization." Testimony before the Secretary of Labor's Taskforce on Excellence in State and Local Government Through Labor-Management Cooperation, Washington, D.C., May 16.

Seelye, Katharine Q. 1995. "The Speaker: Urging Students to Read With a Little Cash." *New York Times*, March 2.

Shanker, Albert. 1994. "The Role of Private Management Companies in the School Reform Movement." Testimony to the Senate Appropriations Committee Subcommittee on Labor, Health and Human Services, Education and Related Agencies, January 25.

Shore, Rima. 1995. *Moving the Ladder: Toward a New Community Vision.* Washington, D.C.: Aspen Institute, Education for a Changing Society Program.

Simon, Herbert A. 1991. "Organizations and Markets." *Journal of Economic Perspectives*, Vol. 5, No. 2, pp. 25-44.

Sizer, Theodore R. 1992. "School Reform: What's Missing." *World Monitor*, November, pp. 20-7.

Solomon, Jolie. 1993. "Mr. Vision, Meet Mr. Reality." *Newsweek*, August 16.

Starr, Paul. 1987. *The Limits of Privatization*. Washington, D.C.: Economic Policy Institute.

Stevenson, Harold W. and James W. Stigler. 1992. *The Learning Gap: Why Our Schools Are Failing and What We Can Learn From Japanese and Chinese Education*. New York: Touchstone.

Stiglitz, Joseph E. et al. 1989. *The Economic Role of the State*. Arnold Heertje, ed. Oxford: Basil Blackwell.

Sutton, Judy. 1992. "Private Investigation." *American School & University* (September), pp. 33-5.

Taylor, Frederick Winslow. 1911. *Principles of Scientific Management*. New York: Harper and Row, 1967 edition.

Thurow, Lester C. 1976. *Generating Inequality*. London: Macmillan.

Toch, Thomas. 1994. "Selling the Schools: Is Private Enterprise the Future of Public Education in America?" *U.S. News & World Report*, May 2.

Traub, James. 1994. "Has Benno Schmidt Learned His Lesson?" *New York Magazine*, October 31.

Tweedie, Jack, Dennis Riley, John E. Chubb and Terry M. Moe. 1990. "Should Market Forces Control Educational Decision Making?" *American Political Science Review* (June), pp. 549-56.

U.S. Department of Education, National Center for Education Statistics. 1994. *Digest of Education Statistics*. NCES 94-115. Washington, D.C.: U.S. Government Printing Office.

U.S. Department of Education, National Center for Educational Statistics. 1994. *NAEP 1992: Trends in Academic Progress: Report in Brief*. Washington, D.C.: U.S. Department of Education, pp. 11-14.

Van Horn, Carl E. 1991. "The Myths and Realities of Privatization." In William T. Gormley Jr., ed., *Privatization and Its Alternatives*. Madison, Wis.: University of Wisconsin Press.

Vickers, John and George Yarrow. 1991. "Economic Perspectives on Privatization." *Journal of Economic Perspectives*, Vol. 5, No. 2, p. 111-32.

Vinovskis, Maris A. 1987. "Family and Schooling in Colonial and Nineteenth Century America." *Journal of Family History*, Vol. 12, No. 1-3, pp. 22-4.

Walberg, Herbert. 1986. *Organizational and Financial Efficiency in the Schools*. Defendant Expert Testimony. Abbott v. Burke, New Jersey Supreme Court, Trenton, New Jersey.

Walsh, Norman J. 1995. "Public Schools, Inc.: Baltimore's Risky Enterprise." *Education and Urban Society* (February), p. 196.

Webb, H. V. 1970. "Performance Contracting: Is It the New Tool for the New Boardsmanship?" *American School Board Journal* (November), pp. 28-36.

Weintraub, Frederick. 1981. "Non-Public Schools in the Education of the Handicapped." In Edward Gaffney, ed., *Private Schools and the Public Good*. South Bend, Ind.: Notre Dame Press.

Weisbrod, Burton A. 1988. *The Nonprofit Economy*. Cambridge, Mass.: Harvard University Press.

Weisbrod, Burton A. 1989. "Rewarding Performance That Is Hard to Measure: The Private Non-Profit Sector." *Science*, May 5.

White, George and Nicholas Morgan. 1992. "A Coordinated Development Program for K-12 Schools." *Phi Delta Kappan* (November), pp. 260-2.

Williams, Lois C. and Lawrence E. Leak. 1995. *The UMBC Evaluation of the Tesseract Program in Baltimore City*. Baltimore, Md.: University of Maryland Baltimore County, Center for Educational Research.

Williamson, Oliver E. 1975. *Markets and Hierarchies: Analysis and Anti-Trust Implications, A Study in the Economics of Internal Organisations*. New York: Free Press.

Wohlferd, G.H. 1972. "Performance Contracting Overview." Report. ERIC Doc. No. EDO79339.

Young, Peter. 1989. "Privatization: Better Services at Less Cost." In Edward H. Crane and David Boaz, eds., *An American Vision: Policies for the '90s*. Washington, D.C.: Cato Institute.

Zlatos, Bill. 1995. "Privatizing Schools Tests Pittsburgh Suburb." *New York Times*, August 30.

INDEX

229

P

Q

THE AUTHORS

CRAIG E. RICHARDS is chairman of the Department of Educational Administration, Teachers College, Columbia University, New York. He received his M.A. in economics and his Ph.D. in education from Stanford University in 1983. He has authored numerous books and research articles in the areas of educational policy and finance. He is currently at work on a new book, *The Ecology of Financial Management* (University of America Press).

RIMA SHORE is a freelance writer specializing in education. She holds a Ph.D. from Columbia University. Her recent projects include *Moving the Ladder: Toward a New Community Vision* (Aspen Institute 1995), *Scaling Up Family Support and Parent Education* (Carnegie Corporation of New York 1996), and *The Current Status of High School Reform* (Carnegie Corporation of New York, forthcoming). She directs a program for immigrant teachers at the Brooklyn College School of Education.

MAX B. SAWICKY, an economist for the Economic Policy Institute, received a Ph.D. from the University of Maryland/College Park. He has worked in the Office of State and Local Finance of the U.S. Treasury Department and the U.S. Advisory Commission on Intergovernmental Relations. He has studied and written about the economics of public finance, with an emphasis on the federal budget, the U.S. federal system, state and local finance, and welfare reform. His reports for the Economic Policy Institute include *The Roots of the Public Sector Fiscal Crisis*, *The Poverty of the New Paradigm*, and *Up From Deficit Reduction*. He is an at-large national board member of Americans for Democratic Action. He resides with his wife and daughter in Silver Spring, Md.

ABOUT EPI

THE ECONOMIC POLICY INSTITUTE was founded in 1986 to widen the debate about policies to achieve healthy economic growth, prosperity, and opportunity in the difficult new era America has entered.

Today, America's economy is threatened by stagnant growth and increasing inequality. Expanding global competition, changes in the nature of work, and rapid technological advances are altering economic reality. Yet many of our policies, attitudes, and institutions are based on assumptions that no longer reflect real world conditions.

Central to the Economic Policy Institute's search for solutions is the exploration of policies that encourage every segment of the American economy (business, labor, government, universities, voluntary organizations, etc.) to work cooperatively to raise productivity and living standards for all Americans. Such an undertaking involves a challenge to conventional views of market behavior and a revival of a cooperative relationship between the public and private sectors.

With the support of leaders from labor, business, and the foundation world, the Institute has sponsored research and public discussion of a wide variety of topics: trade and fiscal policies; trends in wages, incomes, and prices; the causes of the productivity slowdown; labor-market problems; rural and urban policies; inflation; state-level economic development strategies; comparative international economic performance; and studies of the overall health of the U.S. manufacturing sector and of specific key industries.

The Institute works with a growing network of innovative economists and other social science researchers in universities and research centers all over the country who are willing to go beyond the conventional wisdom in considering strategies for public policy.

Founding scholars of the Institute include Jeff Faux, EPI president; Lester Thurow, Sloan School of Management, MIT; Ray Marshall, former U.S. secretary of labor, professor at the LBJ School of Public Affairs, University of Texas; Barry Bluestone, University of Massachusetts-Boston; Robert Reich, U.S. secretary of labor; and Robert Kuttner, author, editor of *The American Prospect,* and columnist for *Business Week* and the Washington Post Writers Group.

For additional information about the Institute, contact EPI at 1660 L Street, NW, Suite 1200, Washington, DC 20036, (202) 775-8810.